Voices From The Kitchen: A Collection of Antebellum and Civil War Era Recipes
From Period Receipt Books

David W. Flowers

ISBN: 9781980344421
ISBN-13:

DEDICATION

To my wife, Monica, for her patience and indulgence
of my hobbies and cooking. She's been known to say "There's not a day goes by
that he doesn't talk about the Civil War or reenacting!"

To my son, David, who has reenacted with me since he was five years old. A good
Pard and great camp-cook in his own right. I have taught him the past, but the
future belongs to him.

To my Mom and Dad who kept us returning to the South for vacations. From that
blessing, I walked the fields of history and breathed it's air. You gave me a life of
learning.

To my Pards in my reenacting unit, Scott's Tennessee Battery. I have learned
much from you fellers and have enjoyed many conversations, laughs, campfires,
cups of coffee and meals.

To Albert Sailhorst, Sergeant, Scott's Tennessee Battery. Died in a hospital at
Chattanooga, Tennessee, December 1862. His grave is presumed to have been
washed away. At present, I have been unable to find any descendants. He died
alone. Thank you for the opportunity to honor you. Deo Vindice.

To my good friend, Lester White (B. B. Battle), whose memory I carry in my heart
and I remember you every day. You would have liked this. Thanks for the fond
memories!

CONTENTS

Pork

Barbeque Shote, Biscuit Sandwiches, Bologna Sausages, Roasted or Baked Ham, Roast A Ham, Fried Liver and Bacon, Etc., Ham Sandwiches, Liver Puddings, Pig's Liver, Pig's Feet and Ears Fricasseed, Roast A Pig, Pork Apple Pie, Pork Cheese, Pork Chops, Pork Cutlets, Pork Olives, Pork Pies, Pork Steaks, Roast A Spare Rib, Roast Pork, Sea Pie, Souse, Boiled Tongue

Chicken and Fowl

Braised Chicken, Braised Turkey, Broiled Chickens, Broiled Fowl and Mushroom Sauce, Capon (Cornish Game Hen), Chicken Currie, Curry Powder, Chicken Cutlets, Chicken Leeky, Chicken Pie, Fowl Pillau, Fricasseed Fowl or Chicken, Fried Chickens, Fried Chicken A La Malabar, Fried Fowl, Minced Turkey or Chicken, Southern Gumbo, Tomato Chicken, Roast Ducks, Turkey Pulled and Grilled, Roast Turkey, White Fricassee

Fish and Seafood

Fried Anchovies, Stewed Carp, Curry of Catfish, Chowder, Cod A La Crème, Boiled Eels, Eels Fried, Fish Salads, Fry Oysters, Oyster Loaves, Roast Oysters, Stewed Oysters, Fried Perch, Ragout Of Fish, Salmon Steaks, Boiled Salmon, Salmon Stewed, Baked Shad, Bake A Shad, Sea Bass With Tomatoes, Trout à-la-Genevoise, Cream Trout

Boiled Artichokes, Boiled Asparagus, Asparagus Loaves, Bacon Salad, Baked Beans, Cabbage A La Crème, Cauliflowers A La Sauce Blanche, Celery Crab Salad, Stewed Celery A La Crème, Cold Slaw, Cranberry Sauce, Cucumbers, Eggs A La Crème, Sauce A La Crème for the Eggs, Eggs and Tomatos, Egg Plant, French Salad For The Summer, French Salad, Gumbo-A West India Dish, Dress Lettuce As Salad, Lettuce Chicken Salad, Dish of Maccaroni, Ochra and Tomatos, Orange Salad, Parsnips, Peach Salad, Stew Green Peas, Polenta, Pork and Beans, Potatoes, Potato Balls, Potatoes Fried or Broiled, Potato Rissouls, Roasted Potatoes, Preserved Pumpkin, Stew Red Cabbage, Salads, Dress Salad, Salad Mixture, Salmagundy, Summer Salad, Spinach and Eggs, Fried Sweet Potatoes, Scolloped Tomatoes, Tomatoes, To Stuff, Vermecelli

Goode Homemade Bread, Brown, or Dyspepsia Bread, Plain Bun,

Carraway Gingerbread, Corn Meal Bread, Corn Muffins, Drop Biscuit, Egg Biscuit, French Bread and Rolls, French Rolls, Hoe Cake, Indian Bread, Pumpkin Bread, Rice Bread, Richer Buns, Rusks, Rye Bread, Sweet Potato Buns, Tavern Biscuit, Tennessee Muffins

Vinegar, Cucumber Vinegar, Garlic Vinegar, Gooseberry Vinegar, Gooseberry Vinegar, Mint Vinegar, Raspberry Vinegar Syrup, Ravigotte Salad Dressing, Salad Dressing for Lettuce, Salad Mixture, Strawberry Vinegar, Sydney Smith's Salad Dressing, Vinegar for Salads

Sauces

Anchovy Sauce, Apple Sauce, Asparagus Sauce, Bechamel, or French White Sauce, Beef Gravy, Egg Sauce, Fish Sauce, Gravy for Roast Meat, Harvey's Sauce, Horseradish Sauce, Mayonnaise, Melted Butter (the French Sauce Blanche), Common Mustard, Peach Sauce, Sauce Robart, Tomata Honey, Turtle Sauce

9 Pickled Dishes   139

An Excellent Pickle, Pickling Apples, Beet Roots, To Pickle Cauliflowers, To Pickle Cucumbers, Pickled Eggs, Pickled Gherkins, Pickled Large Green Peppers, Fine Lemon Pickle, Mangoes, Pickled Mushrooms, To Pickle Onions, Onions Pickled White, Peach Pickles, To Pickle Peppers, Radish Pods, To Pickle Tomatoes, Pickled Walnuts

10 Holidays   147

Christmas

Egg Nog, Molasses Candy, Blanc Mange, Hen's Nest, Mince Pie, Mulled Wine

Valentine's Day

Kisses, Bola D' Amour-Love Cakes

Easter

Roast Ham

Thanksgiving

Turkey Roast, Chestnut Sauce

11 Dishes the Soldiers Ate   154

Boiled Pork and Bean Soup, Beef Stew, To Cook Bacon, Frying Bacon, Bacon German Style, Beans for Breakfast, Beef Soup With Desiccated Mixed Vegetables, To Prepare Coffee, Brazilian Stew, Bubble and Squeek, Corned Beef and Cabbage, To Boil Hominy, To Fry Hominy, Pea Soup, Pork Soup With Vegetables, To Make Tea, Hardtack Pudding

INTRODUCTION

"People have no variety in war times, but they make up for that lack in exquisite cooking"
-Mary Boykin Chesnut, January 22, 1864. "A Diary From Dixie".

The American Civil War created many shortages and hardships, including a strain on the food supply. Prices for necessities as flour, sugar, coffee, bread, meats, etc., reflected this strain. Yet, households of all economic means were able to sustain themselves, albeit by tightening their belts and making do with what they could get. Hence, the simplicity of the above quote speaks volumes to the lives of those trying to survive the war years.

This book is for both the novice and experienced cook alike. It is for those who appreciate history or have a curiosity of what daily household life was like in the middle of a great Civil War. These recipes are also for the Civil War reenactor who wants to taste the memories of our ancestors and cook for their "Pards". Above all, these recipes are meant to be cooked in the kitchens of the readers; so this book is for everyone. I have strived to write a labor of love in order that the culinary history of our ancestors would be remembered, appreciated and perpetuated.

This book is broken down, by chapter, to cover most culinary experiences. It begins as the day begins, with breakfast. As the day progresses, soups, main courses, side dishes and salads would need to be prepared and served. No meal would be complete without breads, desserts, and drinks. Since a portion of these recipes call for the addition of ketchup, salad dressing or sauce, those recipes have been included as well. An enjoyable treat at the dining table or in the picnic basket is the addition of pickled vegetables or eggs. It is my thought that I have included everything necessary to give the reader the information needed to prepare daily meals of their choosing. Unfortunately, my research as led me to a host of recipes that are simply too numerous to include without having a book so thick that it would be impractical to read without getting a feeling of repetition. Thus, I have kept it short, which made it difficult to decide which recipes to keep and which to discard. I also kept a chapter on a few choice holidays, with happy vignettes from the time period. I hope these stories further give life to the people who lived during the Civil War.

I would be remiss if I did not include a chapter on the foods eaten by the soldiers in the field. For this, I relied on quotations regarding eating rats, mussels and the shortages of military rations. I also relied on *Camp Fires and Camp Cooking; or, Culinary Hints for the Soldier* , written by Federal Capt. James R. Sanderson. In his book, Capt. Sanderson sets out to provide the inexperienced soldier, in the newly ascribed duties as cook both for himself and for his "messmates", with methods of cooking and some recipes. I also felt it necessary to present a chapter regarding perfumes, hair oils, soaps and sachets. It is my opinion that such subjects are underrepresented in scholarly works and are under-utilized in the reenacting community.

Finally, I have included is a list of definitions and measurements. This is integral to the intention of this book, so as to encourage these recipes to be prepared. I find it difficult to cook anything in a "slow oven", for example, if I have no knowledge of the temperature of such an oven. The same holds true for measurements of the time and some ingredients.

I have also made a point to include quotations and stories from soldiers and citizens in order to give "life" to each chapter. As these quotes and stories are read, I desire that the reader think about that person, what they were feeling, what they sacrificed and the pangs that shuddered through their bodies, while persevering in the fight for the things they individually believed in. In your heart, honor them by remembering that they had families that loved them and mourned their absence at the supper table and beyond.

My family has been in America since the 1600's, settling first in North Carolina, then in Tennessee. On my branch of the family, I am the first to have not been born in the South.

Growing up, I held in my heart the importance of spending time with my Grandparents, Marshall and Lula Mae, so I listened, with hungry ears, to the stories of Southern life that they told me. I ate the foods that they lovingly cooked. I believe, in their hearts, they knew that they were passing down the history of their lives and foods to an appreciative youth; someone who would carry on with their traditions and memories.

While I was in the First grade, my Dad took our family back to Tennessee for vacation. Before we left, he regaled me with stories of the Great Civil War! To a wide-eyed boy of six years old, stories of soldiers, my Great-great Grandfather Henry V. Flowers (Sergeant, Company A, 6th Tennessee Cavalry,

Federal) and great battles, were a captivating adventure! My father's stories and subsequent family trips to Pleasant Hill, Tennessee, led to the next forty-seven years worth of interest, study, travel and Civil War reenacting. I have spent a life, since then, curious about battles, soldiers and the minutia of life in the 1860's.

Having cooking as another hobby, I grew curious about the culinary history of the Civil War era. I knew what the soldiers ate; that is fairly common knowledge among people who study the War for Southern Independence. So, I took my curiosity to the next level and began to research the foods cooked and eaten on the "Home Front". From that curiosity and research, I started writing a feature article called "Corporal's Kitchen" for my reenacting unit's (Scott's Tennessee Battery) monthly newsletter. From those writings, this work has been conceived and born.

In addition to my writings, my wife, son and reenacting Pards have indulged me in my practice of cooking some of these recipes. My intention in writing the "Corporal's Kitchen" articles, this book and in actually cooking such foods, is to educate by taste and smell! It is my desire that you use these recipes, read the quotes and stories. I want you to think about the hardships that the soldiers that I have quoted have endured. I want you to taste the foods that they have longed for and dreamt of as they were far from their warm homes, fighting a war.

It is my belief that both the experienced cook as well as novice can find these recipes useful. Every recipe comes from an original, "period correct" source. Nothing is made up or altered by me. This is not a stereotypical "Souvenir Shop" type "Hillbilly" cookbook. This book provides period sources for every recipe and quotations to support authenticity. No recipe is contrived by me or taken from a "Hillbilly Cooking" type book. No recipe post-dates the Civil War. I have strived for authenticity in order to be educationally accurate, thus giving you the product that you expect and pay for. It is my pride, as an historian, that compels me to be honest.

Be advised, however, that due to the fact that we now have genetically modified foods, "farm raised" game and fish, meats that have received antibiotics and processed feeds, that our modern food is different that it was over 150 years ago. For example, our tomatoes are not the same, flour and corn meal are processed differently, our water has additives in it, chickens and pigs are fed scientifically produced feeds and are not left to either forage naturally or to be fed grains produced by the farmer. Our fruits, vegetables, meat, poultry and fish have all been bred, or otherwise altered, to be disease resistant and to produce larger quantities at a faster rate. All of these things affect taste. They are not the same as they were when the guns fired at Shiloh.

The same holds true for our cookware and method of cooking. Today's spatulas are plastic, our cookware is Teflon-coated and our stoves rely on either gas or electricity. The days of cast iron, tin or copper cookware as a form of common use are gone. The need to have a keen eye when cooking with a wood fire in a stove or hearth has been replaced with a knob and automatic timer.

To the best of our modern abilities and with a passion for the things that I write and teach, I hope you cook these foods, smelling and tasting the culinary experiences of those who sacrificed to make this country great! I desire that you and your families create great meals and memories together and pass on our great American history!

With all of that said, I wish to reiterate my thanks to my wife Monica, son David, my Dad and Mom Wayne and Melody Flowers and to my Pards in Scott's Tennessee Battery. A special thanks to my good friend and Pard, Bruce Kindig, for his advice in formatting and publishing, as well as his encouragement and kind words. If it were not for him inviting me to reenact with Scott's Battery, I would not have had the great friends that I have now. Another special thanks to another good friend and Pard, Ed Reiter, for sharing his love of camp cooking and cast iron cooking. I appreciate his advice over the years and I compliment him as a fine cook and a great maker of cobblers! I also appreciate his expertise in assisting with the photograph for the book cover!

"In the following, and indeed all other receipts, though the quantities may be as accurately set down as possible, yet much must be left to the discretion of the persons who use them." Maria J. Moss, "The Poetical Cookbook", 1864.

<u>Notes on Font and Spelling</u>

All direct quotes from soldiers and civilians are in italics with quotation marks. All other text in italics reflect an author's note.

In quotations and in all recipes, I have kept the spelling as I found it from the original source. This was done in order to preserve the integrity of the original writing and to illustrate to the reader what may have been either common spellings or errors (i.e from diary/letter writing) of the day in which they were written.

1 BREAKFASTS

"The news of Forrest's victory is confirmed. I went out with some others and bought a peacock for our breakfast in the morning."-Pvt. Martin Van Buren Oldham, Company G of the 9th Tennessee Infantry, May 5, 1863, Camp near Chattanooga, TN. From diary entry.

Beef Cakes
From "Directions for Cookery, in its Various Branches" By Eliza Leslie, 1840

Take some cold roast beef that has been under-done, and mince it very fine. Mix with it grated bread crumbs, and a little chopped onion and parsley. Season it with pepper and salt, and moisten it with some beef-dripping and a little walnut or onion pickle. Some scraped cold tongue or ham will be found an improvement. Make it into broad flat cakes, and spread a coat of mashed potato thinly on the top and bottom of each. Lay a small bit of butter on the top of every cake, and set them in an oven to warm and brown.

Beef cakes are frequently a breakfast dish.

Any other cold fresh meat may be prepared in the same manner.

Cold roast beef may be cut into slices, seasoned with salt

and pepper, broiled a few minutes over a clear fire, and

served up hot with a little butter spread on them.

Beefsteak Pie

From "The Great Western Cook Book, or Table Receipts,
Adapted to Western Housewifery", By Anna Maria
Collins, 1857

Take a large beefsteak, fry it slightly in very hot lard, cut it up, and let it cool. Line your pan with rich pie-crust, put in a layer of beef, salt, pepper, and catsup, then lay on some potatoes sliced very thin, with some very fine-chopped onions, a little parsley, then a layer of beef, then, again, potatoes; cover it with crust. Take the gravy that the steak was fried in, put into it a cup of cream and a lump of butter, say an ounce, well rubbed in browned flour; let it simmer a minute or two, then make a hole in the middle of the top crust, and pour in the gravy; if too thick, add a gill of water.
Bake very slowly, and be very sure not to have it too brown.

Beignets

From "The Practical Housekeeper; A Cyclopedia of Domestic
Economy", By Elizabeth Fries Ellet, 1857

Mix and work well together half a pound of flour, and two ounces of butter, or three table-spoonfuls of sweet oil, and make it into a batter with some warm water; then mix into the batter a couple of raw eggs, keeping the yolk of one for browning. The materials may thus be made of any degree of consistence, so as to act as thick batter, or as thin paste by the addition of a little flour; and being made into small balls, are spread with the remaining yolk of egg, powdered usually with sugar, and fried in hot lard; and, when ready to be served, put them for a moment on a hair sieve to drain off the fat.
If made solely with paste, without mince of any kind, they should have an-other egg, and the batter be more continually beaten, so as to render the beignets light; then, when prepared for dressing, take a spoonful of the batter formed into a ball, and drop it into the boiling lard. A large dishful will be fried in six or seven minutes.

Broiled Rashers of Bacon (a Breakfast Dish)

From "The Book of Household Management", By Isabella Beeton, 1861

Before purchasing bacon, ascertain that it is perfectly free from rust, which may easily be detected by its yellow colour; and for broiling, the streaked part of the thick flank, is generally the most esteemed. Cut it into thin slices, take off the

rind, and broil over a nice clear fire; turn it 2 or 3 times, and serve very hot. Should there be any cold bacon left from the previous day, it answers very well for breakfast, cut into slices, and broiled or fried.
Time-3 or 4 minutes.

The song "Dixie" was written by minstrel Daniel Decatur Emmett circa 1859, quickly growing in popularity, to become the accepted unofficial "National Anthem" of the Southern Confederacy. It was played to great cheering at the inauguration of President Jefferson Davis and throughout the war to inspire troops. Abraham Lincoln is quoted as saying "I have always thought 'Dixie' one of the best tunes I have ever heard. Our adversaries over the way attempted to appropriate it, but I insisted yesterday that we fairly captured it...I now request the band to favor me with its performance." (April 10, 1865). One of the lesser used verses (at today's Civil War reenactments) goes like this:

"There's buckwheat cakes and Injun batter,
Makes you fat or a little fatter
Look away! Look away! Look away!
Dixie Land!"

Buckwheat Cakes Wet with Water
From "Miss Beecher's Domestic Receipt Book", By Catharine Esther Beecher, 1850

Take a quart of buckwheat flour, and nearly an even tablespoonful of salt. Stir in warm water, till it is the consistency of thin batter. Beat it thoroughly. Add two tablespoonfuls of yeast, if distillery, or twice as much if home-brewed.

Set the batter where it will be a little warm through the night. Some persons never stir them after they have risen, but take them out carefully with a large spoon.
Add a teaspoonful of pearlash in the morning, if they are sour. Sift it over the surface, and stir it well.
Some persons like to add one or two tablespoonfuls of molasses, to give them a brown color, and more sweetness of taste.

Buttered Eggs
From "A New System of Domestic Cookery", By
Maria Eliza Ketelby Rundell, 1807

Beat four or five eggs, yolk and white together, put a quarter of a pound of butter in a basin, and then put that in boiling water, stir it till melted, then pour that butter and the eggs into a sauce-pan; keep a basin in your hand, just hold the sauce-pan in the other over a slow part of the fire, shaking it one way, as it begins to warm; pour it into a basin, and back, then hold it again over the fire, stirring it constantly in the sauce-pan, and pouring it into the basin, more perfectly to mix the egg and butter, until they shall be hot without boiling. Serve on toasted bread; or in a basin, to eat with salt fish, or red herrings.

Cod Omlette
From "The Practical Housekeeper; A Cyclopedia of Domestic Economy", By
Elizabeth Fries Ellet, 1857

Break into small pieces the thickest parts of a dressed cod, season it with a little grated nutmeg and a little pounded mace, beat up six eggs well and mix with it, forming it into a paste, fry it as an omelette, and serve as hot as possible.

Dough Nuts
From "Directions for Cookery, in its Various Branches" By Eliza Leslie, 1840

Take two deep dishes, and sift three quarters of a pound of flour into each. Make a hole in the centre of one of them, and pour in a wine glass of the best brewer's yeast; mix the flour gradually into it, wetting it with lukewarm milk; cover it, and set it by the fire to rise for about two hours. This is setting a sponge. In the mean time, cut up five ounces of butter into the other dish of flour, and rub it fine with your hands; add half a pound of powdered sugar, a tea-spoonful of powdered cinnamon, a grated nutmeg, a table-spoonful of rose water, and a half pint of milk. Beat three eggs very light, and stir them hard into the mixture. Then when, the sponge is perfectly light, add it to the other ingredients, mixing them all thoroughly with a knife. Cover it, and set it again by the fire for another hour. When, it is quite light, flour your paste-board, turn out the lump of dough, and cut it into thick diamond shaped cakes with a jagging iron. If you find the dough so soft as to be unmanageable, mix in a little more flour; but not else. Have ready a skillet of boiling lard; put the dough-nuts into it, and fry them brown; and when cool grate loaf-sugar over them. They should be eaten quite fresh, as next day they will be tough and heavy; therefore it is best to make no more than you want for immediate use. The New York Oley Koeks are dough-nuts with currants and raisins in them.

Dough Nuts-A Yankee Cake
From "The Virginia Housewife", By Mary Randolph, 1836

Dry half a pound of good brown sugar, pound it and mix it with two pounds of flour, and sift it; add two spoonsful of yeast, and as much new milk as will make it like bread: when well risen, knead in half a pound of butter, make it in cakes the size of a half dollar, and fry them a light brown in boiling lard.

Eggs, To Fry Extra Nice
From "Dr. Chase's Recipes; or, Information for Everybody", By Dr. Alvin Wood Chase, 1864

Three eggs; flour 1 table-spoon; milk 1 cup.
Beat the eggs and flour together, Then stir in the milk. Have a skillet with a proper amount of butter in it, made hot, for frying this mixture; then pour it in, and when one side is done brown, turn it over, cooking rather slowly; if a larger quantity is needed, it will require a little salt stirred in, but for this amount, the salt in the butter in which you fry it, seasons it very nicely.

Fricasseed Eggs
From "Directions for Cookery, in its Various Branches" By Eliza Leslie, 1840

Take a dozen eggs, and boil them six or seven minutes, or till they are just hard enough to peel and slice without breaking. Then put them into a pan of cold water while you prepare some grated bread-crumbs, (seasoned with pepper, salt and nutmeg,) and beat the yolks of two or three raw eggs very light. Take the boiled eggs out of the water, and having peeled off the shells, slice the eggs, dust a little flour over them, and dip them first into the beaten egg, and then into the bread-crumbs so as to cover them well on both sides. Have ready in a frying-pan some boiling lard; put the sliced eggs into it, and fry them on both sides. Serve them up at the breakfast table, garnished with small sprigs of parsley that has been fried in the same lard after the eggs were taken out.

Griddle Cake

From "The New England Economical Housekeeper", by Esther Allen
Howland, 1845

Rub three ounces of butter into a pound of flour with a little salt, moisten it
with sweet buttermilk to make it into a paste, roll it out, and cut the cakes with
the cover of your dredging-box and put them upon a griddle to bake.

Ham and Eggs Fried

From "The Practical Housekeeper; A Cyclopedia of Domestic Economy", By
Elizabeth Fries Ellet, 1857

Out some nice slices of ham, put them in a frying-pan; cover them with hot
water, and set the pan over the fire. Let it boil up once or twice; then take out
the slices and throw out the water; put a bit of lard in the pan; dip the slices in
wheat flour or finely rolled crackers, and when the fat is hot, put them into the
pan; sprinkle a little popper over; when both sides are a fine brown, take them
on a steak dish; put a little boiling water into the pan, and put it in the dish with
the meat. Now put a bit of lard the size of a large egg into the pan; add a salt-
spoon ful to it; let it become hot; break six or eight eggs carefully into a bowl;
then slip them into the hot lard; set the pan over a gentle fire. When the white
be gins to set, pass a knife-blade, so as to divide an equal quantity of white to
each yolk; cut it entirely through to the pan, that they may cook the more
quickly, When done, take each one up with a skimmer spoon, and lay them in a
chain around the edge of the meat on the dish. Fried eggs should not be turned
in the pan.
Spinach boiled and pressed free from water, and chopped small, may be put on
the centre of a steak dish; lay the fried ham on it; pour the gravy over; place the
fried eggs around it. Vinegar may be eaten with the spinach.

Ham Omelet

From "Directions for Cookery, in its Various Branches" By Eliza Leslie, 1840

Take six ounces of cold coiled ham, and mince it very fine, adding a little
pepper. Beat separately the whites and yolks of six eggs, and then mix them
together add to them gradually the minced ham. Beat the whole very hard, and
do not let it stand a moment after it is thoroughly mixed. Have ready some
boiling lard in a frying-pan, and put in the omelet immediately. Fry it about ten
minutes or a quarter of an hour. When done, put it on a hot dish, trim off the

edges, and fold it over in a half moon. Send it to table hot, and covered. It is eaten at breakfast.

If you wish a soft omelet, (not to fold over,) fry it a shorter time, and serve it in a deep dish, to be helped with a spoon.

A similar omelet may be made of the lean of a cold smoked tongue.

Irish Pancakes

From "A New System of Domestic Cookery", By Maria Eliza
Ketelby Rundell, 1807

Beat eight yolks and four whites of eggs, strain them into a pint of cream, put a grated nutmeg, and sugar to your taste; set three ounces of fresh butter on the fire, stir it, and as it warms pour it to the cream, which should be warm when the eggs are put to it: then mix smooth almost half a pint of flour. Fry the pancakes very thin; the first with a bit of butter, but not the others. Serve several, on one another.

To Make Mush

From "The Virginia Housewife", By Mary Randolph, 1836

Put a lump of butter the size of an egg into a quart of water, make it sufficiently thick with corn meal and a little salt; it must be mixed perfectly smooth--stir it constantly till done enough.

Omelette

From "The Great Western Cook Book, or Table Receipts, Adapted
to Western Housewifery", By Anna Maria Collins, 1857

Break five or six eggs into a basin, and beat them well; add half a tea-spoonful of salt, two drachms of onions, chopped fine, or three drachms of parsley; beat it up well with the eggs. Then take four ounces of fresh butter, break half of it into little bits, and put it into the omelette. Put the other half into a fryingpan, and when it is melted, pour in the omelette, and stir it with a spoon till it begins to set. Turn it up all around the edges, and when it is a nice brown, it is done. Turn it out on a hot dish.

Omelette Aux Confitures, or Jam Omelet
From "The Book of Household Management", By Isabella Beeton, 1861

6 eggs, 4 oz. of butter, 3 tablespoonfuls of apricot, strawberry, or any jam that may be preferred.

Make the omelet by recipe No. 1459 (see "To Make A Plain Sweet Omelet"), only instead of doubling it over, leave it flat in the pan. When quite firm, and nicely brown on one side, turn it carefully on to a hot dish, spread over the middle of it the jam, and fold the omelet over on each side; sprinkle sifted sugar over, and serve very quickly. A pretty dish of small omelets may be made by dividing the batter into 3 or 4 portions, and frying them separately; they should then be spread each one with a different kind of preserve, and the omelets rolled over. Always sprinkle sweet omelets with sifted sugar before being sent to table.

Time-4 to 6 minutes.

To Make A Plain Sweet Omlete
From "The Book of Household Management", By Isabella Beeton, 1861

6 eggs, 4 oz. of butter, 2 oz. of sifted sugar.

Break the eggs into a basin, omitting the whites of 3; whisk them well, adding the sugar and 2 oz. of the butter, which should be broken into small pieces, and stir all these ingredients well together. Make the remainder of the butter quite hot in a small frying-pan, and when it commences to bubble, pour in the eggs, &c. Keep stirring them until they begin to set; then turn the edges of the omelet over, to make it an oval shape, and finish cooking it. To brown the top, hold the pan before the fire, or use a salamander, and turn it carefully on to a very hot dish: sprinkle sifted sugar over, and serve.

Time-From 4 to 6 minutes.

To Make Pancakes
From "The Book of Household Management", By Isabella Beeton, 1861

Eggs, flour, milk; to every egg allow 1 oz. of flour, about 1 gill of milk, 1/8 saltspoonful of salt.

Ascertain that the eggs are fresh; break each one separately in a cup; whisk them well, put them into a basin, with the flour, salt, and a few drops of milk, and beat the whole to a perfectly smooth batter; then add by degrees the remainder of the milk. The proportion of this latter ingredient must be regulated by the size of the eggs, &c. &c.; but the batter, when ready for frying, should be of the consistency of thick cream. Place a small frying-pan on the fire to get hot; let it be delicately clean, or the pancakes will stick, and, when quite hot, put into it a small piece of butter, allowing about 1/2 oz. to each pancake. When it is melted, pour in the batter, about 1/2 teacupful to a pan 5 inches in diameter, and fry it for about 4 minutes, or until it is nicely brown on one side. By only pouring in a small quantity of batter, and so making the pancakes thin, the necessity of turning them (an operation rather difficult to unskilful cooks) is obviated. When the pancake is done, sprinkle over it some pounded sugar, roll it up in the pan, and take it out with a large slice, and place it on a dish before the fire. Proceed in this manner until sufficient are cooked for a dish; then send them quickly to table, and continue to send in a further quantity, as pancakes are never good unless eaten almost immediately they come from the frying-pan. The batter may be flavoured with a little grated lemon-rind, or the pancakes may have preserve rolled in them instead of sugar. Send sifted sugar and a cut lemon to table with them. To render the pancakes very light, the yolks and whites of the eggs should be beaten separately, and the whites added the last thing to the batter before frying.

Time-from 4 to 6 minutes for a pancake that does not require turning; from 6 to 8 minutes for a thicker one.

Pork Cheese (an Excellent Breakfast Dish)

From "The Book of Household Management", By Isabella Beeton, 1861

2 lbs. of cold roast pork, pepper and salt to taste, 1 dessertspoonful of minced parsley, 4 leaves of sage, a very small bunch of savoury herbs, 2 blades of pounded mace, a little nutmeg, ½ teaspoonful of minced lemon-peel; good strong gravy, sufficient to fill the mould.

Cut, but do not chop, the pork into fine pieces, and allow ¼ lb. of fat to each pound of lean. Season with pepper and salt; pound well the spices, and chop finely the parsley, sage, herbs, and lemon-peel, and mix the whole nicely together. Put it into a mould, fill up with good strong well-flavoured gravy, and bake rather more than one hour. When cold, turn it out of the mould.

Scotch Eggs

From "A New System of Domestic Cookery", By
Maria Eliza Ketelby Rundell, 1807

Boil hard five pullets eggs, and without removing the white, cover completely with a fine relishing forcemeat, in which, let scraped ham, or chopped anchovy bear a due proportion. Fry of a beautiful yellow brown, and serve with a good gravy in the dish.

Waffles
From "Directions for Cookery, in its Various Branches" By Eliza Leslie, 1840

Put two pints of rich milk into separate pans. Cut up and melt in one of them a quarter of a pound of butter, warming it slightly; then, when it is melted, stir it about, and set it away to cool. Beat eight eggs till very light, and mix them gradually into the other pan of milk, alternately with half a pound of flour. Then mix in by degrees the milk that has the butter in it. Lastly, stir in a large table-spoonful of strong fresh yeast. Cover the pan, and set it near the fire to rise. When the batter is quite light, heat your waffle-iron, by putting it among the coals of a clear bright fire; grease the inside with butter tied in a rag, and then put in some batter. Shut the iron closely, and when the waffle is done on one side, turn the iron on the other. Take the cake out by slipping a knife underneath; and then heat and grease the iron for another waffle. Send them to table quite hot, four or six on a plate; having buttered them and strewed over each a mixture of powdered cinnamon, and white sugar. Or you may send the sugar and cinnamon in a little glass bowl.
In buying waffle-irons, do not choose those broad shallow ones that are to hold four at a time; as the waffles baked in them are too small, too thin, and are never of a good shape. The common sort that bake but two at once are much the best.

Wonders, or Crullers
From "Directions for Cookery, in its Various Branches" By Eliza Leslie, 1840

Rub half a pound of butter into two pounds of sifted flour, mixing in three quarters of a pound of powdered sugar. Add a tea-spoonful of powdered cinnamon, and a grated nutmeg, with a large table-spoonful of rose water. Beat six eggs very light, and stir them into the mixture. Mix it with a knife into a soft paste. Then put it on the paste-board, and roll it out into a sheet an inch thick. If you find it too soft, knead in a little more flour, and roll it out over again. Cut it into long slips with a jagging iron, or with a sharp knife, and twist them into various fantastic shapes. Have ready on hot coals, a skillet of boiling lard; put in the crullers and fry them of a light brown, turning them occasionally by means of a knife and fork. Take them out one by one on a perforated skimmer, that the lard may drain off through the holes. Spread them out on a large dish, and when cold grate white sugar over them.

They will keep a week or more.

2. SOUPS

"The bacon was rusty and very slimy, the soup was a slop and filled with white worms a half inch long"- Lt. Randolph Shotwell, Confederate Prisoner at Ft. Deleware. Shotwell led the sharpshooters of a regiment in Pickett's Charge at Gettysburg, being promoted to Lieutenant for his gallant conduct. He was captured in 1864 and remained a prisoner for the remainder of the war.

Asparagus Soup
From "The Great Western Cook Book, or Table Receipts, Adapted to Western Housewifery", By Anna Maria Collins, 1857

This is made with the points of asparagus, in the same manner as the green pease soup. Let half the asparagus be rubbed through a sieve, and the other half be cut in pieces about an inch long, and boiled till done enough, and sent up in the soup. To make two quarts, there must be a pint of heads to thicken it, and half a pint cut in. Take care to preserve these green, and a little crisp. This soup is sometimes made, by adding the asparagus heads to common pease soup.

Barley Soup
From "The Book of Household Management", By Isabella Beeton, 1861

2 lbs. of shin of beef, 1/4 lb. of pearl barley, a large bunch of parsley, 4 onions, 6 potatoes, salt and pepper, 4 quarts of water.
Put in all the ingredients, and simmer gently for 3 hours.

Bean Soup
From "Directions for Cookery, in its Various Branches" By Eliza Leslie, 1840

Put two quarts of dried white beans into soak the night before you make the soup, which should be put on as early in the day as possible.

Take five pounds of the lean of fresh beef--the coarse pieces will do. Cut them up, and put them into your soup-pot with the bones belonging to them, (which should be broken to pieces,) and a pound of bacon cut very small. If you have the remains of a piece of beef that has been roasted the day before, and so much under-done that the juices remain in it, you may put it into the pot, and its bones along with it. Season the meat with pepper and salt, and pour on it six quarts of water. As soon as it boils take off the scum, and put in the beans (having first drained them) and a head of celery cut small, or a table-spoonful of pounded celery-seed. Boil it slowly till the meat is done to shreds, and the beans all dissolved. Then strain it through a cullender into the tureen, and put into it small squares of toasted bread with the crust cut off.

Some prefer it with the beans boiled soft, but not quite dissolved. In this case, do not strain it; but take out the meat and bones with a fork before you send it to table.

Beef Soup
From "The Virginia Housewife", By Mary Randolph, 1836

Take the hind shin of beef, cut off all the flesh off the leg-bone, which must be taken away entirely, or the soup will be greasy. Wash the meat clean and lay it in a pot, sprinkle over it one small table-spoonful of pounded black pepper, and two of salt; three onions the size of a hen's egg, cut small, six small carrots scraped and cut up, two small turnips pared and cut into dice; pour on three quarts of water, cover the pot close, and keep it gently and steadily boiling five hours, which will leave about three pints of clear soup; do not let the pot boil over, but take off the scum carefully, as it rises. When it has boiled four hours, put in a small bundle of thyme and parsley, and a pint of celery cut small, or a tea-spoonful of celery seed pounded. These latter ingredients would lose their delicate flavour if boiled too much. Just before you take it up, brown it in the following manner: put a small table-spoonful of nice brown sugar into an iron skillet, set it on the fire and stir it till it melts and looks very dark, pour into it a ladle full of the soup, a little at a time; stirring it all the while. Strain this browning and mix it well with the soup; take out the bundle of thyme and parsley, put the nicest pieces of meat in your tureen, and pour on the soup and vegetables; put in some toasted bread cut in dice, and serve it up.

Bread Soup
From "The Book of Household Management", By Isabella Beeton, 1861

1 lb. of bread crusts, 2 oz. butter, 1 quart of common stock.
Boil the bread crusts in the stock with the butter; beat the whole with a spoon, and keep it boiling till the bread and stock are well mixed. Season with a little salt.

Cabbage Soup
From "The Book of Household Management", By Isabella Beeton, 1861

1 large cabbage, 3 carrots, 2 onions, 4 or 5 slices of lean bacon, salt and pepper to taste, 2 quarts of medium stock No. 105 (See "Medium Stock").
Scald the cabbage, exit it up and drain it. Line the stewpan with the bacon, put in the cabbage, carrots, and onions; moisten with skimmings from the stock, and simmer very gently, till the cabbage is tender; add the stock, stew softly for half an hour, and carefully skim off every particle of fat. Season and serve.

Catfish Soup
From "The Virginia Housewife", By Mary Randolph, 1836

2 large or 4 small white catfish that have been caught in deep water, 1 pound of lean bacon, 1 large onion cut up, 1 handful of parsley chopped, small pepper, salt, yelks of 4 fresh eggs, 1 large spoonful of butter, 2 large spoonfuls of flour, 1/2 pint of rich milk.
Instructions Take the catfish, cut off the heads, and skin and clean the bodies; cut each in three parts, put them in a pot, with the bacon, onion, parsley, some pepper and salt, pour in a sufficient quantity of water, and stew them till the fish are quite tender but not broken; beat the yelks, add to them the butter, flour, and milk; make all these warm and thicken the soup, take out the bacon, and put some of the fish in your tureen, pour in the soup, and serve it up.

Chicken Soup
From "The Lady's Receipt-Book; a Useful Companion for Large or Small Families", By Eliza Leslie, 1847

Cut up two large fine fowls, as if carving them for the table, and wash the pieces in cold water. Take half a dozen thin slices of cold ham, and lay them in a soup-pot, mixed among the pieces of chicken. Season them with a very little cayenne, a little nutmeg, and a few blades of mace, but no salt, as the ham will make it salt enough. Add a head of celery, split and cut into long bits, a quarter of a pound of butter, divided in two, and rolled in flour. Pour on three quarts of milk. Set the soup-pot over the fire, and let it boil rather slowly, skimming it well. When it has boiled an hour, put in some small round dumplings, made of half a pound of flour mixed with a quarter of a pound of butter; divide this dough into equal portions, and roll them in your hands into little balls about the size of a large hickory nut. The soup must boil till the flesh of the fowls is loose on the bones, but not till it drops off. Stir in, at the last, the beaten yolks of three or four eggs; and let the soup remain about five minutes longer over the fire. Then take it up. Cut off from the bones the flesh of the fowls, and divide it into mouthfuls. Cut up the slices of ham in the same manner. Mince the livers and gizzards. Put the bits of fowl and ham in the bottom of a large tureen, and pour the soup upon it.

This soup will be found excellent, and may be made of large old fowls, that cannot be cooked in any other way. If they are so old that when the soup is finished they still continue tough, remove them entirely, and do not serve them up in it.

Similar soup may be made of a large old turkey.

Also of four rabbits.

Clear Gravy Soup
From "Directions for Cookery, in its Various Branches" By Eliza Leslie, 1840

Having well buttered the inside of a nicely tinned stew-pot, cut half a pound of ham into slices, and lay them at the bottom, with three pounds of the lean of fresh beef, and as much veal, cut from the bones, which you must afterward break to pieces, and lay on the meat. Cover the pan closely, and set it over a quick fire. When the meat begins to stick to the pan, turn it; and when there is a nice brown glaze at the bottom, cover the meat with cold water. Watch it well, and when it is just coming to a boil, put in half a pint of cold water. This will cause the scum to rise. Skim it well, and then pour in another half pint of cold water; skim it again; pour in cold water as before, half a pint at a time, and repeat this till no more scum rises. In skimming, carefully avoid stirring the soup, as that will injure its clearness.

In the mean time prepare your vegetables. Peel off the outer skin of three large white onions and slice them. Pare three large turnips, and slice them also. Wash clean and cut into small pieces three carrots, and three large heads of celery. If you cannot obtain fresh celery, substitute a large table-spoonful of celery seed, tied up in a bit of clear muslin. Put the vegetables into the soup, and then place the pot on one side of the fire, where the heat is not so great as in the middle. Let it boil gently for four hours. Then strain the soup through a fine towel or linen bag into a large stone pan, but do not squeeze the bag, or the soup will be cloudy, and look dull instead of clear. In pouring it into the straining cloth, be careful not to disturb the ingredients at the bottom of the soup-pot.

This soup should be of a fine clear amber colour. If not perfectly bright after straining, you may clarify it in this manner. Put it into the stew-pan. Break the whites of two eggs into a basin, carefully avoiding the smallest particle of the yolk. Beat the white of egg to a stiff froth, and then mix it gradually with the soup. Set it over the fire, and stir it till it boils briskly. Then take it off, and set it beside the fire to settle for ten minutes. Strain it then through a clean napkin, and it will be fit for use. But it is better to have the soup clear by making it carefully, than to depend on clarifying it afterward, as the white of egg weakens the taste.

In making this (which is quite a show-soup) it is customary to reverse the general rule, and pour in cold water.

Dried Pea Soup
From "The Virginia Housewife", By Mary Randolph, 1836

Take one quart of split peas, or Lima beans, which are better; put them in three quarts of very soft water with three onions chopped up, pepper and salt; boil them two hours; mash them well and pass them through a sieve; return the liquid into the pot, thicken it with a large piece of butter and flour, put in some slices of nice salt pork, and a large tea-spoonful of celery seed pounded; boil it till the pork is done, and serve it up; have some toasted bread cut into dice and fried in butter, which must be put in the tureen before you pour in the soup.

French Vegetable Soup
From "Miss Beecher's Domestic Receipt Book", By Catharine Esther Beecher, 1850

Take a leg of lamb, of moderate size, and four quarts water. Of potatoes, carrots, cabbage, onions, tomatoes, and turnips take a tea-cup full of each, chopped fine. Salt and black pepper to your taste.
Wash the lamb, and put it into the four quarts of cold water. When the scum rises take it off carefully with a skimmer. After having pared and chopped the vegetables, put them into the soup. Carrots require the most boiling, and should be put in first; onions require the least boiling, and are to be put in the last.
This soup requires about three hours to boil.

French White Soup
From "The Lady's Receipt-Book; a Useful Companion for Large or Small Families", By Eliza Leslie, 1847

Boil a knuckle of veal and four calves' feet in five quarts of water, with three onions sliced, a bunch of sweet herbs, four heads of white celery cut small, a table-spoonful of whole pepper, and a *small* tea-spoonful of salt, adding five or six large blades of mace. Let it boil very slowly, till the meat is in rags and has dropped from the bone, and till the gristle has quite dissolved. Skim it well while boiling. When done, strain it through a sieve into a tureen, or a deep white-ware pan. Next day, take off all the fat, and put the jelly (for such it ought to be) into a clean soup-pot with two ounces of vermicelli, and set it over the fire. When the vermicelli is dissolved, stir in, gradually, a pint of thick cream, while the soup is quite hot; but do not let it come to a boil after the cream is in, lest it should curdle. Cut up one or two French rolls in the bottom of a tureen, pour in the soup, and send it to table.

Giblet Soup
From "A New System of Domestic Cookery", By Maria Eliza Ketelby Rundell, 1807

Scald and clean three or four sets of goose or duck giblets. set them to stew, with a pound or two of gravy-beef, scrag of mutton, or the bone of a knuckle of veal; an ox-tail, or some shanks of mutton; with three onions, a large bunch of sweet herbs, a ten-spoonful of white pepper, and a large spoonful of salt. Put five pints of water, and simmer till the gizzards (which must be each in four pieces) are quite tender: skim nicely, and add a quarter of a pint of cream, two tea-spoonfuls of mushroom-powder, and an ounce of butter mixed with a desert-spoonful of flour. Let it boil a few minutes, and serve with the giblets. It may be seasoned, instead of cream, with two glasses of sherry or Madeira, a large spoonful of ketchup. and some Cayenne. When in the tureen, add salt.

Gravy Soup
From "The Virginia Housewife", By Mary Randolph, 1836

Get eight pounds of coarse lean beef--wash it clean and lay it in your pot, put in the same ingredients as for the shin soup, with the same quantity of water, and follow the process directed for that. Strain the soup through a sieve, and serve it up clear, with nothing more than toasted bread in it; two table-spoonsful of mushroom catsup will add a fine flavour to the soup.

Hare or Rabbit Soup
From "The Virginia Housewife", By Mary Randolph, 1836

Cut up two hares, put them into a pot with a piece of bacon, two onions chopped, a bundle of thyme and parsley, which must be taken out before the soup is thickened, add pepper, salt, pounded cloves, and mace, put in a sufficient quantity of water, stew it gently three hours, thicken with a large spoonful of butter, and one of brown flour, with a glass of red wine; boil it a few minutes longer, and serve it up with the nicest parts of the hares. Squirrels make soup equally good, done the same way.

Jenny Lind's Soup
From "The Practical Housekeeper; A Cyclopedia of Domestic Economy", By Elizabeth Fries Ellet, 1857

Make about three quarts of stock, which strain through a fine sieve into a middle-size stewpan; set it to boil; add to it three ounces of sago; boil gently twenty minutes; skim; just previous to serving break four fresh eggs, and place the yolk, entirely free from the white, into a basin, beat them well with a spoon; add to it a gill of cream; take the pan from the fire, pour in the yolks, stir quickly for one minute, serve immediately; do not let it boil, or it will curdle, and would not be fit to be partaken of. The stock being previously seasoned, it only requires the addition of half a teaspoonful of sugar, a little more salt, pepper, nutmeg; also thyme, parsley, and bay-leaf will agreeably vary the flavor without interfering with the quality.

Medium Stock (Referred to as #105)
From "The Book of Household Management", By Isabella Beeton, 1861

4 lbs. of shin of beef, or 4 lbs. of knuckle of veal, or 2 lbs. of each; any bones, trimmings of poultry, or fresh meat, 1/2 a lb. of lean bacon or ham, 2 oz. of butter, 2 large onions, each stuck with 3 cloves; 1 turnip, 3 carrots, 1/2 a leek, 1 head of celery, 2 oz. of salt, 1/2 a teaspoonful of whole pepper, 1 large blade of mace, 1 small bunch of savoury herbs, 4 quarts and 1/2 pint of cold water.
Cut up the meat and bacon or ham into pieces about 3 inches square; rub the butter on the bottom of the stewpan; put in 1/2 a pint of water, the meat, and all the other ingredients. Cover the stewpan, and place it on a sharp fire, occasionally stirring its contents. When the bottom of the pan becomes covered with a pale, jelly-like substance, add 4 quarts of cold water, and simmer very gently for 5 hours. As we have said before, do not let it boil quickly. Skim off every particle of grease whilst it is doing, and strain it through a fine hair sieve. This is the basis of many of the soups afterwards mentioned, and will be found quite strong enough for ordinary purposes.
Time-5-1/2 hours.

Mock Turtle Soup
From "The Great Western Cook Book, or Table Receipts, Adapted to Western Housewifery", By Anna Maria Collins, 1857

Take the upper from the lower part of a calf's head, and put both in a gallon of water and boil till tender.
Strain the liquor, let it stand till next day, and take off the fat. Hang it over the fire three-quarters of an hour before serving it, and season it with salt, cloves, pepper, mace, and sweet herbs, tied in a bag. Add half a pint of rich gravy. Darken it with browned flour or fried sugar. Then put in the yolks of eight eggs boiled hard, the juice of two lemons, and force-meat balls. When ready to serve, add half a pint of wine.

Onion Soup
From "A New System of Domestic Cookery", By
Maria Eliza Ketelby Rundell, 1807

Into the water that has boiled a leg or neck of mutton, put carrots, turnips, and (if you have one) a shank-bone, and simmer two hours. Strain it on six onions, first sliced and fried of a light brown; simmer three hours, skim it carefully, and serve. Put into it a little roll, or fried bread.

Onion Soup
From "The Virginia Housewife", By Mary Randolph, 1836

Chop up twelve large onions, boil them in three quarts of milk and water equally mixed, put in a bit of veal or fowl, and a piece of bacon with pepper and salt. When the onions are boiled to pulp, thicken it with a large spoonful of butter mixed with one of flour. Take out the meat, and serve it up with toasted bread cut in small pieces in the soup.

Ox-Tail Soup
From "The Book of Household Management", By Isabella Beeton, 1861

2 ox-tails 2 slices of ham 1 ounce of butter 2 carrots 2 turnips 3 onions 1 leek 1 head of celery 1 bunch of savoury herbs 1 bay-leaf 12 whole peppercorns 4 cloves 1 tablespoonful of salt 2 tablespoonfuls of ketchup 1/2 glass of port wine 3 quarts of water
Instructions Cut up the tails, separating them at the joints; wash them, and put them in a stewpan, with the butter. Cut the vegetables in slices, and add them, with the peppercorns and herbs. Put in 1/2 pint of water, and stir it over a sharp fire till the juices are drawn. Fill up the stewpan with the water, and, when boiling, add the salt. Skim well, and simmer very gently for 4 hours, or until the tails are tender. Take them out, skim and strain the soup, thicken with flour, and flavour with the ketchup and port wine. Put back the tails, simmer for 5 minutes, and serve. Time: 4 1/2 hours. Seasonable in winter. Sufficient for 10 persons.

Oyster Soup
From "The Virginia Housewife", By Mary Randolph, 1836

Wash and drain two quarts of oysters, put them on with three quarts of water, three onions chopped up, two or three slices of lean ham, pepper and salt; boil it till reduced one-half, strain it through a sieve, return the liquid into the pot, put in one quart of fresh oysters, boil it till they are sufficiently done, and thicken the soup with four spoonsful of flour, two gills of rich cream, and the yelks of six new laid eggs beaten well; boil it a few minutes after the thickening is put in. Take care that it does not curdle, and that the flour is not in lumps; serve it up with the last oysters that were put in. If the flavour of thyme be agreeable, you may put in a little, but take care that it does not boil in it long enough to discolour the soup.

Porridge
From "The Practical Housekeeper; A Cyclopedia of Domestic Economy", By Elizabeth Fries Ellet, 1857

When children are delicate, porridge is often preferable to bread and milk. Put two table-spoonfuls of grits or oatmeal in the milk saucepan, which moisten with half a pint of milk; let it boil ten minutes, keeping well stirred, add a small piece of butter and a little sugar, and it is ready for use.

Pot-Au-Feu
From "The Practical Housekeeper; A Cyclopedia of Domestic Economy", By Elizabeth Fries Ellet, 1857

This is by far the most wholesome of all soups. Take three pounds of good rump of beef, of any part free from bone and not too fat; put it into an earthen fire-proof pot, with three quarts of water, one large carrot, two turnips, two leeks, a head of celery, and one burnt onion; season, and let the soup boil slowly, skimming it from time to time, for at least five hours; then strain it through a fine sieve, and pour it over thin slices of bread to serve. The meat and vegetables make a dish which is afterwards served. Thus cooked, the beef becomes tender and juicy, and is excellent cold.

Potato Soup Miagre
From "The Practical Housekeeper; A Cyclopedia of Domestic Economy", By Elizabeth Fries Ellet, 1857

Take some large, mealy potatoes; peel and cut them into small slices with an onion; boil them in three pints of water till tender, and then pulp them through a colander; add a small piece of butter, a little cayenne pepper and salt, and, just before the soup is served, two spoonfuls of good cream. The soup must not be allowed to boil after the cream has been put into it.

Stew Soup of Salt Meat

From: "The Book of Household Management", By Isabella Beeton, Published Originally By S. O. Beeton in 24 Monthly Parts 1859-1861, First Published in a Bound Edition 1861

Any pieces of salt beef or pork, say 2 lbs.; 4 carrots, 4 parsnips, 4 turnips, 4 potatoes, 1 cabbage, 2 oz. of oatmeal or ground rice, seasoning of salt and pepper, 2 quarts of water.
Cut up the meat small, add the water, and let it simmer for 2 3/4 hours. Now add the vegetables, cut in thin small slices; season, and boil for 1 hour. Thicken with the oatmeal, and serve.
Note-If rice is used instead of oatmeal, put it in with the vegetables.

Soupe á La Jardiniere

From "The Great Western Cook Book, or Table Receipts, Adapted to Western Housewifery", By Anna Maria Collins, 1857

Wash a leg of lamb or veal, of moderate size, and put it into four quarts of cold water. Boil it gently, and when the scum rises, take it off carefully. Take of potatoes, carrots, cabbage, onions, tomatoes, and turnips, a tea-cupful of each, chopped fine. Add salt and pepper to your taste. Carrots should be put in first, as they require most time for boiling, and onions last.
This soup must be boiled three hours.

Soupe À La Julienne

From "Directions for Cookery, in its Various Branches" By Eliza Leslie, 1840

Make a gravy soup as in the preceding receipt (Clear Gravy Soup), and strain it before you put in the vegetables. Cut some turnips and carrots into ribands, and some onions and celery into lozenges or long diamond-shaped pieces. Boil them separately. When the vegetables are thoroughly boiled, put them with the soup into the tureen, and then lay gently on the top some small squares of toasted bread without crust; taking care that they do not crumble down and disturb the brightness of the soup, which should be of a clear amber colour.

Tomato Soup
From "The Practical Housekeeper; A Cyclopedia of Domestic Economy", By Elizabeth Fries Ellet, 1857

Stew half a peck of tomatoes slowly an hour and a half in a pint of water; pass them through a tamis; add half a gallon of veal or mutton broth. Pass through a tamis enough stale bread to thicken the soup. Fry twelve onions brown, and strain them the same way. Add them to the soup with a bunch of fine herbs, and seasoning to taste. Boil up well, and serve.

Turnip Soup
From "A New System of Domestic Cookery", By Maria Eliza Ketelby Rundell, 1807

Take off a knuckle of veal all the meat that can be made into cutlets, &c. and set the remainder on to stew with an onion, a bunch of herbs, a blade of mace, and five pints of water; cover it close; and let it do on a slow fire, four or five hours at least. Strain it, and set it by till next day; then take the fat and sediment from it, and simmer it with turnips cut into small dice till tender, seasoning it with salt and pepper. Before serving, rub down half a spoonful of flour with half a pint of good cream, and the size of a walnut of butter. Let a small roll simmer in the soup till wet through, and serve this with it. It should be as thick as middling cream.

Vegetable Soup
From "A New System of Domestic Cookery", By Maria Eliza Ketelby Rundell, 1807

Pare and slice five or six cucumbers; and add to these the inside of as many cos-lettuces, a sprig or two of mint, two or three onions, some pepper and salt, a pint and a half of young peas, and a little parsley. Put these, with half a pound of fresh butter, into a sauce-pan, to stew in their own liquor, near a gentle fire, half an hour; then pour two quarts of boiling-water to the vegetables, and stew them two hours; rub down a little flour into a tea-cupful of water, boil it with the rest fifteen or twenty minutes, and serve it.

Vermicelle Soup

From "The Great Western Cook Book, or Table Receipts, Adapted
to Western Housewifery", By Anna Maria Collins, 1857

Take a nice fowl and a shin of veal, two carrots, a turnip and an onion, a little
salt, and put them into four quarts of water. Boil this three hours. Put into it
two teacups full of vermicelli, and boil it an hour. Before serving, take out the
bones and vegetables.

White Stock (To be Used in the Preparation of White Soups)
From "The Book of Household Management", By Isabella Beeton, 1861

4 lbs. of knuckle of veal, any poultry trimmings, 4 slices of lean ham, 1 carrot, 2
onions, 1 head of celery, 12 white peppercorns, 1 oz. of salt, 1 blade of mace, 1
oz. butter, 4 quarts of water.
Cut up the veal, and put it with the bones and trimmings of poultry, and the
ham, into the stewpan, which has been rubbed with the butter. Moisten with
1/2 a pint of water, and simmer till the gravy begins to flow. Then add the 4
quarts of water and the remainder of the ingredients; simmer for 5 hours. After
skimming and straining it carefully through a very fine hair sieve, it will be
ready for use.
Time-5-1/2 hours.
Note-When stronger stock is desired, double the quantity of veal, or
put in an old fowl. The liquor in which a young turkey has been boiled,
is an excellent addition to all white stock or soups.

Winter Hotch-Potch (Scotch Soup)
From "The Cook's Oracle; and Housekeeper's Manual", By William Kitchiner,
1830

Take the best end of a neck or loin of mutton; cut it into neat chops; cut four
carrots, and as many turnips into slices; put on four quarts of water, with half
the carrots and turnips, and a whole one of each, with a pound of dried green
pease, which must be put to soak the night before; let it boil two hours, then
take out the whole carrot and turnip; bruise and return them; put in the meat,
and the rest of the carrot and turnip, some pepper and salt, and boil slowly
three-quarters of an hour; a short time before serving, add an onion cut small
and a head of celery.

3. MAIN COURSES

Beef

"Times are very hard here — not much to eat and what we have is not good by any means. The bread is very sorry, the beef quite poor, and you may be sure that one becomes worn out on such diet." –Sgt. William Duncan Cole, Co. F, 38th Alabama Infantry, Dec. 15, 1863, Dalton, Georgia. Letter to his wife

A Nice Little Dish of Beef
From "The Virginia Housewife", By Mary Randolph, 1836

Mince cold roast beef, fat and lean, very fine, add chopped onion, pepper, salt, and a little good gravy, fill scollop shells two parts full, and fill them up with potatos mashed smooth with cream, put a bit of butter on the top, and set them in an oven to brown.

Baked Beef
From "Directions for Cookery, in its Various Branches" By Eliza Leslie, 1840

This is a plain family dish, and is never provided for company.
Take a nice but not a fat piece of fresh beef. Wash it, rub it with salt, and place it on a trivet in a deep block tin or iron pan. Pour a little water into the bottom, and put under and round the trivet a sufficiency of pared potatoes, either white or sweet ones. Put it into a hot oven, and let it bake till thoroughly done,

basting it frequently with its own gravy. Then transfer it to a hot dish, and serve up the potatoes in another. Skim the gravy, and send it to table in a boat.

Or you may boil the potatoes, mash them with milk, and put them into the bottom of the pan about half an hour before the meat is done baking. Press down the mashed potatoes hard with the back of a spoon, score them in cross lines over the top, and let them, brown under the meat, serving them up laid round it.

Instead of potatoes, you may put in the bottom of the pan what is called a Yorkshire pudding, to be baked under the meat.

To make this pudding,--stir gradually four table-spoonfuls of flour into a pint of milk, adding a salt-spoon of salt. Beat three eggs very light, and mix them gradually with the milk and flour. See that the batter is not lumpy. Do not put the pudding under the meat at first, as if baked too long it will be hard and solid. After the meat has baked till the pan is quite hot and well greased with the drippings, you may put in the batter; having continued stirring it till the last moment.

If the pudding is so spread over the pan as to be but an inch thick, it will require about two hours baking, and need not be turned. If it is thicker than an inch, you must (after it is brown on the top) loosen it in the pan, by inserting a knife beneath it, and having cut it across into four pieces, turn them all nicely that the other side may be equally done. But this pudding is lighter and better if laid so thin as not to require turning.

When you serve up the beef lay the pieces of pudding round it, to be eaten with the meat.

Veal may be baked in this manner with potatoes or a pudding. Also fresh pork.

A la Mode Beef

From "Miss Beecher's Domestic Receipt Book", By Catharine Esther Beecher, 1850

Take a round of beef, cut it full of holes entirely through it, roll strips of raw salt pork in a seasoning made of thyme, cloves, and pepper and salt, half a teaspoonful of each; then draw these strips through the holes in the beef.

Put some small onions, say half a dozen, with a quarter of a pound of butter into a sauce-pan with two great spoonfuls of milk and stew them till soft, put your beef and these onions in a pot, (you can stew the onions in the pot instead of the sauce-pan if you prefer it,) pour on hot water just enough to cover it, and let it cook slowly four or five hours. Just before taking it up, add a pint of wine, either Port or Claret. The onions can be cooked separately if preferred.

Beef A-La-Daube
From "The Virginia Housewife", By Mary Randolph, 1836

Get a round of beef, lard it well, and put it in a Dutch oven; cut the meat from a shin of beef, or any coarse piece in thin slices, put round the sides and over the top some slices of bacon, salt, pepper, onion, thyme, parsley, cellery tops, or seed pounded, and some carrots cut small, strew the pieces of beef over, cover it with water, let it stew very gently till perfectly done, take out the round, strain the gravy, let it stand to be cold, take off the grease carefully, beat the whites of four eggs, mix a little water with them, put them to the gravy, let it boil till it looks clear, strain it, and when cold, put it over the beef.

Beef à-la-Vingrette
From "A New System of Domestic Cookery", By Maria Eliza Ketelby Rundell, 1807

Cut a slice of underdone boiled beef three inches thick, and a litle fat; stew it in half a pint of water, a glass of white wine, a bunch of sweet herbs, an onion, and a bay-leaf: season it with three cloves pounded, and pepper, till the liquor is nearly wasted away, turning it once. When cold, serve it. Strain off the gravy, and mix it with a little vinegar for sauce.

Beef Olives
From "The Book of Household Management", By Isabella Beeton, 1861

2 lbs. of rump-steak, 1 egg, 1 tablespoonful of minced savoury herbs, pepper and salt to taste, 1 pint of stock, No. 105 (see "Medium Stock" recipe), 2 or 3 slices of bacon, 2 tablespoonfuls of any store sauce, a slight thickening of butter and flour.
Have the steaks cut rather thin, slightly beat them to make them level, cut them into 6 or 7 pieces, brush over with egg, and sprinkle with herbs, which should be very finely minced; season with pepper and salt, and roll up the pieces tightly, and fasten with a small skewer. Put the stock in a stewpan that will exactly hold them, for by being pressed together, they will keep their shape better; lay in the rolls of meat, cover them with the bacon, cut in thin slices, and over that put a piece of paper. Stew them very gently for full 2 hours; for the slower they are done the better. Take them out, remove the skewers, thicken the gravy with butter and flour, and flavour with any store sauce that may be preferred. Give one boil, pour over the meat, and serve.
Time-2 hours.

Brisket of Beef Baked
From "The Virginia Housewife", By Mary Randolph, 1836

Bone a brisket of beef, and make holes in it with a sharp knife about an inch apart, fill them alternately with fat bacon, parsley and oysters, all chopped small and seasoned with pounded cloves and nutmeg, pepper and salt, dredge it well with flour, lay it in a pan with a pint of red wine and a large spoonful of lemon pickle; bake it three hours, take the fat from the gravy and strain it; serve it up garnished with green pickles.

Broiled Rump Steaks with Onion Gravy
From "The Complete Cook", By J. M. Sanderson, 1864

Peel and slice two large onions, put them into a quart stew-pan, with two table-spoonfuls of water; cover the stew-pan close, set it on a slow fire till the water has boiled away, and the onions have got a little browned, then add half a pint of good broth, and boil the onions till they are tender; strain the broth from them, and chop them very fine, and season with mushroom catsup, pepper, and salt; put the onion into it, and let it boil gently for five minutes, pour it into the dish, and lay it over a broiled rump steak. If instead of broth you use good beef gravy, it will be superlative. Stewed cucumber is another agreeable accompaniment to rump steaks.

Bubble and Squeak (New Receipt)
From "The Practical Housekeeper; A Cyclopedia of Domestic Economy", By Elizabeth Fries Ellet, 1857

Cut into pieces, convenient for frying, cold, roast or boiled beef; pepper, salt, and fry them; when done, lay them on a hot drainer, and while the meat is draining from the fat used in frying them, have in readiness a cabbage already boiled in two waters; chop it small, and put it in the frying-pan with some butter, add a little pepper and salt, keep stirring it, that all of it may be equally done. When taken from the fire, sprinkle over the cabbage a very little vinegar, only enough to give it a slight acid taste. Place the cabbage in the centre of the dish; and arrange the slices of meat neatly around it.

To Fry Calf's Feet
From "Directions for Cookery, in its Various Branches", By Eliza Leslie, 1840

Having first boiled them till tender, cut them in two, and (having taken out the large bones) season the feet with pepper and salt, and dredge them well with flour. Strew some chopped parsley or sweet marjoram over them, and fry them of a light brown in lard or butter. Serve them up with parsley-sauce.

Calf's Liver and Bacon
From "The Book of Household Management", By Isabella Beeton, 1861

2 or 3 lbs. of liver, bacon, pepper and salt to taste, a small piece of butter, flour, 2 tablespoonfuls of lemon-juice, 1/4 pint of water.
Cut the liver in thin slices, and cut as many slices of bacon as there are of liver; fry the bacon first, and put that on a hot dish before the fire. Fry the liver in the fat which comes from the bacon, after seasoning it with pepper and salt and dredging over it a very little flour. Turn the liver occasionally to prevent its burning, and when done, lay it round the dish with a piece of bacon between each. Pour away the bacon fat, put in a small piece of butter, dredge in a little flour, add the lemon-juice and water, give one boil, and pour it in the middle of the dish. It may be garnished with slices of cut lemon, or forcemeat balls.
Time-According to the thickness of the slices, from 5 to 10 minutes.

Calf's Liver Aux Fines Herbes & Sauce Piquante
From "The Book of Household Management", By Isabella Beeton, 1861

A calf's liver, flour, a bunch of savoury herbs, including parsley; when liked, 2 minced shalots; 1 teaspoonful of flour, 1 tablespoonful of vinegar, 1 tablespoonful of lemon-juice, pepper and salt to taste, 1/4 pint water.
Procure a calf's liver as white as possible, and cut it into slices of a good and equal shape. Dip them in flour, and fry them of a good colour in a little butter. When they are done, put them on a dish, which keep hot before the fire. Mince the herbs very fine, put them in the frying-pan with a little more butter; add the remaining ingredients, simmer gently until the herbs are done, and pour over the liver.
Time-According to the thickness of the slices, from 5 to 10 minutes.

To Corn Beef In Hot Weather
From "The Virginia Housewife", By Mary Randolph, 1836

Take a piece of thin brisket or plate, cut out the ribs nicely, rub it on both sides well with two large spoonsful of pounded saltpetre; pour on it a gill of molasses and a quart of salt; rub them both in; put it in a vessel just large enough to hold it, but not tight, for the bloody brine must run off as it makes, or the meat will spoil. Let it be well covered, top, bottom and sides, with the molasses and salt. In four days you may boil it, tied up in a cloth with the salt, &c. about it: when done, take the skin off nicely, and serve it up. If you have an ice-house or refrigerator, it will be best to keep it there. A fillet or breast of veal, and a leg or rack of mutton, are excellent done in the same way.

To Boil Corned or Salted Beef
From "Directions for Cookery, in its Various Branches" By Eliza Leslie, 1840

The best piece is the round. You may either boil it whole, or divide it into two, or even three pieces if it is large, taking care that each piece shall have a portion of the fat. Wash it well; and, if very salt, soak it in two waters. Skewer it up tightly and in a good compact shape, wrapping the flap piece firmly round it. Tie it round with broad strong tape, or with a strip of coarse linen. Put it into a large pot, and cover it well with water. It will be found a convenience to lay it on a fish drainer.

Hang it over a moderate fire that it may heat gradually all through. Carefully take off the scum as it rises, and when no more appears, keep the pot closely covered, and let it boil slowly and regularly, with the fire at an equal temperature. Allow three hours and a half to a piece weighing about twelve pounds, and from that to four or five hours in proportion to the size. Turn the meat twice in the pot while it is boiling. Put in some carrots and turnips about two hours after the meat. Many persons boil cabbage in the same pot with the beef, but it is a much nicer way to do the greens in a separate vessel, lest they become saturated with the liquid fat. Cauliflower or brocoli (which are frequent accompaniments to corned beef) should never be boiled with it.

Wash the cabbage in cold water, removing the outside leaves, and cutting the stalk close. Examine all the leaves carefully, lest insects should be lodged among them. If the cabbage is large, divide it into quarters. Put it into a pot of boiling water with a handful of salt, and boil it till the stalk is quite tender. Half an hour will generally be sufficient for a small young cabbage; an hour for a large full-grown one. Drain it well before you dish it. If boiled separately from the meat, have ready some melted butter to eat with it.

Should you find the beef under-done, you may reboil it next day; putting it into boiling-water and letting it simmer for half an hour or more, according to its size.

Cold corned beef will keep very well for some days wrapped in several folds of a thick linen cloth, and set away in a cool dry place.

In carving a round of beef, slice it horizontally and very thin. Do not help any one to the outside pieces, as they are generally too hard and salt. French mustard is very nice with corned beef. [Footnote: French mustard is made of the very best mustard powder, diluted with vinegar, and flavoured with minced tarragon leaves, and a minced clove of garlic; all mixed with a wooden spoon.]

This receipt will apply equally to any piece of corned beef, except that being less solid than the round, they will, in proportion to their weight, require rather less time to boil.

In dishing the meat, remove the wooden skewers and substitute plated or silver ones.

Many persons think it best (and they are most probably right) to stew corned beef rather than to boil it. If you intend to stew it, put no more water in the pot than will barely cover the meat, and keep it gently simmering over a slow fire for four, five, or six hours, according to the size of the piece.

Fillet of Beef Saute
From "The Practical Housekeeper; A Cyclopedia of Domestic Economy", By Elizabeth Fries Ellet, 1857

After having cut the fillet in slices, put two ounces of butter into a clean frying-pan, which set upon the fire, and when melted, lay in the meat, seasoned with a salt-spoonful of salt, and half that quantity of pepper to each piece; turn them over three or four times whilst cooking, and, when done, dress upon your dish, with either anchovy or maitre d'hotel butter.

Forcemeat Balls
From "The Virginia Housewife", By Mary Randolph, 1836

Take half a pound of veal, and half a pound of suet cut fine, and beat in a marble mortar or wooden bowl; add a few sweet herbs shred fine, a little mace pounded fine, a small nutmeg grated, a little lemon peel, some pepper and salt, and the yelks of two eggs; mix them well together, and make them into balls and long pieces--then roll them in flour, and fry them brown. If they are for the use of white sauce, do not fry them, but put them in a sauce-pan of hot water and let them boil a few minutes.

A Fricandeau of Beef
From "A New System of Domestic Cookery", By
Maria Eliza Ketelby Rundell, 1807

Take a nice bit of lean beef; lard it with bacon seasoned with pepper, salt, cloves, mace, and allspice. Put it into a stew-pan with a pint of broth, a glass of white wine, a bundle of parsley, all sorts of sweet herbs, a clove of garlick, a shalot or two, four cloves, pepper, and salt. When the meat is become tender, cover it close: skim the sauce well, and strain it: set it on the fire, and let it boil till it is reduced to a glaze. Glaze the larded side with this, and serve the meat on sorrel-sauce.

To Fry Beef Steaks
From "Directions for Cookery, in its Various Branches" By Eliza Leslie, 1840

Beef-steaks for frying should be cut thinner than for broiling. Take them from the ribs or sirloin, and remove the bone. Beat them to make them tender. Season them with salt and pepper.

Put some fresh butter, or nice beef-dripping into a frying pan, and hold it over a clear bright fire till it boils and has done hissing. Then put in the steaks, and (if you like them) some sliced onions. Fry them about a quarter of an hour, turning them frequently. Steaks, when fried, should be thoroughly done. After they are browned, cover them with a large plate to keep in the juices, Have ready a hot dish, and when they are done, take out the steaks and onions and lay them in it with another dish on the top, to keep them hot while you give the gravy in the pan another boil up over the fire. You may add to it a spoonful of mushroom catchup. Pour the gravy over the steakes, and send them to table as hot as possible.

Mutton chops may be fried in this manner.

Broiled Ox-Tail (an Entrée)
From "The Book of Household Management", By Isabella Beeton, 1861

2 tails, 1-1/2 pint of stock, No. 105 (see recipe for "Medium Stock"), salt and cayenne to taste, bread crumbs, 1 egg.

Joint and cut up the tails into convenient-sized pieces, and put them into a stewpan, with the stock, cayenne, and salt, and, if liked very savoury, a bunch of sweet herbs. Let them simmer gently for about 2-1/2 hours; then take them out, drain them, and let them cool.

Beat an egg upon a plate; dip in each piece of tail, and, afterwards, throw them into a dish of bread crumbs; broil them over a clear fire, until of a brownish colour on both sides, and serve with a good gravy, or any sauce that may be preferred.

Time-About 2-1/2 hours.

Ox Tails A La Jardiniere

From "The Practical Housekeeper; A Cyclopedia of Domestic Economy", By
Elizabeth Fries Ellet, 1857

Cut and cook two ox tails as directed for soup, but just before they are done,
skim well, and take out the pieces of tails, which put upon a dish; then in
another stewpan put two ounces of butter, to which, when melted, add three
ounces of flour, stirring it over the fire until forming a brownish roux
(thickening), then mix by degrees two quarts of the stock the tails were boiled
in, and boil all together ten minutes; then put in the tails, with one carrot and
two turnips (cut into small dice, or any other shape, with a vegetable cutter),
and about thirty button onions; let the whole simmer very gently upon the
corner of the fire, keeping it well skimmed, until the vegetables are tender, and
the sauce sufficiently thick to adhere to the back of the spoon; dress the meat
upon a dish, re-duce the sauce, which pour over and serve.

To Roast Beef

From "Directions for Cookery, in its Various Branches" By Eliza Leslie, 1840

The fire should be prepared at least half an hour before the beef is put down,
and it should be large, steady, clear, and bright, with plenty of fine hot coals at
the bottom.

The best apparatus for the purpose is the well-known roaster frequently called a
tin-kitchen.

Wash the meat in cold water, and then wipe it dry, and rub it with salt. Take
care not to run the spit through the best parts of it. It is customary with some
cooks to tie blank paper over the fat, to prevent it from melting and wasting too
fast.

Put it evenly into the roaster, and do not set it too near the fire, lest the outside
of the meat should be burned before the inside is heated.

Put some nice beef-dripping or some lard into the pan or bottom of the roaster,
and as soon as it melts begin to baste the beef with it; taking up the liquid with
a long spoon, and pouring it over the meat so as to let it trickle down again,
into the pan. Repeat this frequently while it is roasting; after a while you can
baste it with its own fat. Turn the spit often, so that the meat may be equally
done on all sides.

Once or twice draw back the roaster, and improve the fire by clearing away the
ashes, bringing forward the hot coals, and putting on fresh fuel at the back.
Should a coal fall into the dripping-pan take it out immediately. An allowance
of about twenty minutes to each pound of meat is the time commonly given for
roasting; but this rule, like most others, admits of exceptions according to
circumstances. Also, some persons like their meat very much done; others
prefer it rare, as it is called. In summer, meat will roast in a shorter time than in

winter.

When the beef is nearly done, and the steam draws towards the fire, remove the paper that has covered the fat part, sprinkle on a little salt, and having basted the meat well with the dripping, pour off nicely (through the spout of the roaster) all the liquid fat from the top of the gravy.

Lastly, dredge the meat very lightly with a little flour, and baste it with fresh butter. This will give it a delicate froth. To the gravy that is now running from the meat add nothing but a tea-cup of boiling water. Skim it, and send it to table in a boat. Serve up with the beef in a small deep plate, scraped horseradish moistened with vinegar.

Fat meat requires more roasting than lean, and meat that has been frozen will take nearly double the usual time.

Basting the meat continually with flour and water is a bad practice, as it gives it a coddled parboiled appearance, and diminishes the flavour.

These directions for roasting beef will apply equally to mutton.

Pickles are generally eaten with roast beef. French mustard is an excellent condiment for it. In carving begin by cutting a slice from the side.

Roast Beef Heart

From "Directions for Cookery, in its Various Branches", By Eliza Leslie, 1840

Cut open the heart, and (having removed the ventricles) soak it in cold water to free it from the blood, Parboil it about ten minutes. Prepare a force-meat of grated bread crumbs, butter or minced suet, sweet marjoram and parsley chopped fine, a little grated lemon-peel, nutmeg, pepper, and salt to your taste, and some yolk of egg to bind the ingredients. Stuff the heart with the force-meat, and secure the opening by tying a string around it. Put it on a spit, and roast it till it is tender throughout. Add to the gravy a piece of butter rolled in flour, and a glass of red wine. Serve up the heart very hot in a covered dish. It chills immediately. Eat currant jelly with it. Boiled beef's heart is frequently used in mince pies.

A Round of Beef Stewed Brown

From "The Lady's Receipt-Book; a Useful Companion for Large or Small Families", By Eliza Leslie, 1847

Take a round of fresh beef; the larger it is the more tender it will be: a small round is always, comparatively, hard and tough. Remove the fat; with a sharp knife make deep cuts or incisions all over the meat, and stuff into them a seasoning of finely minced onions, mixed with powdered mace, nutmeg, and a little pepper and salt. Then go all over the meat with the drippings or cold gravy

34

of roast beef, and dredge it slightly with flour. Have ready an iron dutch-oven and its lid, well heated by standing up both lid and oven before the fire. Then put the meat into the oven, cover it, and let it brown on all sides. Have ready, cut into small pieces, two turnips; four carrots; four oyster plants or salsify; three stalks of celery; two small onions; and two large tomatoes, or a large table-spoonful of tomato catchup. After the meat is browned, raise it up, and place the vegetables underneath it, and pour on three half-pints of water, or more if the round is very large. Let it cook slowly in the oven, with a regular fire, for several hours, till it is entirely done all through; taking care to keep it closely covered. After the meat is taken out, place it on a large hot dish, with the vegetables round it. Cover it, and keep it hot while you thicken the gravy with a small tea-spoonful of flour, and the beaten yolk of an egg. Simmer this gravy a few minutes, then put it into a sauce-boat, and serve it up with the meat. What is left will be very good stewed over again the next day, with fresh vegetables; letting the meat cook no longer than till the vegetables are sufficiently done. Observe this rule with all stews, soups, hashes, &c., when cooked the second time.

Spiced Beef

From "The Practical Housekeeper; A Cyclopedia of Domestic Economy", By Elizabeth Fries Ellet, 1857

A joint from the round, rump, or flank, from ten to fourteen pounds, is the usual weight of the piece intended to be thus dressed. Make a mixture of the following ingredients, and let them be well amalgamated; pound finely as much mace as will quite fill a teaspoon, grind a nutmeg to powder, and add it, also two spoonfuls of cloves, one-fourth of that quantity of cayenne pepper, and half a pound of coarse brown sugar; rub the beef well with this mixture for three days, turning it each day once; add three-quarters of a pound of salt, and then continue rubbing well each day, for ten days more; at the expiration of that time dip it into some cold clear spring water, twice or thrice, secure it into a handsome shape, put it into a stewpan with a quart of good beef broth, let it come to a boil, skim as the scum rises, and as soon as it boils put in three carrots cut in slices, a bundle of sweet herbs, a little parsley, and an onion; stew gently four hours.

If it is intended to serve this dish cold, let it remain until it is cool in the liquor in which it was boiled, but take the precaution to put the meat into a clean pan, and pour the liquor over it.

Staffordshire Beef-Steaks
From "A New System of Domestic Cookery", By
Maria Eliza Ketelby Rundell, 1807

Beat them a little with a rolling-pin, flour and season, then fry with sliced onion
of a fine light brown; lay the steaks into a stew-pan, and pour as much boiling
water over them as will serve for sauce: stew them very gently half an hour, and
add a spoonful of ketchup, or walnut-liquor, before you serve.

To Stew A Beef's Heart
From "Directions for Cookery, in its Various Branches" By Eliza Leslie, 1840

Clean the heart, and cut it lengthways into large pieces. Put them into a pot
with a little salt and pepper, and cover them with cold water. Parboil them for a
quarter of an hour, carefully skimming off the blood that rises to the top. Then
take them out, cut them, into mouthfuls, and having strained the liquid, return
them to it, adding a head or two of chopped celery, a few sliced onions, a dozen
potatoes pared and quartered, and a piece of butter rolled in flour. Season with
whole pepper, and a few cloves if you like. Let it stew slowly till all the pieces of
heart and the vegetables are quite tender.
You may stew a beef's kidney in the same manner.
The heart and liver of a calf make a good dish cooked as above.

Stewed Rump of Beef
From "The Book of Household Management", By Isabella Beeton, 1861

1/2 rump of beef, sufficient stock to cover it (No. 105, see "Medium Stock"
recipe), 4 tablespoonfuls of vinegar, 2 tablespoonfuls of ketchup, 1 large bunch
of savoury herbs, 2 onions, 12 cloves, pepper and salt to taste, thickening of
butter and flour, 1 glass of port wine.
Cut out the bone, sprinkle the meat with a little cayenne (this must be sparingly
used), and bind and tie it firmly up with tape; put it into a stewpan with
sufficient stock to cover it, and add vinegar, ketchup, herbs, onions, cloves, and
seasoning in the above proportion, and simmer very gently for 4 or 5 hours, or
until the meat is perfectly tender, which may be ascertained by piercing it with
a thin skewer. When done, remove the tape, lay it into a deep dish, which keep
hot; strain and skim the gravy, thicken it with butter and flour, add a glass of
port wine and any flavouring to make the gravy rich and palatable; let it boil up,
pour over the meat, and serve. This dish may be very much enriched by
garnishing with forcemeat balls, or filling up the space whence the bone is

taken with a good forcemeat; sliced carrots, turnips, and onions boiled with the meat, are also a great improvement, and, where expense is not objected to, it may be glazed. This, however, is not necessary where a good gravy is poured round and over the meat.

Time-1/2 rump stewed gently from 4 to 5 hours.

To Stew Smoked Beef
From "The Lady's Receipt-Book; a Useful Companion for Large or Small Families", By Eliza Leslie, 1847

The dried beef, for this purpose, must be fresh and of the very best quality. Cut it (or rather shave it) into very thin, small slices, with as little fat as possible. Put the beef into a skillet, and fill up with boiling water. Cover it, and let it soak or steep till the water is cold. Then drain off that water, and pour on some more, but merely enough to cover the chipped beef, which you may season with a little pepper. Set it over the fire, and (keeping on the cover) let it stew for a quarter of an hour. Then roll a few bits of butter in a little flour, and add it to the beef, with the yolk of one or two beaten eggs. Let it stew five minutes longer. Take it up on a hot dish, and send it to the breakfast or tea-table. Cold ham may be sliced thin, and stewed in the same manner.

Dried venison also.

To Stuff and Roast a Calf's Liver
From "The Virginia Housewife", By Mary Randolph, 1836

Take a fresh calf's liver, and having made a hole in it with a large knife run in lengthways, but not quite through, have ready a forced meat, or stuffing made of part of the liver parboiled, fat of bacon minced very fine, and sweet herbs powdered; add to these some grated bread and spice finely powdered, with pepper and salt. With this stuffing fill the hole in the liver, which must be larded with fat bacon, and then roasted, flouring it well, and basting with butter till it is enough. This is to be served up hot, with gravy sauce having a little wine in it.

Veal Chops
From "The Virginia Housewife", By Mary Randolph, 1836

Take the best end of a rack of veal, cut it in chops, with one bone in each, leave the small end of the bone bare two inches, beat them flat, and prepare them with eggs and crumbs, as the cutlets, butter some half-sheets of white paper, wrap one round each chop, skewer it well, leaving the bare bone out, broil them till done, and take care the paper does not burn; have nice white sauce in a boat.

Veal Cutlets

From "The Virginia Housewife", By Mary Randolph, 1836

Cut them from the fillet, put them in a stew pan with a piece of nice pork, a clove of garlic, a bundle of thyme and parsley, pepper and salt, cover them with water and let them stew ten or fifteen minutes, lay them on a dish, and when cold cover them well with the crumb of stale bread finely grated, mixed with the leaves of parsley chopped very small, some pepper, salt and grated nutmeg; press these on the veal with a knife, and when a little dried, turn it and do the same to the other side; put a good quantity of lard in a pan, when it boils lay the cutlets in carefully that the crumbs may not fall; fry them a little brown, lay them on a strainer to drain off the grease, do the same with the crumbs that have fallen in the pan: while this is doing, simmer the water they were boiled in to half a pint, strain it and thicken with four ounces of butter and a little browned flour; add a gill of wine and one of mushroom catsup, put in the cutlets and crumbs, and stew till tender; add forcemeat balls.

Pork

"Our "mess" is composed of six good fellows, among whom is "Dan," the "baby of the regiment," or the "infant" as some are pleased to call him. He is about six feet and three inches in height, and weighs about three hundred pounds. He has the peculiar faculty of purchasing chicken and pigs without money, looking upon such locomotive property, when brought within his reach, as the gifts of providence. This morning he accidentally, as he says, let an axe slip from his hand, and struck a fat pig on the head. Fresh pork was on the bill of fare for dinner, and the neighbors wondered where the soldiers got so much pork. But the "mess" will pay for the pig, and "Dan" will learn, before we meet the Yankees, that one of the duties of a good soldier is to respect, and protect private property, even though it be in the form of a trespassing pig."-Corporal John G. Law, "Hickory Rifles", May 6, 1861, at Randolph, Tennessee. From his diary.

To Barbeque Shote
From "The Virginia Housewife", By Mary Randolph, 1836

This is the name given in the southern states to a fat young hog, which, when the head and feet are taken off, and it is cut into four quarters, will weigh six pounds per quarter. Take a fore-quarter, make several incisions between the ribs, and stuff it with rich forcemeat; put it in a pan with a pint of water, two cloves of garlic, pepper, salt, two gills of red wine, and two of mushroom catsup, bake it, and thicken the gravy with batter and brown flour; it must be jointed, and the ribs cut across before it is cooked; or it cannot be carved well; lay it in the dish with the ribs uppermost; if it be not sufficiently brown, add a little burnt sugar to the gravy, garnish with balls.

Biscuit Sandwiches
From "The Lady's Receipt-Book; a Useful Companion for Large or Small Families", By Eliza Leslie, 1847

Split some light soft milk biscuits (or small French rolls) and butter them. Cover the lower half thickly with grated ham, or smoked tongue; pressing it down upon the butter. Then put on the upper half or lid; pressing that on, to make it stick. Pile the biscuits handsomely in a pyramid upon a flat dish, and place among them, at regular distances, green sprigs of pepper-grass, corn-salad, water-cresses, or curled parsley, allowing four or six to each biscuit. Put in the sprigs between the upper and lower halves of the biscuits, so that they may stick out at the edges.
To make more space for the grated ham, you may scoop out a little of the inside of the upper-half of each milk biscuit or roll. They should be fresh, of that day's baking.
This is a nice supper-dish.

Bologna Sausages
From "Directions for Cookery, in its Various Branches" By Eliza Leslie, 1840

Take ten pounds of beef, and four pounds of pork; two-thirds of the meat should be lean, and only one third fat. Chop it very fine, and mix it well together. Then season it with six ounces of fine salt, one ounce of black pepper, half an ounce of cayenne, one table-spoonful of powdered cloves; and one clove or garlic minced very fine.
Have ready some large skins nicely cleaned and prepared, (they

should be beef-skins,) and wash them in salt and vinegar. Fill them with the above mixture, and secure the ends by tying them with packthread or fine twine. Make a brine of salt and water strong enough to bear up an egg. Put the sausages into it, and' let them lie for three weeks, turning them daily. Then take them out, wipe them dry, hang them up and smoke them. Before you put them away rub them all over with, sweet oil, Keep them in ashes. That of vine-twigs is best for them.

You may fry them or not before you eat them.

Bologna Sausages

From "The Virginia Housewife" By Mrs. Mary Randolph, 1836

Take one pound of bacon fat and lean, one ditto veal, do., pork, do., suet, chop all fine, season highly: fill the skins, prick and boil them an hour, and hang them to dry grated bread or boiled rice may be added: clean the skins with salt and vinegar.

I should think all of the meat should be ground up. "Fill the skins" refers to stuffing the sausage casing. Also note that "do" means "ditto".

Roasted or Baked Ham

From "The Great Western Cook Book, or Table Receipts, Adapted to Western Housewifery", By Anna Maria Collins, 1857

Parboil a ham, if very salt, change the water, draw off the skin, set it before the fire, or on a stove, for at least half an hour, let the fire be very moderate, then set it off, baste it with a small lump of butter, grate a stale cracker thickly over it, sprinkle it with wine, or a little sweetened vinegar, put it back, let it roast slowly for an hour, and then serve it with sauce.

Champagne wine sauce is very fashionable with roasted or baked ham.

To Roast A Ham

From "Directions for Cookery, in its Various Branches" By Eliza

Leslie, 1840

Take a very fine ham (a Westphalia one if you can procure it) and soak it in lukewarm water for a day or two, changing the water frequently. The day before you intend cooking it, take the ham out of the water, and (having removed the skin) trim it nicely, and pour over it a bottle of Madeira or sherry. Let it steep till next morning, frequently during the day washing the wine over it. Put it on the spit in time to allow at least six hours for slowly roasting it. Baste it continually with hot water. When it is done, dredge it all over with fine bread-raspings shaken on through the top of the dredging box; and set it before the fire to brown.

For gravy, take the wine in which the ham was steeped, and add to it the essence or juice which flowed from the meat when taken from the spit. Squeeze in the juice of two lemons. Put it into a sauce-pan, and boil and skim it. Send it to table in a boat. Cover the shank of the ham (which should have been sawed short) with bunches of double parsley, and ornament it with a cluster of flowers cut out with a penknife from raw carrots, beets, and turnips; and made to imitate marygolds, and red and white roses.

"The next house we got to we bought a ham, a peck of meal, a peck of sweet potatoes and some turnips."- Pvt. Louis Leon, Company C, First North Carolina Regiment, February 6, 1863, from his diary.

Fried Liver and Bacon, Etc.
From "The Practical Housekeeper; A Cyclopedia of Domestic Economy", By Elizabeth Fries Ellet, 1857

Cut the liver rather thin, say about half an inch thick, but first soak it in warm water about one hour; chop a quantity of parsley, season it with pepper, and lay it thick upon the liver; cut slices of bacon, and fry both together, but put the bacon first into the pan; add a little lemon-pickle to the gravy made by pouring the fat out of the pan, flour-ing, and adding boiling water, or:--Out the liver in handsome pieces, lard them very nicely, and chop some parsley and spread it over the surface with a little pepper and salt; put a small piece of butter well mixed with flour in the bottom of a stewpan, and put in the liver, and allow it to stew gently in its own juices until it is done enough.

Ham Sandwiches
From "Directions for Cookery, in its Various Branches", By Eliza Leslie, 1840

Cut some thin slices of bread very neatly, having slightly buttered them; and, if you choose, spread on a very little mustard. Have ready some very thin slices of cold boiled ham, and lay one between two slices of bread. You may either roll them up, or lay them flat on the plates. They are used at supper, or at luncheon. You may substitute for the ham, cold smoked tongue, shred or grated.

Liver Puddings
From "Directions for Cookery, in its Various Branches" By Eliza Leslie, 1840

Boil some pigs' livers. When cold, mince them, and season them with pepper, salt, and some sage and sweet marjoram rubbed fine. You may add some powdered cloves. Have ready some large skins nicely cleaned, and fill them with the mixture, tying up the ends securely. Prick them with a fork to prevent their bursting; put them into hot water, and boil them slowly for about an hour. They will require no farther cooking before you eat them. Keep them in stone jars closely covered. They are eaten cold at breakfast or supper, cut into slices an inch thick or more; or they may be cut into large pieces, and broiled or fried.

Pig's Liver (a Savoury and Economical Dish)
From "The Book of Household Management", By Isabella Beeton, 1861

The liver and lights of a pig, 6 or 7 slices of bacon, potatoes, 1 large bunch of parsley, 2 onions, 2 sage-leaves, pepper and salt to taste, a little broth or water.
Slice the liver and lights, and wash these perfectly clean, and parboil the potatoes; mince the parsley and sage, and chop the onion rather small. Put the meat, potatoes, and bacon into a deep tin dish, in alternate layers, with a sprinkling of the herbs, and a seasoning of pepper and salt between each; pour on a little water or broth, and bake in a moderately-heated oven for 2 hours.

Pig's Feet and Ears Fricasseed

From "A New System of Domestic
Cookery", By Maria Eliza Ketelby Rundell,
1807

Put no vinegar into the pickle, if to be dressed with cream. Cut the
feet and ears into neat bits, and boil them in a little milk; then pour
that from them, and simmer in a little veal-broth, with a bit of
onion, mace, and lemon-peel. Before you serve, add a little cream,
flour, butter, and salt.

To Roast A Pig

From "The Virginia Housewife", By Mary Randolph, 1836

The pig must be very fat, nicely cleaned, and not too large to lie in
the dish; chop the liver fine and mix it with crumbs of bread,
chopped onion and parsley, with pepper and salt, make it into a
paste with butter and an egg, stuff the body well with it, and sew it
up, spit it, and have a clear fire to roast it; baste with salt and water
at first, then rub it frequently with a lump of lard wrapped in a piece
of clean linen; this will make it much more crisp than basting it
from the dripping pan. When the pig is done, take off the head,
separate the face from the chop, cut both in two and take off the
ears, take out the stuffing, split the pig in two parts lengthways, lay
it in the dish with the head, ears, and feet, which have been cut off,
placed on each side, put the stuffing in a bowl with a glass of wine,
and as much dripping as will make it sufficiently liquid, put some of
it under the pig, and serve the rest in a boat.

Pork Apple Pie

From "The Great Western Cookbook" By A. M. Collins,
1851

Make your crust in the usual way; spread it over a large, deep plate;

cut some slices of fat pork, very thin, also some slices of apples; place a layer of apples, and then of pork, with a very little allspice, and pepper, and sugar between--three or four layers of each--with crust over the top. Bake one hour.

Pork Cheese

From "Directions for Cookery, in its Various Branches" By Eliza Leslie, 1840

Take the heads, tongues, and feet of young fresh pork, or any other pieces that are convenient. Having removed the skin, boil them till all the meat is quite tender, and can be easily stripped from the bones. Then chop it small, and season it with salt and black pepper to your taste, and if you choose, some beaten cloves. Add sage-leaves and sweet marjoram, minced fine, or rubbed to powder. Mix the whole very well together with your hands. Put it into deep pans, with straight sides, (the shape of a cheese,) press it down hard and closely with a plate that will fit the pan; putting the under side of the plate next to the meat, and placing a heavy weight on it. In two or three days it will be fit for use, and you may turn it out of the pan. Send it to table cut in slices, and use mustard and vinegar with it. It is generally eaten at supper or breakfast.

Pork Chops

From "The Great Western Cookbook" By A. M. Collins, 1851

Cut them about half an inch thick, trim them neatly, beat them flat, put them into a stewpan with a bit of butter or lard. Let them have one fry; then beat two eggs with a little salt, and add to them some sage and onion, chopped fine; dip the chops in, one at a time, then sprinkle them with bread-crumbs, or flour, and fry them in hot lard till brown.

Pork Chops

From "The Practical Housekeeper; A Cyclopedia of Domestic Economy", By Elizabeth Fries Ellet, 1857

Perhaps few things of a simple nature, and served in a plain way, are better than a hot pork chop, cut about half an inch thick, trimmed neatly, and broiled upon the gridiron.

or:--Marinade the cutlets four hours in oil with an onion in slices, parsley, bay-leaf, pepper, and salt; fry them in the marinade; serve with tomato sauce.

Pork Cutlets
From "The Practical Housekeeper; A Cyclopedia of Domestic Economy", By Elizabeth Fries Ellet, 1857

Cut them from a small delicate loin of pork, bone, and trim them neatly, fry them a light brown, put into a small stewpan a little vinegar, and eschalot chopped very finely, two table-spoonfuls of tomato sauce, and sufficient brown gravy to make it tasty; stew the cutlets in the sauce five minutes, and send them to table dished handsomely; if the cutlets are broiled they may be dipped in yolk of egg and bread-crumbs, and broiled over a clear fire, and served with tomato sauce, or sauce Robert.

Pork Olives
From "The Lady's Receipt-Book; a Useful Companion for Large or Small Families", By Eliza Leslie, 1847

Cut slices from a fillet or leg of cold fresh pork. Make a force-meat in the usual manner, only substituting for sweet herbs some sage-leaves chopped fine. When the slices are covered with the force-meat, and rolled up and tied round, stew them slowly either in cold gravy left of the pork, or in fresh lard. Drain them well before they go to table. Serve them up on a bed of mashed turnips or potatoes, or of mashed sweet potatoes, if in season.

Pork Pies (Warwickshire Recipe)
From "The Book of Household Management", By Isabella Beeton, 1861

For the crust, 5 lbs. of lard to 14 lbs. of flour, milk, and water. For filling the pies, to every 3 lbs. of meat allow 1 oz. of salt, 2-1/4 oz. of pepper, a small quantity of cayenne, 1 pint of water.

Rub into the flour a portion of the lard; the remainder put with sufficient milk and water to mix the crust, and boil this gently for 1/4 hour. Pour it boiling on the flour, and knead and beat it till perfectly smooth. Now raise the crust in either a round or oval form, cut up the pork into pieces the size of a nut, season it in the above proportion, and press it compactly into the pie, in alternate layers of fat and lean, and pour in a small quantity of water; lay on the lid, cut the edges smoothly round, and pinch them together. Bake in a brick oven, which should be slow, as the meat is very solid. Very frequently, the inexperienced cook finds much difficulty in raising the crust. She should bear in mind that it must not be allowed to get cold, or it will fall immediately: to prevent this, the operation should be performed as near the fire as possible. As considerable dexterity and expertness are necessary to raise the crust with the hand only, a glass bottle or small jar may be placed in the middle of the paste, and the crust moulded on this; but be particular that it is kept warm the whole time.

Pork Steaks
From "A New System of Domestic Cookery", By
Maria Eliza Ketelby Rundell, 1807

Cut them from a loin or neck, and of middling thickness; pepper and broil them, turning them often; when nearly done, put on salt, rub a bit of butter over, and serve the moment they are taken off the fire, a few at a time.

To Roast A Spare Rib
From "The Great Western Cook Book, or Table Receipts, Adapted
to Western Housewifery", By Anna Maria Collins, 1857

Rub your ribs with salt, pepper, and sage, set the bone side next the fire, bake very slowly, put a lump of butter and some water in a dripping pan, dredge on a little flour, and baste it frequently; when it is pretty well done on that side, turn it around, and so continue until it is done; it will take two hours, at least, to roast thoroughly, and is very fine when well done.

Roast Pork
From "A Plain Cookery Book for the Working Classes", By Charles Elme
Francatelli, 1852

Leg of pork, 6 onions, 12 sage leaves, 6 ounces of bread, potatoes, butter, pepper, salt
Let us suppose, or rather hope, that you may sometimes have a leg of pork to cook for your dinner; it will eat all the better if it is scored all over by cutting the rind, or rather slitting it crosswise, at short distances, with the point of a sharp knife; it is to be well sprinkled all over with salt, and allowed to absorb the seasoning during some hours previously to its being cooked. Prepare some

stuffing as follows: Chop the onions and sage leaves fine, fry these with a bit of butter, pepper, and salt, for five minutes; then add the bread soaked in water; stir all together on the fire for five minutes, and use this stuffing to fill up a hole or pocket, which you will make by running the point of a knife down between the rind and the flesh of the joint of pork; secure this by sewing it up, or else fasten it securely in with a small wooden skewer or twig. The joint of pork, so far prepared, must then be placed upon a trivet in a baking-dish containing plenty of peeled potatoes, and, if possible, a few apples for the children; add half a pint of water, pepper and salt, and if the joint happens to be a leg, it will require about two hours to bake it.

A Sea Pie
From "The Virginia Housewife", By Mary Randolph, 1836

Lay at the bottom of a small Dutch oven some slices of boiled pork or salt beef, then potatos and onions cut in slices, salt, pepper, thyme and parsley shred fine, some crackers soaked, and a layer of fowls cut up, or slices of veal; cover them with a paste not too rich, put another layer of each article, and cover them with paste until the oven is full; put a little butter between each layer, pour in water till it reaches the top crust, to which you must add wine, catsup of any kind you please, and some pounded cloves; let it stew until there is just gravy enough left; serve it in a deep dish and pour the gravy on.

To Make Paste for the Pie
Pour half a pound of butter or dripping, boiling hot, into a quart of flour, add as much water as will make it a paste, work it and roll it well before you use it. It is quite a savoury paste.

Souse
From "The Practical Housekeeper; A Cyclopedia of Domestic Economy", By Elizabeth Fries Ellet, 1857

Take pigs' ears and feet, clean them thoroughly, then soak them in salt and water, for several days. Boil them tender and split them, they are then good fried. If you wish to souse them when cold, turn boiling vinegar on them, spice with peppercorns and mace. Cloves improve the taste, but turn them a dark color. Add a little salt They will keep good pickled five or six weeks. Fry them in lard.

Boiled Tongue
From "The Book of Household Management", By Isabella Beeton, 1861

1 tongue, a bunch of savoury herbs, water.

In choosing a tongue, ascertain how long it has been dried or pickled, and select one with a smooth skin, which denotes its being young and tender. If a dried one, and rather hard, soak it at least for 12 hours previous to cooking it; if, however, it is fresh from the pickle, 2 or 3 hours will be sufficient for it to remain in sock. Put the tongue in a stewpan with plenty of cold water and a bunch of savoury herbs; let it gradually come to a boil, skim well and simmer very gently until tender. Peel off the skin, garnish with tufts of cauliflowers or Brussels sprouts, and serve. Boiled tongue is frequently sent to table with boiled poultry, instead of ham, and is, by many persons, preferred. If to serve cold, peel it, fasten it down to a piece of board by sticking a fork through the root, and another through the top, to straighten it. When cold, glaze it, and put a paper ruche round the root, and garnish with tufts of parsley.

Time-A large smoked tongue, 4 to 4-1/2 hours; a small one, 2-1/2 to 3 hours. A large unsmoked tongue, 3 to 3-1/2 hours; a small one, 2 to 2-1/2 hours.

Chicken and Fowl

"Fetch some 15teen pounds of flour and some dried fruit and some butter and some chickens and I will pay for the flour for I have to pay one dollar for one pound here and am glad to get it at that for we only get enough for two little snacks a day and we eat it at one time." - James Andrew James, T. B. Ferguson's (South Carolina) Battery, Camp near Dalton, Georgia, January 18, 1864. Letter to his father.

Braised Chicken
From "The Great Western Cook Book, or Table Receipts, Adapted to Western Housewifery", By Anna Maria Collins, 1857

If not convenient to roast, put a little bacon in a stewpan, then a chicken, an onion, half a carrot, some celery, two cloves, one table-spoonful of salt, a little pepper, and a quart of water; let it simmer till tender. After draining it well, dish up, take the string off, and pour over it any sauce you like. A most excellent dish.

Braised Turkey
From "The Great Western Cook Book, or Table Receipts, Adapted to Western Housewifery", By Anna Maria Collins, 1857

Take two carrots, one onion, and one turnip, cut them in thin slices, with a little celery and parsley; lay three sheets of paper on the table, on these spread your vegetables, and pour over them two or three table-spoonsful of oil. Your turkey must be trussed; cover the breast with thin slices of bacon, and lay the back of the bird on the vegetables; a few slices of lemon on the breast to keep it white; tie the paper round with string, then put some paper over the breast and legs also, to keep them from burning. Roast it three hours, at a pretty good distance from the fire.

Broiled Chickens

From "Directions for Cookery, in its Various Branches" By Eliza Leslie, 1840

Split a pair of chickens down the back, and beat them flat, Wipe the inside, season them with pepper and salt, and let them, lie while you prepare some beaten yolk of egg and grated bread-crumbs. Wash the outside of the chickens all over with the egg, and then strew on the bread-crumbs. Have ready a hot gridiron over a bed of bright coals. Lay the chickens on it with the inside downwards, or next the fire. Broil them about three quarters of an hour, keeping them covered with a plate. Just before you take them up, lay some small pieces of butter on them.

In preparing chickens for broiling, you may parboil them about ten minutes, to ensure their being sufficiently cooked; as it is difficult to broil the thick parts thoroughly without burning the rest.

Broiled Fowl and Mushroom Sauce

From "The Book of Household Management", By Isabella Beeton, 1861

A large fowl, seasoning, to taste, of pepper and salt, 2 handfuls of button mushrooms, 1 slice of lean ham, 3/4 pint of thickened gravy, 1 teaspoonful of lemon-juice, 1/2 teaspoonful of pounded sugar.

Cut the fowl into quarters, roast it until three-parts done, and keep it well basted whilst at the fire. Take the fowl up, broil it for a few minutes over a clear fire, and season it with pepper and salt. Have ready some mushroom sauce made in the following manner. Put the mushrooms into a stewpan with a small piece of butter, the ham, a seasoning of pepper and salt, and the gravy; simmer these gently for ½ hour, add the lemon-juice and sugar, dish the fowl, and pour the sauce round them.

Time-To roast the fowl, 35 minutes; to broil it, 10 to 15 minutes.

Capon (Cornish Game Hen)

From "A Poetical Cook-Book", By Maria J. Moss 1864

Take a quart of white wine, season the capon with salt, cloves, and whole pepper, a few shallots, and then put the capon in an earthen pan; you must take care it has not room to shake; it must be covered close, and done over a slow charcoal fire.

Chicken Currie
From "A New System of Domestic Cookery", By Maria Eliza
Ketelby Rundell, 1807

Cut up the chickens raw, slice onions, and fry both in butter with great care, of a fine light brown; or if you use chickens that have been dressed, fry only the onions. Lay the joints, cut into two or three pieces each, into a stew-pan; with a veal or mutton gravy, and a clove or two of garlick. Simmer till the chicken is quite tender. Half an hour before you serve it, rub smooth a spoonful or two of currie-powder (see following recipe), a spoonful of flour, and an ounce of butter; and add this, with four large spoonfuls of cream, to the stew. Salt to your taste. When serving, squeeze in a little lemon.
Slices of under-done veal, or rabbit, turkey, &c. make excellent currie.

To Prepare Curry Powder
From "Miss Beecher's Domestic Receipt Book", By Catharine
Esther Beecher, 1850

One ounce of ginger, one ounce of mustard, one of pepper, three of coriander seed, three of tumeric, half an ounce of cardamums, quarter of an ounce of Cayenne pepper, quarter of an ounce of cinnamon, and quarter of an ounce of cummin seed. Pound them fine, sift them, and cork them tight in a bottle.

Chicken Cutlets (an Entrée)
From "The Book of Household Management", By Isabella Beeton, 1861

2 chickens; seasoning to taste of salt, white pepper, and cayenne; 2 blades of pounded mace, egg and bread crumbs, clarified butter, 1 strip of lemon-rind, 2 carrots, 1 onion, 2 tablespoonfuls of mushroom ketchup, thickening of butter and flour, 1 egg.
Remove the breast and leg bones of the chickens; cut the meat into neat pieces after having skinned it, and season the cutlets with pepper, salt, pounded mace, and cayenne. Put the bones, trimmings, &c., into a stewpan with 1 pint of

water, adding carrots, onions, and lemon-peel in the above proportion; stew gently for 1-1/2 hour, and strain the gravy. Thicken it with butter and flour, add the ketchup and 1 egg well beaten; stir it over the fire, and bring it to the simmering-point, but do not allow it to boil. In the mean time, egg and bread-crumb the cutlets, and give them a few drops of clarified butter; fry them a delicate brown, ccasionally turning them; arrange them pyramidically on the dish, and pour over them the sauce.

Time-10 minutes to fry the cutlets.

Chicken Leeky
From "A Plain Cookery Book for the Working Classes", 1852

1 old hen or cock 1 pound of Patna rice 12 leeks cut in pieces peppercorns salt Instructions I hope that at some odd times you may afford yourselves an old hen or cock; and when this occurs, this is the way in which I recommend that it be cooked, viz.: First pluck, draw, singe off the hairs, and tie the fowl up in a plump shape; next, put it into a boiling-pot with a gallon of water, and the rice, leeks, some peppercorns and salt to season; boil the whole very gently for three hours, and divide the fowl to be eaten with the soup, which will prove not only nourishing but invigorating to the system.

Chicken Pie
From "The Great Western Cook Book, or Table Receipts, Adapted to Western Housewifery", By Anna Maria Collins, 1857

Carve, neatly, two young chickens, simmer them in salt and water at least half an hour. Lay a deep pan, or dish, with rich crust, put the chicken in with small pieces of pork, an ounce of butter, a tea-spoonful of black pepper, and half a nutmeg; sprinkle a little flour, or grated cracker, over the surface, pour the liquor, in which the fowl was boiled, over the whole, and bake it in a brisk oven or stove.

"Well Mother, I want you to raise a big gobbler for me when I get home. Tell Aunt Neely to hold herself in readiness to make me a good chicken pie." - Archibald Alexander Rudder, Co. C, 6th Tennessee Infantry (Federal), near Cassville, Georgia, May 23, 1864. Letter to his father.

Fowl Pillau

Based on M. Soyer's Recipe (an Indian Dish)
From "The Book of Household Management", By Isabella Beeton, 1861

Ingredients 1 pound of rice 2 ounces of butter a fowl 2 quarts of stock or good broth 40 cardamum-seeds 1/2 ounce of coriander-seed 1/4 ounce of cloves 1/4 ounce of allspice 1/4 ounce of mace 1/4 ounce of cinnamon 1/2 ounce of peppercorns 4 onions 6 thin slices of bacon 2 hard-boiled eggs Instructions Well wash 1 pound of the best Patna rice, put it into a frying-pan with the butter, which keep moving over a slow fire until the rice is lightly browned. Truss the fowl as for boiling, put it into a stewpan with the stock or broth; pound the spices and seeds thoroughly in a mortar, tie them in a piece of muslin, and put them in with the fowl. Let it boil slowly until it is nearly done; then add the rice, which should stew until quite tender and almost dry; cut the onions into slices, sprinkle them with flour, and fry, without breaking them, of a nice brown colour. Have ready the slices of bacon curled and grilled, and the eggs boiled hard. Lay the fowl in the form of a pyramid upon a dish, smother with the rice, garnish with the bacon, fried onions, and the hard-boiled eggs cut into quarters, and serve very hot. Before taking the rice out, remove the spices. Time: 1/2 hour to stew the fowl without the rice; 1/2 hour with it. Sufficient for 4 or 5 persons. Seasonable at any time.

Fricasseed Fowl or Chicken (an Entree)
From "The Book of Household Management", By Isabella Beeton, 1861

2 small fowls or 1 large one, 3 oz. of butter, a bunch of parsley and green onions, 1 clove, 2 blades of mace, 1 shalot, 1 bay-leaf, salt and white pepper to taste, 1/4 pint of cream, the yolks of 3 eggs.
Choose a couple of fat plump chickens, and, after drawing, singeing, and washing them, skin, and carve them into joints; blanch these in boiling water for 2 or 3 minutes; take them out, and immerse them in cold water to render them white. Put the trimmings, with the necks and legs, into a stewpan; add the parsley, onions, clove, mace, shalot, bay-leaf, and a seasoning of pepper and salt; pour to these the water that the chickens were blanched in, and simmer gently for rather more than 1 hour. Have ready another stewpan; put in the joints of fowl, with the above proportion of butter; dredge them with flour, let them get hot, but do not brown them much; then moisten the fricassee with the gravy made from the trimmings, &c., and stew very gently for 1/2 hour. Lift the fowl into another stewpan, skim the sauce, reduce it quickly over the fire, by letting it boil fast, and strain it over them. Add the cream, and a seasoning of pounded mace and cayenne; let it boil up, and when ready to serve, stir to it the well-beaten yolks of 3 eggs: these should not be put in till the last moment, and the sauce should be made hot, but must not boil, or it will instantly curdle. A

few button-mushrooms stewed with the fowl are by many persons considered an improvement.

Time-1 hour to make the gravy, 1/2 hour to simmer the fowl.

Fried Chickens
From "The Virginia Housewife", By Mary Randolph, 1836

Cut them up as for the fricassee, dredge them well with flour, sprinkle them with salt, put them into a good quantity of boiling lard, and fry them a light brown; fry small pieces of mush and a quantity of parsley nicely picked, to be served in the dish with the chickens; take half a pint of rich milk, add to it a small bit of butter, with pepper, salt, and chopped parsley; stew it a little, and pour it over the chickens, and then garnish with the fried parsley.

Fried Chicken A La Malabar
From "The Practical Housekeeper; A Cyclopedia of Domestic Economy", By Elizabeth Fries Ellet, 1857

The Indian receipts for cooking chicken are very numerous; we select the following. Cut up the fowl as for a stew, removing the joints carefully and carving the body into handsome shapes; remove all moisture with a clean dry cloth, and powder every part with curry; fry it in fresh butter, to which half a teaspoonful of curry has been added, a pale brown; cut into small pieces two or three onions, and fry in clear butter, sufficient to keep the pan from burning; but not more than should be absorbed by the onion after some time frying. It is as well here to say, that as onions are frequently used in the curried poultry by the Indian cooks, they employ the following method, When to be cut small, they slice the onions and then separate them into rings, cutting these rings into the sizes they may require, which, if a little more labor, yet presents a better appearance; when they are fried sufficiently to have absorbed the grease in the pan without in any degree having been burned, spread them over the chicken and serve; a whole lemon should be sent to table with them.

Fried Fowl
From "The Practical Housekeeper; A Cyclopedia of Domestic Economy", By Elizabeth Fries Ellet, 1857

When you have cut the pieces as before, put them into a basin with a little salt and pepper, a spoonful of oil, and two of vinegar, and a little chopped eschalot; stir them well in it, and let remain for half an hour; have ready a quantity of batter, and take a fork and dip each piece one after the other into it, and then let it drop into the frying-pan, in which is sufficient hot fat to cover them; fry a nice color, and serve in the form of a pyramid, with fried parsley over, or any sauce you like under.

Minced Turkey or Chicken
From "The Lady's Receipt-Book; a Useful Companion for Large or Small Families", By Eliza Leslie, 1847

Take a cold turkey, or one or two cold fowls; remove all the skin, and cut the flesh from the bones. Then mince it fine, with two or three thin slices of cold smoked tongue, and from half a pint to a pint of button mushrooms well chopped. Add some mace and nutmeg, and put the whole into a stew-pan, with a piece of fresh butter rolled in flour, and sufficient cream to moisten it well. Let it stew ten minutes. Then serve it up in a deep dish.
Instead of mushrooms, you may mix two or three dozen oysters, chopped, and seasoned with pepper and powdered mace.

Southern Gumbo (Mrs. L.'s Receipt)
From "Miss Beecher's Domestic Receipt Book", By Catharine Esther Beecher, 1850

This is a favorite dish at the South and West, and is made in a variety of ways. The following is a very fine receipt, furnished by a lady, who has had an extensive opportunity for selection.
Fry one chicken, when cut up, to a light brown, and also two slices of bacon. Pour on to them three quarts of boiling water. Add one onion and some sweet herbs, tied in a rag. Simmer them gently three hours and a half. Strain off the liquor, take off the fat, and then put the ham and chicken, cut into small pieces, into the liquor. Add half a tea-cup of *ochre*, cut up; if dry, the same quantity; also half a tea-cup of rice. Boil all half an hour, and just before serving add a glass of wine and a dozen oysters, with their juice. Ochra is a fine vegetable, especially for soups, and is easily cultivated. It is sliced and dried for soups in winter.

Tomato Chicken
From "The Lady's Receipt-Book; a Useful Companion for Large or Small Families", By Eliza Leslie, 1847

Take four small chickens or two large ones, and cut them up as for carving. Put them into a stew-pan, with one or two large slices of cold boiled ham cut into little bits; eight or ten large tomatoes; an onion sliced; a bunch of pot-herbs, (cut up;) a small green pepper, (the seeds and veins first extracted;) half a dozen blades of mace; a table-spoonful of lard, or of fresh butter rolled in flour; and two pounded crackers, or a handful of grated bread-crumbs. Add a tumbler or half a pint of water. Cover the sauce-pan closely with a cloth beneath the lid; set it on hot coals, or over a moderate fire; and let it stew slowly till the chickens are thoroughly done, and the tomatoes entirely dissolved. Turn it out into a deep dish.

Rabbits may be stewed in this manner.

Also, veal steaks, cut thin and small.

Roast Ducks
From "Miss Beecher's Domestic Receipt Book", By Catharine Esther Beecher, 1850

Wash the ducks, and stuff them with a dressing made with mashed potatoes, wet with milk, and chopped onions, sage, pepper, salt, and a little butter, to suit your taste. Reserve the inwards to make the gravy, as is directed for turkeys, except it should be seasoned with sage and chopped onions. They will cook in about an hour. Ducks are to be cooked rare. Baste them with salt water, and before taking up, dredge on a little flour and let it brown.

Green peas and stewed cranberries are good accompaniments.

Canvass-back ducks are cooked without stuffing.

Wild ducks must be soaked in salt and water the night previous, to remove the fishy taste, and then in the morning put in fresh water, which should be changed once or twice.

Turkey Pulled and Grilled
From "The Practical Housekeeper; A Cyclopedia of Domestic Economy", By Elizabeth Fries Ellet, 1857

Is a mode of preparing the remains of cold turkey, by mincing the white meat and fricasseeing it with white sauce; the legs being scored, peppered, and salted, broiled, and sent up over the mince.

Or devilled, as thus:--On the rump, gizzard, and a drumstick, put salt, pepper, and cayenne. Let them be broiled, and brought to table as hot as possible; cut them in small pieces; pour over them a ladle of mustard, ditto of melted butter, a spoonful of soy, ditto of lemon-juice, and some of the gravy out of the dish; mix quickly and hand round. It forms an admirable relish; fowls may be treated in the same manner.

Roast Turkey
From "Miss Beecher's Domestic Receipt Book", By
Catharine Esther Beecher, 1850

Wash the outside and inside very clean. Take bread crumbs, grated or chopped, about enough to fill the turkey, chop a bit of salt pork, the size of a good egg, and mix it in, with butter, the size of an egg, pepper, salt, and sweet herbs to your taste. Then beat up an egg and work in. Fill the crop and the body, sew them up, and tie the legs and wings, and spit them. Set it where it will gradually heat, and turn it once or twice, while heating, for fifteen minutes. Then put it up to the fire, and allow about twenty-five minutes for each pound. Turkey must be cooked very thoroughly. It must roast slowly at first, and be often basted with butter on a fork. Dredge it with flour just before taking it up, and let it brown.

Put the inwards in a skillet to boil for two hours, chop them up, season them, use the liquor they are boiled in for gravy, and thicken it with brown flour, and a bit of butter, the size of a hen's egg. This is the giblet sauce. Take the drippings, say half a pint, thickened with a paste, made of a tablespoonful of brown, or white flour, and let it simmer five minutes, and then use it for thin gravy.

White Fricassee
From "The Lady's Receipt-Book; a Useful Companion for Large or Small Families", By Eliza Leslie, 1847

Cut a pair of chickens into pieces, as for carving; and wash them through two or three waters. Then lay them in a large pan, sprinkle them slightly with salt, and fill up the pan with boiling water. Cover it, and let the chickens stand for half an hour. Then put them immediately into a stew-pan; adding a few blades of mace, and a few whole pepper-corns, and a handful of celery, split thin and chopped finely; also, a small white onion sliced. Pour on cold milk and water (mixed in equal portions) sufficient to cover the chickens well. Cover the stew-pan, set it over the fire, and let it stew till the chickens are thoroughly done, and quite tender. While the chickens are stewing, prepare, in a smaller sauce-pan, a gravy or sauce made as follows:--Mix two tea-spoonfuls of flour with as much cold water as will make it like a batter, and stir it till quite smooth and free from lumps. Then add to it, gradually, half a pint of boiling milk. Next put in a quarter of a pound of fresh butter, cut into small pieces. Set it over hot coals, and stir it till it comes to a boil, and the butter is well melted and mixed throughout. Then take it off the fire, and, while it is hot, stir in a glass of madeira or sherry, and four table-spoonfuls of rich cream, and some grated nutmeg. Lastly, take the chickens out of the stew-pan, and pour off all the liquor, &c. Return the chicken to the stew-pan, and pour over it, hot, the above-

mentioned gravy. Cover the pan closely, and let it stand in a hot place, or in a kettle of boiling water for ten minutes. Then send it to table in a covered dish. To the taste of many persons, this fricassee will be improved by adding to the chicken, while stewing, some small, thin slices of cold boiled ham.
Rabbits or veal may be fricasseed in the above manner.

Fish and Seafood

"Reader, did you ever eat a mussel? Well, we did, at Shelbyville.....We tried frying them, but the longer they fried the tougher they got. They were a little too large to swallow whole. Then we stewed them, and after a while we boiled them, and then we baked them, but every flank movement we would make on those mussels the more invulnerable they would get. We tried cutting them up with a hatchet, but they were so slick and tough the hatchet would not cut them. Well, we cooked them, and buttered them, and salted them, and peppered them, and battered them. They looked good, and smelt good, and tasted good; at least the fixings we put on them did, and we ate the mussels. I went to sleep that night. I dreamed that my stomach was four grindstones, and that they turned in four directions, according to the four corners of the earth. I awoke to hear four men yell out, "O, save, O, save me from eating any more mussels!"-Pvt. Sam Watkins, Co, H, 1st Tennessee Infantry.

Fried Anchovies
From "The Book of Household Management", By Isabella Beeton, 1861

1 tablespoonful of oil, 1/2 a glass of white wine, sufficient flour to thicken; 12 anchovies.
Mix the oil and wine together, with sufficient flour to make them into a thickish paste; cleanse the anchovies, wipe them, dip them in the paste, and fry of a nice brown colour.
Time-1/2 hour.

Stewed Carp
From "A New System of Domestic Cookery", By Maria Eliza Ketelby Rundell, 1807

Scale and clean, take care of the roe, &c. lay the fish in a stewpan, with a rich beef gravy, an onion, eight cloves, a desert spoonful of Jamaica pepper, the same, of black, a fourth part of the quantity of gravy of port, (cyder may do); simmer close covered; when nearly done add two anchovies chopped line, a desert spoonful of made mustard, and some fine walnut ketchup, a bit of butter rolled in flour, shake it, and let the gravy boil a few minutes. Serve with sippets of fried bread, the roe fried, and a good deal of horse-radish and lemon.

To Make A Curry of Catfish
From "The Virginia Housewife", By Mary Randolph, 1836

Take the white channel catfish, cut off their heads, skin and clean them, cut them in pieces four inches long, put as many as will be sufficient for a dish into a stew pan with a quart of water, two onions, and chopped parsley; let them stew gently till the water is reduced to half a pint, take the fish out and lay them on a dish, cover them to keep them hot, rub a spoonful of butter into one of flour, add a large tea-spoonful of curry powder, thicken the gravy with it, shake it over the fire a few minutes, and pour it over the fish; be careful to have the gravy smooth.

Chowder
From "The Great Western Cook Book, or Table Receipts, Adapted to Western Housewifery", By Anna Maria Collins, 1857

Cut the fish in pieces of an inch thick and two inches square. Take half a dozen large slices of salt pork, and lay in the bottom of an iron pot, and fry till crisped. Take the pork out of the fat, and chop it fine. Put in the pot a layer of fish, a layer of split crackers, some of the chopped pork, black and red pepper, and onion chopped fine, then another layer of fish, split crackers, &c. Continue this till all the fish is used. Barely cover the fish with water, and slowly stew it till it is tender. Then take out the fish, and thicken the gravy with pounded cracker, and season it with mushroom catsup, and the juice of a lemon. Pour the gravy over the fish, after it has boiled up once. Garnish it with slices of lemon.

Cod A La Creme
From "The Book of Household Management", By Isabella Beeton, 1861

1 large slice of cod, 1 oz. of butter, 1 chopped shalot, a little minced parsley, 1/4 teacupful of white stock, 1/4 pint of milk or cream, flour to thicken, cayenne and lemon-juice to taste, 1/4 teaspoonful of powdered sugar.
Boil the cod, and while hot, break it into flakes; put the butter, shalot, parsley,

and stock into a stewpan, and let them boil for 5 minutes. Stir in sufficient flour to thicken, and pour to it the milk or cream. Simmer for 10 minutes, add the cayenne and sugar, and, when liked, a little lemon-juice. Put the fish in the sauce to warm gradually, but do not let it boil. Serve in a dish garnished with croŭtons.

Time-Rather more than 1/2 hour.

Boiled Eels

From "The Book of Household Management", By Isabella Beeton, 1861

4 small eels, sufficient water to cover them; a large bunch of parsley.
Choose small eels for boiling; put them in a stewpan with the parsley, and just sufficient water to cover them; simmer till tender. Take them out, pour a little parsley and butter over them, and serve some in a tureen.

Time-1/2 hour.

Eels Fried

From "The Practical Housekeeper; A Cyclopedia of Domestic Economy", By Elizabeth Fries Ellet, 1857

Cut your eels into pieces three inches long, trim them, dip the pieces into flour, egg over with a paste-brush, and throw them into some bread-crumbs; fry in hot lard as directed for fried soles.

Fish Salads

From "The Practical Housekeeper; A Cyclopedia of Domestic Economy", By Elizabeth Fries Ellet, 1857

All fish salads are made from the remains of fish from a previous dinner, especially turbot and salmon; but for fillets of soles they must be dressed thus: --When filleted, melt an ounce of butter in a saucepan, lay the fillets in, season with pepper and salt, and the juice of half a lemon; saute them on a slow fire until done, which may be from four to five minutes, and put by to get cold; cut in middle-sized pieces and use as lobster.

To Fry Oysters

From "The Virginia Housewife", By Mary Randolph, 1836

Take a quarter of a hundred of large oysters, wash them and roll them in grated bread, with pepper and salt, and fry them a light brown; if you choose, you may add a little parsley, shred fine. They are a proper garnish for calves' head, or most made dishes.

Oyster Loaves
From "The Lady's Receipt-Book; a Useful Companion for Large or Small Families", By Eliza Leslie, 1847

Take some tall fresh rolls, or small loaves. Cut nicely a round or oval hole in the top of each, saving the pieces that come off. Then carefully scoop out the crumb from the inside, leaving the crust standing. Have ready a sufficient quantity of large fresh oysters. Put the oysters with one-fourth of their liquor into a stew-pan; adding the bread-crumbs; a large piece of fresh butter; some powdered nutmeg; and a few blades of mace. Stew them about ten minutes. Then stir in two or three large table-spoonfuls of cream; take them off just as they are coming to a boil. If cooked too long the oysters will become tough and shrivelled, and the cream will curdle. Fill the inside of your scooped loaves with the oysters, reserving as many large oysters as you have loaves. Place the bit of upper-crust carefully on the top of each, so as to cover the whole. Arrange them on a dish, and lay on each lid one of the large oysters kept out for the purpose. These ornamental oysters must be well drained from any liquid that is about them.

Roast Oysters
From "The Great Western Cook Book, or Table Receipts, Adapted to Western Housewifery", By Anna Maria Collins, 1857

Roast your oysters over a clear, hot fire, till they are done dry, do not burn them, but turn them out in a plate, without their liquor, then put some butter, pepper, and a little vinegar over them.

"I have been here about two weeks and have been enjoying the oysters & fish very much as it is the first opportunity I have had of getting any of late." –Dr. Charles Abram Rutledge, Assistant Surgeon, Confederate States Army, Savannah, Georgia, March 14, 1863. Letter to his sister, Henrietta.

Stewed Oysters
From "The Practical Housekeeper; A Cyclopedia of Domestic Economy", By Elizabeth Fries Ellet, 1857

The oysters should be bearded and rinsed in their own liquor, which should then be strained and thickened with flour and butter, and placed with the oysters in a stewpan; add mace, lemon-peel cut into threads, some white pepper whole; these ingredients had better be confined in a piece of muslin. The stew must simmer only; if it is suffered to boil, the oysters will become hard; serve with sippets of bread. This may be varied by adding a glass of wine to the liquor, before the oysters are put in and warmed.

Fried Perch

From "Directions for Cookery, in its Various Branches" By Eliza Leslie, 1840

Having cleaned the fish and dried them, with a cloth, lay them, side by side, on a board or large dish; sprinkle them with salt, and dredge them with flour. After a while turn them, and salt and dredge the other side. Put some lard or fresh beef-dripping into a frying-pan, and hold it over the fire. When the lard boils, put in the fish and fry them of a yellowish brown. Send to table with them in a boat, melted butter flavoured with anchovy.
Flounders or other small fish may be fried in the same manner.
You may know when the lard or dripping is hot enough, by dipping in the tail of one of the fish. If it becomes crisp immediately, the lard is in a proper state for frying. Or you may try it with a piece of stale bread which will become brown directly, if the lard is in order.
There should always be enough of lard to cover the fish entirely. After they have fried five minutes on one side, turn them and fry them five minutes on the other. Skim the lard or dripping always before you put in the fish.

Ragout Of Fish

From "The Practical Housekeeper; A Cyclopedia of Domestic Economy", By Elizabeth Fries Ellet, 1857

Take carp, perch, pike, and eels; clean and scale them well, and cut them into pieces for serving; put in your stewpan a good-sized piece of butter, let it fry to a pale brown, fry some flour in it, and add a quart or two of good bouillon with a glass or two of red wine, and a few cloves and onions. When boiling put your ragoût into it, let it well boil, and add some lemon-juice before serving it up.

Salmon Steaks

From "Directions for Cookery, in its Various Branches" By Eliza Leslie, 1840

Split the salmon and take out the bone as nicely as possible, without mangling the flesh. Then cut it into fillets or steaks about an inch thick. Dry them lightly in a cloth, and dredge them with flour. Take care not to squeeze or press them. Have ready some clear bright coals, such as are fit for beef-steaks. Let the gridiron be clean and bright, and rub the bars with chalk to prevent the fish from sticking. Broil the slices thoroughly, turning them with steak tongs. Send them to table hot, wrapped in the folds of a napkin that has been heated. Serve up with them anchovy, or prawn, or lobster sauce.

Many epicures consider this the best way of cooking salmon.

Another way, perhaps still nicer, is to take some pieces of white paper and butter them well. Wrap in each a slice of salmon, securing the paper around them, with a string or pins. Lay them on a gridiron, and broil them over a clear but moderate fire, till thoroughly done. Take off the paper, and send the cutlets to table hot, garnished with fried parsley.

Serve up with them prawn or lobster sauce in a boat.

Boiled Salmon
From "A Poetical Cookbook, By Maria J. Moss, 1864

Put on a fish-kettle, with spring water enough to well cover the salmon you are going to dress, or the salmon will neither look nor taste well (boil the liver in a separate saucepan). When the water boils put in a handful of salt, take off the scum as soon as it rises; have the fish well washed, put it in, and if it is thick, let it boil very gently. Salmon requires as much boiling as meat; about a quarter of an hour to a pound of meat; but practice can only perfect the cook in dressing salmon.

A quarter of a salmon will take as long boiling as half a one. You must consider the thickness, not the weight.

Obs.: The thinnest part of the fish is the fattest, and if you have a "grand gourmand" at table, ask him if he is for thick or thin.

Lobster sauce and rye bread should be eaten with boiled salmon.

Fresh Salmon Stewed
From "The Lady's Receipt-Book; a Useful Companion for Large or Small Families", By Eliza Leslie, 1847

Having cleaned and washed the fish, cut it into round slices or fillets, rather more than an inch in thickness. Lay them in a large dish; sprinkling a very little salt evenly over the slices; and in half an hour turn them on the other side. Let them rest another half hour; then wash, drain, and wipe them dry with a clean towel. Spread some of the best fresh butter thickly over the strainer of a large fish-kettle; and lay the pieces of salmon upon it. Cover them nearly all over with very thin slices of fresh lemon, from which the seeds have been removed. Intersperse among the lemon a few slices of shalots, or very small mild onions; a few sprigs of parsley and some whole pepper-corns. Set the kettle over a large bed of live coals; and spread very hot ashes thickly over the lid; which must be previously well-heated on the inside by standing it up before the fire. The heat should be regularly kept up, while the fish is stewing, both above and below it. It will require an hour to cook thoroughly. When dishing it, remove the sliced lemon, shalots, parsley, &c., leaving them in the bottom of the kettle. Put a cover over the fish, and set the dish that contains it over a large vessel of hot water, while you are preparing the sauce. For this sauce, mix thoroughly a quarter of a pound of fresh butter with a table-spoonful of flour. Put it into a quart tin vessel with a lid, and add a table-spoonful of water, and the seasoning that was left in the bottom of the fish-kettle. Cover the vessel closely, and set it in a larger sauce-pan or pot of boiling water. Shake it about over the fire till it comes to a boil. If you set it down on hot coals the butter will oil. When it has boiled, remove the lemon, onion, &c.; pour the sauce into a sauce-boat, and send it to table with the stewed fish, garnished with sprigs of curled parsley. This is a French mode of cooking salmon.

Fresh cod, or halibut, may be stewed in the same manner.

Baked Shad

From "Directions for Cookery, in its Various Branches" By Eliza Leslie, 1840

Keep on the head and fins. Make a force-meat or stuffing of grated bread crumbs, cold boiled ham or bacon minced fine, sweet marjoram, pepper, salt, and a little powdered mace or cloves. Moisten it with beaten yolk of egg. Stuff the inside of the fish with it, reserving a little to rub over the outside, having first rubbed the fish all over with yolk of egg. Lay the fish in a deep pan, putting its tail to its mouth. Pour into the bottom of the pan a little water, and add a jill of port wine, and a piece of butter rolled in flour. Bake it well, and when it is done, send it to table with the gravy poured round it. Garnish with slices of lemon.

Any fish may be baked in the same manner.

A large fish of ten or twelve pounds weight, will require about 2 hours baking.

During the battle of Five Forks, at Hatcher's Run, April 1, 1865, three Confederate generals, George Pickett, Fitzhugh Lee and Thomas L Rosser, enjoyed a meal and gathering known as a "Shad Bake". To bake the shad (a local herring) they were attached to boards, which were then stuck in the ground around a fire, then eating them. The winter had been a cold one, with provisions scarce and limited, and the shad provided the men with brief respite to combat duties. The main problem was that two miles away, Pickett's troops were being mercilessly beaten in what would become considered as the "Waterloo" of the Confederacy.

"Some time was spent over lunch," recalled Gen. Rosser, "during which no firing was heard... We concluded that the enemy was not in much of a hurry to find us as Five Forks." Five Forks was the crucial crossroads which, that morning, Robert E Lee had ordered Pickett to hold at all costs. The generals at the Shad Bake were unaware of the intensity of the fighting that began shortly after 4pm, because the wooded area they were in muffled the sound of gunfire.

Pickett was a flamboyant character, with long locks of hair flowing down. But he'd had some previous experience when it came to avoiding battle. On July 3rd of 1863, during the battle of Gettysburg, specifically as 'Pickett's Charge" was taking place, he stayed well to the rear of his advancing troops. Before the Battle of Five Forks, Pickett informed no one of his intention to attend the shad bake, and when he did arrive on the scene of the battle, he found that 2,400 of his soldiers had been captured.

After the battle, Gen. Lee was compelled to retreat. Before Lee's surrender a week later, he said of Pickett: "I thought that man was no longer with the army". After the war, Pickett became an insurance salesman.

To Bake A Shad
From "The Virginia Housewife", By Mary Randolph, 1836

The shad is a very indifferent fish unless it be large and fat; when you get a good one, prepare it nicely, put some forcemeat inside, and lay it at full length in a pan with a pint of water, a gill of red wine, one of mushroom catsup, a little pepper, vinegar, salt, a few cloves of garlic, and six cloves: stew it gently till the gravy is sufficiently reduced; there should always be a fish-slice with holes to lay the fish on, for the convenience of dishing without breaking it; when the fish is taken up, slip it carefully into the dish; thicken the gravy with butter and brown flour, and pour over it.

Sea Bass With Tomatoes
From "The Lady's Receipt-Book; a Useful Companion for Large or Small Families", By Eliza Leslie, 1847

Take three large fine sea-bass, or black-fish. Cut off their heads and tails, and fry the fish in plenty of lard till about half done. Have ready a pint of tomatoes, that have been pickled cold in vinegar flavoured with a muslin bag of mixed spices. Drain the tomatoes well from the vinegar; skin them, and mash them in a pan; dredging them with about as much flour as would fill a large table-spoon heaped up. Pour the mixture over the fish while in the frying pan; and continue frying till they are thoroughly done.
Cutlets of halibut may be fried in this manner with tomatoes: also, any other pan-fish.
Beef-steaks or lamb-chops are excellent fried thus with tomatoes.

Trout à-la-Genevoise
From "A New System of Domestic Cookery", By Maria Eliza Ketelby Rundell, 1807

Clean the fish very well; put it into your stewpan, adding half Champaign and half Moselle, or Rhenish, or Sherry wine. Season it with pepper, salt, an onion, a few cloves stuck in it, and a small bunch of parsley and thyme; put it in a crust of French bread; set it on a quick fire. When the fish is done, take the bread out, bruise it, and then thicken the sauce; add flour and a little butter, and let it boil up. See that your sauce is of a proper thickness. Lay your fish on the dish, and pour the sauce over it. Serve it with sliced lemon and fried bread.

Cream Trout
From "The Lady's Receipt-Book; a Useful Companion for Large or Small Families", By Eliza Leslie, 1847

Having prepared the trout very nicely, and cut off the heads and tails, put the fish into boiling water that has been slightly salted, and simmer them for five minutes. Then take them out, and lay them to drain. Put them into a stew-pan, and season them well with powdered mace, nutmeg, and a little cayenne, all mixed together. Put in as much rich cream as will cover the fish, adding some bits of the fresh yellow rind of a small lemon. Keep the pan covered, and let the fish stew for about ten minutes after it has begun to simmer. Then dish the fish, and keep them hot till you have finished the sauce. Mix, very smoothly, a small tea-spoonful of arrow-root with a little milk, and stir it into the cream. Then add the juice of the lemon. Pour the sauce over the fish, and then send them to table.
Turbot or sheep's-head fish may be dressed as above; of course it will require a

large proportion of seasoning, &c., and longer time to cook.
Carp is very nice stewed in this manner.

4. SIDE DISHES AND SALADS

"I went to a man's corn field and pillaged some corn today the first time I ever did the like. I was hungry." -Pvt. Martin Van Buren Oldham, Company G of the 9th Tennessee Infantry, September 2, 1863, Lookout Mountain, TN. From diary entry.

Boiled Artichokes
From "The Book of Household Management", By Isabella Beeton, 1861

To each 1/2 gallon of water, allow 1 heaped tablespoonful of salt, a piece of soda the size of a shilling; artichokes.
Wash the artichokes well in several waters; see that no insects remain about them, and trim away the leaves at the bottom. Cut off the stems and put them into *boiling* water, to which have been added salt and soda in the above proportion. Keep the saucepan uncovered, and let them boil quickly until tender; ascertain when they are done by thrusting a fork in them, or by trying if the leaves can be easily removed. Take them out, let them drain for a minute or two, and serve in a napkin, or with a little white sauce poured over. A tureen of melted butter should accompany them. This vegetable, unlike any other, is considered better for being gathered two or three days; but they must be well soaked and washed previous to dressing.

Boiled Asparagus
From "The Book of Household Management", By Isabella Beeton, 1861

To each 1/2 gallon of water allow 1 heaped tablespoonful of salt; asparagus. Asparagus should be dressed as soon as possible after it is cut, although it may be kept for a day or two by putting the stalks into cold water; yet, to be good, like every other vegetable, it cannot be cooked too fresh. Scrape the white part of the stems, beginning from the head, and throw them into cold water; then tie them into bundles of about 20 each, keeping the heads all one way, and cut the stalks evenly, that they may all be the same length; put them into boiling water, with salt in the above proportion; keep them boiling quickly until tender, with the saucepan uncovered. When the asparagus is done, dish it upon toast, which should be dipped in the water it was cooked in, and leave the white ends outwards each war, with the points meeting in the middle. Serve with a tureen of melted butter.
Time-15 to 18 minutes after the water boils.

Asparagus Loaves
From "The Practical Housekeeper; A Cyclopedia of
Domestic Economy", By Elizabeth Fries Ellet, 1857

Boil three bunches of asparagus; cut off the tops of two bunches when tender, leaving two inches of the white stalk on the rest, and keeping it warm; stew the tops in a pint of new milk, with three tablespoonfuls of butter, rubbed in flour, the yolks of three eggs, nutmeg and mace; when it boils put the mixture into loaves of rolls, with the crumb scooped out; put on the tops of the rolls; make holes in the tops, and stick in the remaining asparagus.

A Bacon Salad
From "A Plain Cookery Book for the Working Classes", By Charles Elme
Francatelli, 1852

Having prepared any kind of salad you may happen to have, such as endive, corn salad, lettuce, celery, mustard and cress, seasoned with beet-root, onions, or shalot; let the salad be cut up into a bowl or basin ready for seasoning in the following manner:--Cut eight ounces of fat bacon into small square pieces the size of a cob-nut, fry these in a frying-pan, and as soon as they are done, pour the whole upon the salad; add two table-spoonfuls of vinegar, pepper and salt to taste. Mix thoroughly.

Baked Beans
From "The Practical Housekeeper; A Cyclopedia of
Domestic Economy", By Elizabeth Fries Ellet, 1857

Soak a quart of dried beans over night, in cold water; drain off the water in the morning and stew for half an hour in a little water, put them in a deep dish, with one pound of salt pork, cut the rind in strips, and place in the centre of the dish. The pork should be sunk a little below the surface of the beans. Bake for three hours and a half. A lump of saleratus should be thrown in while the beans are boiling, and a pint of water be added, when they are put into the bake-pan.

Cabbage A La Creme
From "The Virginia Housewife", By Mary Randolph, 1836

Take two good heads of cabbage, cut out the stalks, boil it tender, with a little salt in the water--have ready one large spoonful of butter, and a small one of flour rubbed into it, half a pint of milk, with pepper and salt; make it hot, put the cabbage in after pressing out the water, and stew it till quite tender.

Cauliflowers A La Sauce Blanche
(Entremets, or Side-dish, to be served with the Second Course.)
From "The Book of Household Management", By Isabella Beeton, 1861

3 cauliflowers, 1/2 pint of sauce blanche, or French melted butter, No. 378 (see "Melted Butter" recipe); 3 oz. of butter; salt and water.
Cleanse the cauliflowers as in the preceding recipe, and cut the stalks off flat at the bottom; boil them until tender in salt and water, to which the above proportion of butter has been added, and be careful to take them up the moment they are done, or they will break, and the appearance of the dish will be spoiled. Drain them well, and dish them in the shape of a large cauliflower. Have ready 1/2 pint of sauce, made by recipe No. 378, pour it over the flowers, and serve hot and quickly.
Time-Small cauliflowers, 12 to 15 minutes, large ones, 20 to 25 minutes, after the water boils.

Celery Crab Salad
From "A Plain Cookery Book for the Working Classes", By Charles Elme Francatelli, 1852

First thoroughly wash and wipe clean, and then cut a stick of celery into a basin; add two ounces of any kind of cheese sliced very thinly, season with a good tea spoonful of made mustard, a table-spoonful of salad oil, ditto of vinegar, with pepper and salt. Mix thoroughly.

Stewed Celery A La Creme
From "The Book of Household Management", By Isabella Beeton, 1861

6 heads of celery; to each 1/2 gallon of water allow 1 heaped tablespoonful of salt, 1 blade of pounded mace, 1/3 pint of cream.
Wash the celery thoroughly; trim, and boil it in salt and water until tender. Put the cream and pounded mace into a stewpan; shake it over the fire until the cream thickens, dish the celery, pour over the sauce, and serve.
Time-Large heads of celery, 25 minutes; small ones, 15 to 20 minutes.

Cold Slaw
From "Directions for Cookery, in its Various Branches" By Eliza Leslie, 1840

Take a nice fresh cabbage, wash and drain it, and cut off all the stalk. Shave down the head into very small slips, with a cabbage cutter, or a very sharp knife. It must be done evenly and nicely. Put it into a deep china dish, and prepare for it the following dressing. Melt in a sauce-pan a quarter of a pound of butter, with half a pint of water, a large table-spoonful of vinegar, a salt-spoon of salt, and a little cayenne. Give this a boil up, and pour it hot upon the cabbage.

Send it to table as soon as it is cold.

Cranberry Sauce

From "The Practical Housekeeper; A Cyclopedia of Domestic Economy", By Elizabeth Fries Ellet, 1857

This sauce is very simply made. A quart of cranberries is washed and stewed with sufficient water to cover them; when they burst mix with them a pound of brown sugar, and stir them well. Before you remove them from the fire, all the berries should have burst. When cold they will be jellied, and if thrown into a form while warm, will turn out whole.

Cucumbers
From "The Complete Cook", By J. M. Sanderson, 1864

May be stewed in the same way as celery, with the addition of some sliced onions; or the cucumbers and onions may be first floured and fried in butter; then add the gravy, and stew till tender; skim off the fat.

Eggs A La Creme
From "The Virginia Housewife", By Mary Randolph, 1836

Boil twelve eggs just hard enough to allow you to cut them in slices--cut some crusts of bread very thin, put them in the bottom and round the sides of a moderately deep dish, place the eggs in, strewing each layer with the stale bread grated, and some pepper and salt.

Sauce A La Crème for the Eggs
From "The Virginia Housewife", By Mary Randolph, 1836

Put a quarter of a pound of butter, with a large table-spoonful of flour rubbed well into it in a sauce pan; add some chopped parsley, a little onion, salt, pepper, nutmeg, and a gill of cream; stir it over the fire until it begins to boil, then pour it over the eggs, cover the top with grated bread, set it in a Dutch oven with a heated top, and when a light brown, send it to table.

Eggs and Tomatos

From "The Virginia Housewife", By Mary Randolph, 1836

Peel the skins from a dozen large tomatos, put four ounces of butter in a frying pan, add some salt, pepper, and a little chopped onion; fry them a few minutes, add the tomatos, and chop them while frying; when nearly done, break in six eggs, stir them quickly, and serve them up.

Egg Plant

From "The Practical Housekeeper; A Cyclopedia of Domestic Economy", By Elizabeth Fries Ellet, 1857

Cut the egg plant in slices half an inch thick, and let it lie for several hours in salted water, to remove the bitter taste. To fry it put the slices in the frying-pan with a small quantity of butter, and turn them when one side is done, Be sure that they are thoroughly cooked. Stuffed egg plant is sometimes preferred to fried. Peel the plant whole, cut it in two, and let it lies in salted water. Then scoop out the inside of the plant, chop it up fine, mixing crumbs of bread, salt and butter with it; fry it, return it to the hollow egg plant, join the cut pieces together, and let them bake awhile in an oven. The best way of cooking is to slice them, dip the slices into egg and bread-crumbs, and fry very brown in butter or lard.

A Family French Salad For The Summer

From "The Practical Housekeeper; A Cyclopedia of Domestic Economy", By Elizabeth Fries Ellet, 1857

Cut up a pound of cold beef into thin slices, which put into a salad-bowl, with about half a pound of white fresh lettuce, cut into pieces similar to the beef, season over with a good teaspoonful of salt, half that quantity of pepper, two spoonfuls of vinegar, and five of good salad oil, stir all together lightly with a fork and spoon, and when well mixed it is ready to serve.

For a change, cabbage-lettuce may be used, or, if in season, a little endive (well washed), or a little celery, or a few gher-kins; also, to vary the seasoning, a little chopped tarragon and chervil, chopped eschalots, or a little scraped garlic, if ap-proved of, but all in proportion, and used with moderation. White haricot beans are also excellent with it. Remains of cold veal, mutton, or lamb may be dress-ed the same way.

French Salad

From "A New System of Domestic Cookery", By Maria Eliza

Ketelby Rundell, 1807

Chop three anchovies, a shalot, and some parsley, small; put them into a bowl with two table-spoonfuls of vinegar, one of oil, a little mustard, and salt. When well mixed, add by degrees some cold roast or boiled meat in very thin slices; put in a few at a time, not exceeding two or three inches long. Shake them in the seasoning, and then put more; cover the bowl close, and let the salad be prepared three hours before it is to be eaten. Garnish with parsley, and a few slices of the fat.

Gumbo-A West India Dish
From "The Virginia Housewife", By Mary Randolph, 1836

Gather young pods of ochra, wash them clean, and put them in a pan with a little water, salt and pepper, stew them till tender, and serve them with melted butter. They are very nutritious, and easy of digestion.

To Dress Lettuce As Salad
From "Directions for Cookery, in its Various Branches" By Eliza Leslie, 1840

Strip off the outer leaves, wash the lettuce, split it in half, and lay it in cold water till dinner time. Then drain it and put it into a salad dish. Have ready two eggs boiled hard, (which they will be in twelve minutes,) and laid in a basin of cold water for five minutes to prevent the whites from turning blue. Cut them in half, and lay them on the lettuce.

Put the yolks of the eggs on a large plate, and with a wooden spoon mash them smooth, mixing with them a table-spoonful of water, and two table-spoonfuls of sweet oil. Then add, by degrees, a salt-spoonful of salt, a tea-spoonful of mustard, and a tea-spoonful of powdered loaf-sugar. When these are all smoothly united, add very gradually three table-spoonfuls of vinegar. The lettuce having been cut up fine on another plate, put it to the dressing, and mix it well.

If you have the dressing for salad made before a dinner, put it into the bottom of the salad dish; then (having cut it up) lay the salad upon it, and let it rest till it is to be eaten, as stirring it will injure it.

You may decorate the top of the salad with slices of red beet, and with the hard white of the eggs cut into rings.

Lettuce Chicken Salad
From "The Lady's Receipt-Book; a Useful Companion for Large or Small Families", By Eliza Leslie, 1847

Having skinned a pair of cold fowls, remove the fat, and carve them as if for eating, cut all the flesh entirely from the bones, and either mince it or divide it into small shreds. Mix with it a little smoked tongue or cold ham, grated rather than chopped. Have ready one or two fine fresh lettuces, picked, washed, drained, and cut small. Put the cut lettuce on a dish, (spreading it evenly,) or into a large bowl, and place upon it the minced chicken in a close heap in the centre. For the dressing, mix together the following ingredients, in the proportion of the yolks of four eggs well beaten; a tea-spoonful of powdered white sugar; a salt-spoon of cayenne; (no salt if you have ham or tongue with the chicken;) two tea-spoonfuls of made mustard; two table-spoonfuls of vinegar, and four table-spoonfuls of salad oil. Stir this mixture well: put it into a small sauce-pan, set it over the fire, and let it boil three minutes, (not more,) stirring it all the time. Then set it to cool. When quite cold, cover with it thickly the heap of chicken in the centre of the salad. To ornament it, have ready half a dozen or more hard-boiled eggs, which after the shell is peeled off, must be thrown directly into a pan of cold water to prevent their turning blue. Cut each egg (white and yolk together) lengthways into four long pieces of equal size and shape; lay the pieces upon the salad all round the heap of chicken, and close to it; placing them so as to follow each other round in a slanting direction, something in the form of a circular wreath of leaves. Have ready, also, some very red cold beet, cut into small cones or points all of equal size; arrange them in a circle upon the lettuce, outside of the circle of cut egg. To be decorated in this manner, the salad should be placed in a dish rather than a bowl. In helping it, give each person a portion of everything, and they will mix them together on their plates.

This salad should be prepared immediately before dinner or supper, as standing long will injure it. The colder it is the better.

A Dish of Maccaroni

From "The Great Western Cook Book, or Table Receipts, Adapted to Western Housewifery", By Anna Maria Collins, 1857

Boil four ounces of maccaroni, till it is quite done, lay it on a sieve to drain; then put it into a saucepan with a gill of cream, a piece of butter about the size of an egg, rolled in flour, stew it a few minutes, and pour it in a plate, lay toasted cheese over it, and send it to the table hot.

Ochra and Tomatos

From "The Virginia Housewife", By Mary Randolph, 1836

Take an equal quantity of each, let the ochra be young, slice it, and skin the tomatos; put them into a pan without water, add a lump of butter, an onion chopped fine, some pepper and salt, and stew them one hour.

Orange Salad

From "The Great Western Cook Book, or Table Receipts, Adapted
to Western Housewifery", By Anna Maria Collins, 1857

Cut the large oranges crosswise, lay them neatly in a glass dish, sprinkle them with two ounces of powdered loaf-sugar, pour over a table-spoonful of brandy, or a glass of wine. This dish ought not to be prepared long before it is required.

Parsnips

From "The Complete Cook", By J. M. Sanderson, 1864

Clean and dress just the same as carrots, they require boiling from one hour to two, according to their size and freshness; they should be drained well, and set on the hob in a dry saucepan to steam; they are sometimes mashed with butter, pepper, salt, and cream, or milk, the same as turnips; they are eaten alone, or with salt beef or salt pork. Sauce, melted butter and vinegar.

Peach Salad

From "The Great Western Cook Book, or Table Receipts, Adapted
to Western Housewifery", By Anna Maria Collins, 1857

Peel four or five ripe, juicy peaches, and slice them neatly, and have each slice as much alike as possible in shape and thickness; lay them in a glass dish, and cover them with loaf-sugar, pour over them a spoonful of brandy or wine; turn them off the top to the bottom, so they may all be seasoned alike.
The most of fruits may be prepared in the same way; but never mix fruits.

To Stew Green Peas

From "A New System of Domestic Cookery", By Maria Eliza
Ketelby Rundell, 1807

Put a quart of peas, a lettuce and an onion both sliced, a bit of butter, pepper, salt, and no more water than hangs round the lettuce from washing. Stew them two hours very gently. When to be served, beat up an egg, and stir it into them: or a bit of flour and butter.
Some think a tea-spoonful of white powdered sugar is an improvement. Gravy may be added, but then there will be less of the flavour of the peas. Chop a bit

of mint, and stew in them.

To Make Polenta
From "The Virginia Housewife", By Mary Randolph, 1836

Put a large spoonful of butter in a quart of water, wet your corn meal with cold water in a bowl, add some salt, and make it quite smooth, then put it in the buttered water when it is hot, let it boil, stirring it continually till done; as soon as you can handle it, make it into a ball, and let it stand till quite cold--then cut it in thin slices, lay them in the bottom of a deep dish so as to cover it, put on it slices of cheese, and on that a few bits of butter; then mush, cheese and butter, until the dish is full; put on the top thin slices of cheese and butter, put the dish in a quick oven; twenty or thirty minutes will bake it.

Pork and Beans
From "Directions for Cookery, in its Various Branches" By Eliza Leslie, 1840

Allow two pounds of pickled pork to two quarts of dried beans. If the meat is very salt put it in soak over night. Put the beans into a pot with cold water, and let them hang all night over the embers of the fire, or set them in the chimney corner, that they may warm as well as soak. Early in the morning rinse them through a cullender. Score the rind of the pork, (which should not be a very fat piece,) and put the meat into a clean pot with the beans, which must be seasoned with pepper. Let them boil slowly together for about two hours, and carefully remove all the scum and fat that rises to the top. Then take them out; lay the pork in a tin pan, and cover the meat with the beans, adding a very little water. Put it into an oven, and bake it four hours.
This is a homely dish, but is by many persons much liked. It is customary to bring it to table in the pan in which it is baked.

"The bean ration was an important factor in the sustenance of the Army, and no edible, I think, was so thoroughly appreciated." - John D. Billings, 10th Massachusetts Volunteer Artillery Battery

Potatoes
From "A Poetical Cookbook, By Maria J. Moss, 1864

Wash them, but do not pare or cut them, unless they are very large. Fill a saucepan half full of potatoes of equal size (or make them so by dividing the larger ones), put to them as much cold water as will cover them about an inch; they are sooner boiled, and more savory than when drowned in water. Most boiled things are spoiled by having too little water; but potatoes are often spoiled by having too much; they must be merely covered, and a little allowed for waste in boiling, so that they may be just covered at the finish. Set them on a moderate fire till they boil; then take them off, and put them by the side of the fire to simmer slowly till they are soft enough to admit a fork. Place no dependence on the usual test of their skins cracking, which, if they are boiled fast, will happen to some potatoes when they are not half done, and the insides quite hard. Then pour the water off--(if you let the potatoes remain in the water a moment after they are done enough, they will become waxy and watery),-- uncover the saucepan, and set it at such a distance from the fire as will secure it from burning; their superfluous moisture will evaporate, and the potatoes will be perfectly dry and mealy.

You may afterwards place a napkin, folded up to the size of the saucepan's diameter, over the potatoes, to keep them hot and mealy till wanted.

This method of managing potatoes is in every respect equal to steaming them, and they are dressed in half the time.

There is such an infinite variety of sorts and sizes of potatoes, it is impossible to say how long they will take doing: the best way is to try them with a fork. Moderate sized potatoes will generally be done enough in fifteen or twenty minutes.

Potato Balls
From "The Virginia Housewife", By Mary Randolph, 1836

Mix mashed potatos with the yelk of an egg, roll them into balls, flour them, or cover them with egg and bread crumbs, fry them in clean dripping, or brown them in a Dutch oven. They are an agreeable vegetable relish, and a supper dish.

Potatoes Fried or Broiled
From "The Complete Cook", By J. M. Sanderson, 1864

Cut cold potatoes into slices a quarter of an inch thick, and fry them brown in a clean dripping-pan. Some people like them shaved in little thin pieces, sprinkled with salt and pepper, and stirred about in the frying-pan till hot through. They are very good fried whole; first dip them in egg and roll them in bread crumbs; they are likewise very good broiled on a gridiron, after being partially boiled. Cold potatoes, which are generally thrown away, are very good when broiled.

Potato Rissouls
From "The Practical Housekeeper; A Cyclopedia of Domestic Economy", By Elizabeth Fries Ellet, 1857

Boil the potatoes floury; mash them, seasoning with salt and a little cayenne; mince parsley very finely and work up with the potatoes, adding eschalot also chopped small; bind with yolk of egg; roll into balls and fry with fresh butter over a clear fire. Meat shred finely, bacon or ham may be added.

Roasted Potatoes
From "Directions for Cookery, in its Various Branches" By Eliza Leslie, 1840

Take large fine potatoes; wash and dry them, and either lay them on the hearth and keep them buried in hot wood ashes, or bake them slowly in a Dutch oven. They will not be done in less than two hours. It will save time to half-boil them before they are roasted. Send them to table with the skins on, and eat them with cold butter and salt. They are introduced with cold meat at supper.
Potatoes keep best buried in sand or earth. They should never be wetted till they are washed for cooking. If you have them in the cellar, see that they are well covered with matting or old carpet, as the frost injures them greatly.

Preserved Pumpkin
From "The Book of Household Management", By Isabella Beeton, 1861

To each lb. of pumpkin allow 1 lb. of roughly pounded loaf sugar, 1 gill of lemon-juice.
Obtain a good sweet pumpkin; halve it, take out the seeds, and pare off the rind; cut it into neat slices, or into pieces about the size of a five-shilling piece. Weigh the pumpkin, put the slices in a pan or deep dish in layers, with the sugar sprinkled between them; pour the lemon-juice over the top, and let the whole remain for 2 or 3 days. Boil altogether, adding 1/4 pint of water to every 3 lbs. of sugar used until the pumpkin becomes tender; then turn the whole into a pan, where let it remain for a week; then drain off the syrup, boil it until it is quite thick; skim, and pour it, boiling, over the pumpkin. A little bruised ginger and lemon-rind, thinly pared, may be boiled in the syrup to flavour the pumpkin.

To Stew Red Cabbage
From "A New System of Domestic Cookery", By Maria Eliza
Ketelby Rundell, 1807

Slice a small, or half a large, red cabbage; wash and put it into a sauce-pan with pepper, salt, no water but what hangs about it, and a piece of butter. Stew till quite tender; and when going to serve, add two or three spoonfuls of vinegar, and give one boil over the fire, Serve it for cold meat, or with sausages on it.

Another way.--Shred the cabbage; wash it; and put it over a slow fire, with slices of onion, pepper and salt, and a little plain gravy. When quite tender, and a few minutes before serving, add a bit of butter rubbed with flour, and two or three spoonfuls of vinegar, and boil up.

Another.--Cut the cabbage very thin; and put it into the stew-pan with a small slice of ham, and half an ounce of butter, at the bottom, half a pint of broth, and a gill of vinegar. Let it stew covered three hours. When it is very tender, add a little more broth, salt, pepper, and. a table-spoonful of pounded sugar. Mix these well, and boil them all till the liquor is wasted; then put it into the dish, and lay fried sausages on it.

Salads
From "The Practical Housekeeper; A Cyclopedia of Domestic Economy", By
Elizabeth Fries Ellet, 1857

Toss-lettuce and blanched endive make the best salad, the green leaves being stripped off, and leaving nothing but the close, white hearts, which, after being washed and placed for an hour or two in cold water, should be wiped quite dry. To this should be added a head or two of celery, a couple of anchovies (which are far preferable to the essence), and several chives, or young onions, all cut small, while the lettuces should be divided lengthwise into quarters, and cut into rather large pieces.

To Dress Salad
From "The Virginia Housewife", By Mary Randolph, 1836

To have this delicate dish in perfection, the lettuce, pepper grass, chervil, cress, &c. should be gathered early in the morning, nicely picked, washed, and laid in cold water, which will be improved by adding ice; just before dinner is ready to be served, drain the water from your salad, cut it into a bowl, giving the proper proportions of each plant; prepare the following mixture to pour over it: boil two fresh eggs ten minutes, put them in water to cool, then take the yelks in a soup plate, pour on them a table spoonful of cold water, rub them with a wooden spoon until they are perfectly dissolved; then add two spoonsful of oil: when well mixed, put in a tea-spoonful of salt, one of powdered sugar, and one of made mustard; when all these are united and quite smooth, stir in two table spoonsful of common, and two of tarragon vinegar; put it over the salad, and garnish the top with the whites of the eggs cut into rings, and lay around the edge of the bowl young scallions, they being the most delicate of the onion tribe.

Salad Mixture

From "The Great Western Cook Book, or Table Receipts, Adapted to Western Housewifery", By Anna Maria Collins, 1857

Boil a couple of eggs fifteen minutes, and put them in a basin of water a few minutes. The yolks must be quite cold and hard. Rub them through a sieve with a wooden spoon, and mix them with a table-spoonful of water or rich cream. Then add two table-spoonsful of oil or melted butter. When these are well mixed, add by degrees a tea-spoonful of salt, or powdered loaf-sugar, the same of mustard, and, when these are smoothly united, add, very gradually, three table-spoonsful of vinegar, and rub it with the other ingredients till it is thoroughly incorporated with them; cut up the white of the egg, and garnish the top with it. This is a good sauce for any kind of salad, and is delicious when mixed with minced turkey or chicken, and celery.
Let the sauce remain in the bottom of the bowl, and do not stir the salad in it till it is to be eaten.

Salmagundy

From "A New System of Domestic Cookery", By Maria Eliza Ketelby Rundell, 1807

Is a beautiful small dish, if in nice shape, and if the colours of the ingredients are varied. For this purpose chop separately the white part of cold chicken or veal, yolks of eggs boiled hard, the whites of eggs; parsley, half a dozen anchovies, beet-root, red pickled cabbage, ham, and grated tongue, or any thing well-flavoured, and of a good colour. Some people like a small proportion of onion, but it may be better omitted. A saucer, large tea-cup, or any other base, must be put into a small dish; then make rows round it wide at bottom, and growing smaller towards the top; choosing such of the ingredients for each row as will most vary the colours. At the top a little sprig of curled parsley may be stuck in; or, without any thing on the dish, the salmagundy may be laid in rows, or put into the half-whites of eggs, which may be made to stand upright by cutting off a little bit at the round end. In the latter case, each half egg has but one ingredient. Curled butter and parsley may be put as garnish between.

Summer Salad
From "The Book of Household Management", By Isabella
Beeton, 1861

3 lettuces, 2 handfuls of mustard-and-cress, 10 young radishes, a few slices of cucumber.

Let the herbs be as fresh as possible for a salad, and, if at all stale or dead-looking, let them lie in water for an hour or two, which will very much refresh them. Wash and carefully pick them over, remove any decayed or wormeaten leaves, and drain them thoroughly by swinging them gently in a clean cloth. With a silver knife, cut the lettuces into small pieces, and the radishes and cucumbers into thin slices; arrange all these ingredients lightly on a dish, with the mustard-and-cress, and pour under, but not over the salad, either of the sauces No. 506, 507, or 508, and do not stir it up until it is to be eaten. It may be garnished with hard-boiled eggs, cut in slices, sliced cucumbers, nasturtiums, cut vegetable-flowers, and many other things that taste will always suggest to make a pretty and elegant dish. In making a good salad, care must be taken to have the herbs freshly gathered, and *thoroughly drained* before the sauce is added to them, or it will be watery and thin. Young spring onions, cut small, are by many persons considered an improvement to salads; but, before these are added, the cook should always consult the taste of her employer. Slices of cold meat or poultry added to a salad make a convenient and quickly-made summer luncheon-dish; or cold fish, flaked, will also be found exceedingly nice, mixed with it.

Spinach and Eggs
From "Directions for Cookery, in its Various Branches" By Eliza Leslie, 1840

Boil the spinach (Chop it fine, and put it into a sauce-pan with a piece of butter and a little pepper and salt. Set it on hot coals, and let it stew five minutes, stirring it all the time.), and drain and press it, but do not chop it. Have ready some eggs poached as follows. Boil in a sauce-pan, and skim some clear spring water, adding to it a table-spoonful of vinegar. Break the eggs separately, and having taken the sauce-pan off the fire, slip the eggs one at a time into it with as much dexterity as you can. Let the sauce-pan stand by the side of the fire till the white is set, and then put it over the fire for two minutes. The yolk should be thinly covered by the white. Take them up with an egg slice, and having trimmed the edges of the whites, lay the eggs on the top of the spinach, which should firstly seasoned with pepper and salt and a little butter, and must be sent to table hot.

Fried Sweet Potatoes

From "Directions for Cookery, in its Various Branches" By Eliza Leslie, 1840

Choose them of the largest size. Half boil them, and then having taken off the skins, cut the potatoes in slices, and fry them in butter, or in nice dripping.
Sweet potatoes are very good stewed with fresh pork, veal, or beef.
The best way to keep them through the cold weather, is to bury them in earth or sand; otherwise they will be scarcely eatable after October.

Scolloped Tomatoes

From "The Lady's Receipt-Book; a Useful Companion for Large or Small Families", By Eliza Leslie, 1847

Take fine large tomatoes, perfectly ripe. Scald them to loosen the skins, and then peel them. Cover the bottom of a deep dish thickly with grated bread-crumbs, adding a few bits of fresh butter. Then put in a layer of tomatoes, seasoned slightly with a little salt and cayenne, and some powdered mace or nutmeg. Cover them with another layer of bread-crumbs and butter. Then another layer of seasoned tomatoes; and proceed thus till the dish is full, finishing at the top with bread-crumbs. Set the dish into a moderate oven, and bake it near three hours.
Tomatoes require long cooking, otherwise they will have a raw taste, that to most persons is unpleasant.

The decades following the Civil War have produced sufficient genetic modifications to the tomato, that our forefathers would have difficulty recognizing our modern fruit! For reenacting and culinary purposes of the accompanying recipes, it is recommended that Heirloom type fruits be used. While grown and used throughout pre-Civil War America, tomatoes weren't as loved as they are today. The Tomato family has among it's cousins the deadly nightshades and other poisonous plants; this relationship caused some to fear the tomato. Even today, the intensely aromatic leaves and stem of the tomato are commonly thought to be toxic, which they are not. American colonists from continental Europe had been using tomatoes for cooking in their settlements, especially in more urban cities along the eastern coast and Mississippi River. But in isolated rural areas, settlers considered the unfamiliar tomato with fear and skepticism. Tomatoes were basically an ornamental garden plant, grown mainly in the south. Wrote Working Farmer editor James Mapes, of Newark, New Jersey, the tomato was "long grown in our gardens as an ornamental plant, under the name of Love Apple, before being used at all as a culinary vegetable. About 1827 or '28, we occasionally heard of its being eaten in French or Spanish families, but seldom if ever by others." The Civil War era, however, was the true turning point of the tomato as an edible. The industrial production of canned vegetables and fruits was increased in order to fulfill contracts to the Federal government to feed the armies. Tomatoes, which could be quickly grown and proved durable during the canning process, were easier to produce and ship to the troops. After the war, public demand for canned goods grew, and tomatoes were being canned more than any other vegetable. This meant more farmers were needed to grow them. Today, we grow, preserve and brag about our tomatoes in gardens, along the garage or in 5 gallon buckets. They are the definition of a great summer treat, eaten like an apple with salt, cut up for sandwiches or made into a sauce. Thanks to the Civil War, tomatoes have sky-rocketed to popularity and are enjoyed to this day!

Tomatoes, To Stuff
From "The Practical Housekeeper; A Cyclopedia of Domestic Economy", By Elizabeth Fries Ellet, 1857

Take some fine tomatoes and scoop the inside out, which should be set aside until required. Chop or mince fine some beef, mutton, or other fresh under-done meat, mix with a little pepper, salt, and a little sweet herbs; or make a forcemeat, and mix with the scoopings of the tomatoes; form into a good consistence, and stuff the inside of the vegetable with the mixture. Set the prepared vegetables in a dish with a little lard in a slow oven, and bake until tender; then serve with the liquor that exudes during the process; but if not brown enough, color by means of a salamander held over the top of each. A good rich beef gravy poured over all, improves the flavor very much. This is the best way to dress these vegetables, and serves also to make cold meat more palatable, in addition to forming a pretty and economical side dish.

To Make Vermecelli
From "The Virginia Housewife", By Mary Randolph, 1836

Beat two or three fresh eggs quite light, make them into a stiff paste with flour, knead it well, and roll it out very thin, cut it in narrow strips, give them a twist, and dry them quickly on tin sheets. It is an excellent ingredient in most soups, particularly those that are thin. Noodles are made in the same manner, only instead of strips they should be cut in tiny squares and dried. They are also good in soups.

5. BREAD AND BISCUITS

President Jefferson Davis asked his nation to spend March 27, 1863 in fasting and prayer for the "Cause". Many viewed such a request to an already starving populace to go without food as an insult. On April 1, a group of poor working women held a meeting in a Baptist church to organize a protest against the rising costs of food. Mary Jackson and Martha Fergussen stirred the audience with tales of rampant speculation and price gouging in the markets. Soon the angry mob agreed to meet the very next day, outside of the Capitol building, to cry for bread and justice from those running the country.

The women arrived at the Capitol around 9 a.m. the next day. They demanded an audience with the governor, John Letcher, but an aide informed them that the governor was too busy. This further angered the women, and soon a mob of hundreds of armed, hungry housewives was left listlessly flowing around the Capitol building. Letcher, hearing the commotion from his office, came down to address the women, but his dismissive words accomplished nothing in the ways of appeasement to their demands. Quietly, the women filed out of the Capitol yard making their way to the market district.

Within an hour, the mob used their axes to loot shops, steal carts and break into storage lockers. As the cries of "bread or blood!" filled the air, they seized a wagon of beef meant for a hospital, and 500 pounds of bacon from a warehouse. Soon Governor Letcher arrived, as did Jefferson Davis himself, who attempted to calm the women by offering them his last loaf of bread. Davis' gesture was not enough for the mob, and a riot guard loaded their weapons before the women finally took their looted goods and retreated to their homes.

To Make Goode Homemade Bread
From "The Book of Household Management", By Isabella Beeton, 1861

1 quartern of flour, 1 large tablespoonful of solid brewer's yeast, or nearly 1 oz. of fresh German yeast, 1-1/4 to 1-1/2 pint of warm milk-and-water.

Put the flour into a large earthenware bowl or deep pan; then, with a strong metal or wooden spoon, hollow out the middle; but do not clear it entirely away from the bottom of the pan, as, in that case, the sponge (or leaven, as it was formerly termed) would stick to it, which it ought not to do. Next take either a large tablespoonful of brewer's yeast which has been rendered solid by mixing it with plenty of cold water, and letting it afterwards stand to settle for a day and night; or nearly an ounce of German yeast; put it into a large basin, and proceed to mix it, so that it shall be as smooth as cream, with 3/4 pint of warm milk-and-water, or with water only; though even a very little milk will much improve the bread. Pour the yeast into the hole made in the flour, and stir into it as much of that which lies round it as will make a thick batter, in which there must be no lumps. Strew plenty of flour on the top; throw a thick clean cloth over, and set it where the air is warm; but do not place it upon the kitchen fender, for it will become too much heated there. Look at it from time to time: when it has been laid for nearly an hour, and when the yeast has risen and broken through the flour, so that bubbles appear in it, you will know that it is ready to be made up into dough. Then place the pan on a strong chair, or dresser, or table, of convenient height; pour into the sponge the remainder of the warm milk-and-water; stir into it as much of the flour as you can with the spoon; then wipe it out clean with your fingers, and lay it aside. Next take plenty of the remaining flour, throw it on the top of the leaven, and begin, with the knuckles of both hands, to knead it well. When the flour is nearly all kneaded in, begin to draw the edges of the dough towards the middle, in order to mix the whole thoroughly; and when it is free from flour and lumps and crumbs, and does not stick to the hands when touched, it will be done, and may again be covered with the cloth, and left to rise a second time. In 3/4 hour look at it, and should it have swollen very much, and begin to crack, it will be light enough to bake. Turn it then on to a paste-board or very clean dresser, and with a large sharp knife divide it in two; make it up quickly into loaves, and dispatch it to the oven: make one or two incisions across the tops of the loaves, as they will rise more easily if this be done. If baked in tins or pans, rub them with a tiny piece of butter laid on a piece of clean paper, to prevent the dough from sticking to them. All bread should be turned upside down, or on its side, as soon as it is drawn from the oven: if this be neglected, the under part of the loaves will become wet and blistered from the steam, which cannot then escape from them. To make the dough without setting a sponge, merely mix the yeast with the greater part of the warm milk-and-water, and wet up the whole of the flour at once after a little salt has been stirred in, proceeding exactly, in every other respect, as in the directions just given. As the dough will soften in the rising, it should be made quite firm at first, or it will be too lithe by the time it is ready for the oven.

Brown, or Dyspepsia Bread
From "The Practical Housekeeper; A Cyclopedia of Domestic Economy", By Elizabeth Fries Ellet, 1857

Take six quarts of wheat meal, rather coarsely ground, one teacup of good yeast, and half a teacup of molasses, mix these with a pint of milk-warm water and a teaspoonful of saleratus. Make a hole in the meal and stir this mixture in the middle till it is like batter. Then proceed as with fine flour bread. Make the dough, when sufficiently light, into four loaves, which will weigh two pounds per loaf when baked. It requires a hotter oven than fine flour bread, and must bake about an hour and a half.

A Good Plain Bun, That May Be Eaten With or Without Toasting and Butter
From "A New System of Domestic Cookery", By Maria Eliza Ketelby Rundell, 1807

Rub four ounces of butter into two pounds of flour, four ounces of sugar, a nutmeg, or not, as you like, a few Jamaica peppers, a desert spoonful of caraways; put a spoonful or two of cream into a cup of yeast, and as much good milk as will make the above into a light paste. Set it to rise by a fire till the oven be ready. They will quickly bake on tins.

Carraway Gingerbread
From "The Lady's Receipt-Book; a Useful Companion for Large or Small Families", By Eliza Leslie, 1847

Cut up half a pound of fresh butter in a pint of West India molasses and warm them together slightly, till the butter is quite soft. Then stir them well, and add, gradually, a pound of good brown sugar, a table-spoonful of powdered cinnamon, and two heaped table-spoonfuls of ground ginger, or three, if the ginger is not very strong. Sift two pounds or two quarts of flour. Beat four eggs till very thick and light, and stir them, gradually, into the mixture, in turn with the flour, and five or six large table-spoonfuls of carraway seeds, a little at a time. Dissolve a very small tea-spoonful of pearlash or soda in as much lukewarm water as will cover it. Then stir it in at the last. Stir all very hard. Transfer it to a buttered tin pan with straight sides, and bake it in a loaf in a moderate oven. It will require a great deal of baking.

Corn Meal Bread
From "The Virginia Housewife", By Mary Randolph, 1836

Rub a piece of butter the size of an egg, into a pint of corn meal—make it a batter with two eggs, and some new milk--add a spoonful of yeast, set it by the fire an hour to rise, butter little pans, and bake it.

Corn Muffins (from the South)
From "Miss Beecher's Domestic Receipt Book", By Catharine Esther Beecher, 1850

One pint of sifted meal, and half a teaspoonful of salt. A teaspoonful of saleratus, in two great spoonfuls of hot water.
Wet the above with sour milk, as thick as for mush or hasty pudding, and bake in buttered rings on a buttered tin.

To Make Drop Biscuit
From "The Virginia Housewife", By Mary Randolph, 1836

Beat eight eggs very light, add to them twelve ounces of flour, and one pound of sugar; when perfectly light, drop them on tin sheets, and bake them in a quick oven.

Egg Biscuit
From "The Practical Housekeeper; A Cyclopedia of Domestic Economy", By Elizabeth Fries Ellet, 1857

One pound of flour; wet nearly all of it to a paste with the whites of two eggs, beat and roll out thin, work in three-quarters of a pound of butter, placing bits on the paste, flouring, folding, and rolling it out again till all is used. Move the rolling pin from you always. Cut out in small squares or with a tumbler, and bake in a quick oven.

French Bread and Rolls
From "The Cook's Oracle; and Housekeeper's Manual", By William Kitchiner, 1830

Take a pint and a half of milk; make it quite warm; half a pint of small-beer yest; add sufficient flour to make it as thick as batter; put it into a pan; cover it over, and keep it warm: when it has risen as high as it will, add a quarter of a pint of warm water, and half an ounce of salt,--mix them well together;--rub into a little flour two ounces of butter; then make your dough, not quite so stiff as for your bread; let it stand for three quarters of an hour, and it will be ready to make into rolls, &c.: let them stand till they have risen, and bake them in a quick oven.

French Rolls
From "Directions for Cookery, in its Various Branches" By Eliza Leslie, 1840

Sift a pound of flour into a pan, and rub into it two ounces of butter; mix in the whites only of three eggs, beaten to a stiff froth, and a table-spoonful of strong yeast; add sufficient milk to make a stiff dough, and a salt-spoonful of salt. Cover it and set it before the fire to rise. It should be light in an hour. Then put it on a paste-board, divide it into rolls, or round cakes; lay them in a floured square pan, and bake them about ten minutes in a quick oven.

Hoe Cake
From "Directions for Cookery, in its Various Branches" By Eliza Leslie, 1840

Beat the whites of three eggs to a stiff froth, and sift into a pan a quart of wheat flour, adding a salt-spoon of salt. Make a hole in the middle, and mix in the white of egg so as to form a thick batter, and then add two table-spoonfuls of the best fresh yeast. Cover it, and let it stand all night. In the morning, take a hoe-iron (such as are made purposely for cakes) and prop it before the fire till, it is well heated. Then flour a tea-saucer, and filling it with batter, shake it about, and clap it to the hoe, (which must be previously greased,) and the batter will adhere, till it is baked. Repeat this with each cake. Keep them hot, and eat them with butter.

Indian Bread
From "Confederate Receipt Book: Over 100 Recipes Adapted to Our Times", 1863

One quart of butter milk, one quart of corn meal, one quart of coarse flour, one cup of molasses, add a little soda and salt.

Pumpkin Bread
From "The Great Western Cookbook" By A. M. Collins, 1851

Take two quarts of sweet pumpkin, stewed dry; two quarts of fine Indian meal, two tea-spoonsful of salt, a table-spoon heaping full of lard, and mix them up with sufficient hot water to make it of the consistence of common corn-meal dough. Set it in a warm place, two hours, to rise, and bake it in a pan, in a moderate oven. It will take an hour and a half to bake.

"Lucy, I would like to eat some of her pumpkin bread, fatty bread, potatoes, baked possum, baked chicken, and other eatables, but I content myself for the present and think how I will do when I get home." --Pvt. James A. Durrett, Co. E, 18th Alabama Infantry, Nov. 12, 1863 in the Chattanooga Valley, Tennessee. Letter to his mother. He was shot through the head and died April 3, 1865 at Spanish Fort, Mobile Alabama

Rice Bread
From "The Book of Household Management", By Isabella Beeton, 1861

To every lb. of rice allow 4 lbs. of wheat flour, nearly 3 tablespoonfuls of yeast, 1/4 oz. of salt. Boil the rice in water until it is quite tender; pour off the water, and put the rice, before it is cold, to the flour. Mix these well together with the yeast, salt, and sufficient warm water to make the whole into a smooth dough; let it rise by the side of the fire, then form it into loaves, and bake them from 1-1/2 to 2 hours, according to their size. If the rice is boiled in milk instead of water, it makes very delicious bread or cakes. When boiled in this manner, it may be mixed with the flour without straining the liquid from it.
Time-1-1/2 to 2 hours.

Richer Buns
From "A New System of Domestic Cookery", By
Maria Eliza Ketelby Rundell, 1807

Mix one pound and a half of dried flour with half a pound of sugar; melt a pound and two ounces of butter in a little warm water; add six spoonfuls of rose-water, and knead the above into a light dough, with half a pint of yeast; then mix five ounces of caraway-comfits in, and put some on them.

Rusks
From "A New System of Domestic Cookery", By
Maria Eliza Ketelby Rundell, 1807

Beat seven eggs well, and mix with half a pint of new milk, in which have been melted four ounces of butter, add to it a quarter of a pint of yeast, and three ounces of sugar, and put them, by degrees, into as much flour as will make a very light paste, rather like a batter, and let it rise before the fire half an hour; then add some more flour, to make it a little stiffer, but not stiff. Work it well, and divide it into small loaves, or cakes about five or six inches wide, and flatten them. When baked and cold, slice them the thickness of rusks, and put them in the oven to brown a little.

Note-The cakes, when first baked, eat deliciously buttered for tea; or, with caraways, to eat cold.

Rye Bread
From "The Lady's Own Cookery Book", By Charlotte Campbell Bury, 1844

Ingredients 1 peck of wheaten flour 6 pounds of rye flour a little salt 1/2 pint of good yeast
Instructions Take the wheaten flour, rye flour, salt, yeast, and as much warm water as will make it into a stiff dough. Let it stand three hours to rise before you put it into the oven. A large loaf will take three hours to bake.

Sweet Potato Buns
From "The Virginia Housewife", By Mary Randolph, 1836

Boil and mash a potato, rub into it as much flour as will make it like bread--add spice and sugar to your taste, with a spoonful of yeast; when it has risen well, work in a piece of butter, bake it in small rolls, to be eaten hot with butter, either for breakfast or tea.

Tavern Biscuit
From "The Virginia Housewife", By Mary Randolph, 1836

To one pound of flour, add half a pound of sugar, half a pound of butter, some mace and nutmeg powdered, and a glass of brandy or wine; wet it with milk, and when well kneaded, roll it thin, cut it in shapes, and bake it quickly.

Tennessee Muffins
From "Directions for Cookery, in its Various Branches" By Eliza Leslie, 1840

Sift three pints of yellow Indian meal, and put one-half into a pan and scald it. Then set it away to get cold. Beat six: eggs, whites and yolks separately. The yolks must be beaten till they become very thick and smooth, and the whites till they are a stiff froth, that stands alone. When the scalded meal is cold, mix it into a batter with the beaten yolk of egg, the remainder of the meal, a salt-spoonful of salt, and, if necessary, a little water. The batter must be quite thick. At the last, stir in, lightly and slowly, the beaten white of egg. Grease your muffin rings, and set them in an oven of the proper heat; put in the batter immediately, as standing will injure it.

Send them to table hot; pull them open, and eat them with butter.

6. DESSERTS

"Margaret, I will tell you that Aunt Milly sent me some provisions by Lee Westmoreland and I have plenty of bread and butter and collards and potatoes yet. I have not eat any of my peaches yet but I have to get some pies made and have some made and if I get in for a regular cook, I can store them myself. And if I didn't get in for a cook, I will go to the camp for I would not be a nurse for fifty dollars a month. But I would rather be a cook than to be at camp for I would not have to stand guard and I would be in a house." - Pvt. Joseph S. Lipe , Co. I, 7th North Carolina Infantry, Nov. 30, 1861, Carolina City Camp Argyle, North Carolina. Letter to his wife, Margaret. During the Battle of Gaines Mill, Joseph was critically wounded (gut shot) on June 27, 1862 and died in the St. Charles Hospital in Richmond on July 2, 1862. The St. Charles Hospital (former St. Charles Hotel) was also known as General Hospital #8.

Almond Cake
From "The Book of Household Management", By Isabella Beeton, 1861

1/2 lb. of sweet almonds, 1 oz. of bitter almonds, 6 eggs, 8 tablespoonfuls of sifted sugar, 5 tablespoonfuls of fine flour, the grated rind of 1 lemon, 3 oz. of butter.
Blanch and pound the almonds to a paste; separate the whites from

the yolks of the eggs; beat the latter, and add them to the almonds. Stir in the sugar, flour, and lemon-rind; add the butter, which should be beaten to a cream; and when all these ingredients are well mixed, put in the whites of the eggs, which should be whisked to a stiff froth. Butter a cake-mould, put in the mixture, and bake in a good oven from 1-1/4 to 1-3/4 hour.

Almond Cheesecakes
From "The Book of Household Management", By Isabella Beeton, 1861

¼ lb. of sweet almonds, 4 bitter ones, 3 eggs, 2 oz. of butter, the rind of 1 lemon, 1 tablespoonful of lemon-juice, 3 oz. of sugar.
Blanch and pound the almonds smoothly in a mortar, with a little rose- or spring-water; stir in the eggs, which should be well beaten, and the butter, which should be warmed; add the grated lemon-peel and juice, sweeten, and stir well until the whole is thoroughly mixed. Line some pattypans with puff-paste, put in the mixture, and bake for 20 minutes, or rather less in a quick oven.
Time: 20 minutes, or rather less.

An Excellent and Cheap Dessert Dish
From "The Virginia Housewife", By Mary Randolph, 1836

Wash a pint of small homony very clean, and boil it tender; add an equal quantity of corn meal, make it into a batter with eggs, milk, and a piece of butter; bake it like batter cakes on a griddle, and eat it with butter and molasses.

An Apple Custard
From "The Virginia Housewife", By Mary Randolph, 1836

Pare and core twelve pippins, slice them tolerably thick, put a pound of loaf sugar in a stew pan, with a pint of water and twelve cloves: boil and skim it, then put in the apples, and stew them till clear, and but little of the syrup remains--lay them in a deep dish, and take out the cloves; when the apples are cold, pour in a quart of rich boiled custard--set it in water, and make it boil till the custard is set—take care the water does not get into it.

Apple Dumplings
From "A Poetical Cookbook, By Maria J. Moss, 1864

Pare and scoop out the core of six large baking apples; put part of a clove and a little grated lemon-peel inside of each, and enclose them in pieces of puff paste; boil them in nets for the purpose, or bits of linen, for an hour. Before serving, cut off a small bit from the top of each, and put a teaspoonful of sugar and a bit of fresh butter; replace the bit of paste, and strew over them pounded loaf sugar.

"CSA stands for corn, salt and apples, the staple of the Confederate soldier," said a Rebel soldier at Gettysburg when asked by a civilian what "CSA" stood for.

Apple Pie
From "A New System of Domestic Cookery", By Maria Eliza Ketelby Rundell, 1807

Pare and core the fruit, having wiped the outside; which, with the cores, boil with a little water till it tastes well; strain, and put a little sugar, and a bit of bruised cinnamon, and simmer again. In the mean time place the apples in a dish, a paste being put round the edge; when one layer is in, sprinkle half the sugar, and shred lemon-peel, and squeeze some juice, or a glass of cyder if the apples have lost their spirit; put in the rest of the apples, sugar, and the liquor that you have boiled. Cover with paste. You may add some butter when cut, if eaten hot; or put quince-marmalade, orange-paste, or cloves, to flavour.

Bread Pudding
From "The Virginia Housewife", By Mary Randolph, 1836

Grate the crumb of a stale loaf, and pour on it a pint of boiling milk--let it stand an hour, then beat it to a pulp; add six eggs, well beaten, half a pound of butter, the same of powdered sugar, half a nutmeg, a glass of brandy, and some grated lemon peel--put a paste in the dish, and bake it.

Child's Feather Cake
From "Miss Beecher's Domestic Receipt
Book", By Catharine Esther Beecher, 1850

Three cups of light dough, Two cups rolled sugar,
Three well-beaten eggs, mixed with the sugar and
butter, Half a cup of warm milk, or a little less, One
teaspoonful of saleratus in two great spoonfuls of
water, and put in the milk, One cup of melted butter,
worked into the sugar, The grated rind and juice of
one lemon.
Work all together, adding the lemon juice just before
putting it in buttered pans.
If you have no lemons, use one nutmeg, and a
tablespoonful of sharp vinegar, added just before
putting it in pans. One and a half, if the vinegar is
weak. Some think this improved by standing to rise
fifteen minutes. Try it.

Columbian Pudding
From "The Lady's Receipt-Book; a Useful Companion for Large or
Small Families", By Eliza Leslie, 1847

Tie up closely in a bit of very thin white muslin, a vanilla bean cut
into pieces; and a broken-up stick of cinnamon. Put this bag with
its contents into half a pint of rich milk, and boil it a long time till
very highly flavoured. Then take out the bag; set the milk near the
fire to keep warm in the pan in which it was boiled, covering it
closely. Slice thin a pound of almond sponge-cake, and lay it in a
deep dish. Pour over it a quart of rich cream, with which you must
mix the vanilla-flavoured milk, and leave the cake to dissolve in it.
Blanch, in scalding water, two ounces of shelled bitter almonds or
peach-kernels; and pound them (one at a time) to a smooth paste in
a marble mortar; pouring on each a few drops of rose-water or
peach-water to prevent their oiling. When the almonds are done, set
them away in a cold place till wanted. Beat eight eggs till very light
and thick; and having stirred together, hard, the dissolved cake and
the cream, add them, gradually, to the mixture in turn with the
almond, and half a pound of powdered loaf sugar, a little at a time
of each. Butter a deep dish, and put in the mixture. Set the pudding
into a brisk oven and bake it well. Have ready a star nicely cut out of
a large piece of candied citron, a number of small stars all of equal

size, as many as there are states in the Union: and a sufficiency of rays or long strips also cut out of citron. The rays should be wide at the bottom and run to a point at the top. As soon as the pudding comes out of the oven, while it is smoking, arrange these decorations. Put the large star in the centre, then the rays so that they will diverge from it, widening off towards the edge of the pudding. Near the edge place the small stars in a circle.
Preserved citron-melon will be still better for this purpose than the dry candied citron.
This is a very fine pudding; suitable for a dinner party, or a Fourth of July dinner.

An Excellent Corn-Meal Pudding

From "The Lady's Receipt-Book; a Useful Companion for Large or Small Families", By Eliza Leslie, 1847

Boil a quart of rich milk, and pour it scalding hot into a large pan. Stir in, gradually, a quart of sifted Indian meal, and a quarter of a pound of fresh butter; adding the grated yellow rind of a lemon or orange. Squeeze the juice upon a quarter of a pound of brown sugar, and stir that in also. Add a large tea-spoonful of powdered cinnamon. Have ready a pound of raisins, seeded, and cut in half, and dredged thickly with wheat flour, to prevent their sinking. Beat six eggs very light, and stir them gradually into the mixture. Lastly, stir in the raisins, a few at a time, and stir the whole very hard. Have ready a large pot of boiling water; dip into it a square pudding-cloth, shake it out, and dredge it with flour. Spread out the cloth in a deep, empty pan, and pour into it the pudding-mixture. Tie it firmly, leaving room for the pudding to swell. Put it into the pot of hot water, and boil it four hours, or five; turning it several times, while boiling; and replenishing the water, as it boils away, with water kept hot, for the purpose, in a kettle. When done, take out the pudding from the pot; dip it, for a minute into cold water, before you untie the cloth; then turn it out into a dish, and send it to table. It should not be taken out of the pot till a minute or two before it is wanted.
Eat it with wine-sauce; or with butter, white sugar nutmeg, and lemon or orange-juice, beaten together to a light cream.
What is left, may be tied again in a cloth, and boiled for an hour, next day.
Instead of butter, you may use a quarter of a pound of beef-suet, minced as fine as possible.

Cracker Pie

From "The Practical Housekeeper; A
Cyclopedia of Domestic Economy", By
Elizabeth Fries Ellet, 1857

One soda biscuit and a half, one teacup of white sugar, one lemon, one teacup of boiling water. Break the biscuit into small bits, pour over them the boiling water, cover, and leave them to swell. Grate the yellow part of the rind of the lemon, add to it the juice and the sugar, mix with the cracker when it is sufficiently swelled; make a nice crust, and prepare as apple pies. Sift sugar over the pies when baked.

Pot Apple Pie

From "The Great Western
Cookbook" By A. M. Collins, 1851

Pare and slice your apples, and put them in a pot. Make your crust of a half a pint of sour milk, sweeten it with a little molasses, add a little allspice, lay it over the top of your apples, leave an opening for the steam to pass through; put a little water to your apple, let it stew slowly, three-quarters of an hour; when done, take up your crust in one dish, spice and sweeten your apple in another; slice your crust, and cover it with your apples. To be eaten with butter, while warm.

"It rained last night every time I was on guard. I came off guard duty at 1am. Went and got some apples"- Diary of Homer Harris Jewett, 1861 (Born in Pella, IA. Served as Private with Co. D, 7th Regiment, Missouri Cavalry, Federal. After the end of the Civil War, Homer moved south into Louisiana and was never heard from again as he went missing after March 9, 1866).

English Curd Pie

From: "Miss Beecher's Domestic Receipt Book'" By Catherine Esther Beecher,
1846

One quart of milk. A bit of rennet to curdle it.
Press out the whey, and put into the curds three eggs, a nutmeg, and a tablespoonful of brandy. Bake it in paste, like custard.
Heat the milk in a stainless steel saucepan and, stirring often, warm it to the required temperature (each recipe varies slightly).

Still stirring, add the rennet (or citric acid), as for ricotta. Cover; let curds form without stirring, keeping the temperature steady.

Using a rubber spatula, break up the curd. This will allow the whey to separate from the curd. A resting period usually follows this step.

Place a sturdy cheesecloth over a bowl. Using a slotted spoon, transfer the curd to a cheesecloth.

Grab the cheesecloth and pull it tight, allowing the whey to drain off into the bowl underneath.

Into the curds, 3 medium eggs, 2 teaspoons nutmeg, and a generous tablespoon of brandy.

Mix well and pour into a pie crust.

Bake at 350* for 30 minutes.

Lafayette Gingerbread
From "A Poetical Cookbook, By Maria J. Moss, 1864

Five eggs, half pound of brown sugar, half pound fresh butter, a pint of sugarhouse molasses, a pound and a half of flour, four tablespoonfuls of ginger, two large sticks of cinnamon, three dozen grains of allspice, three dozen of cloves, juice and grated peel of two lemons. Stir the butter and sugar to a cream; beat the eggs very well; pour the molasses at once into the butter and sugar. Add the ginger and other spice, and stir all well together. Put in the eggs and flour alternately, stirring all the time. Stir the whole very hard, and put in the lemon at the last. When the whole is mixed, stir it till very light. Butter an earthen pan, or a thick tin or iron one, and put the gingerbread in it. Bake it in a moderate oven an hour or more, according to its thickness, or you may bake it in small cakes or little tins.

Molasses Cake
From "The Lady's Receipt-Book; a Useful Companion for Large or Small Families", By Eliza Leslie, 1847

Cut up a quarter of pound of fresh butter into a pint of West India molasses. Warm it just sufficiently to soften the butter, and make it mix easily. Stir it well into the molasses, and add a tablespoonful of powdered cinnamon. Beat three eggs very light, and stir them, gradually, into the mixture, in turn with barely enough of sifted flour (not more than a pint and a half) to make it about as thick as pound-cake batter. Add, at the last, a small or level tea-spoonful of pearlash, or a full one of soda, dissolved in a very little warm water. Butter some small tin cake-pans, or patty-pans, put in the mixture, and set them immediately into the oven, which must not be too hot, as all cakes made with molasses are peculiarly liable to scorch on the outside.

Pilgrim Cake
From "Miss Beecher's Domestic Receipt Book", By Catharine Esther Beecher, 1850

Rub two spoonfuls of butter into a quart of flour, and wet it to dough with cold water. Rake open a place in the hottest part of the hearth, roll out the dough into a cake an inch thick, flour it well both sides, and lay it on hot ashes. Cover it with hot ashes, and then with coals. When cooked, wipe off the ashes, and it will be very sweet and good.

The Kentucky corn cake, and common dough, can be baked the same way. This method was used by our pilgrim and pioneer forefathers.

Plum Cake
From "The Complete Cook", By J. M. Sanderson, 1864

A quartern of dough, half a pound of moist sugar, half a pound of butter, a tea-cup full of cream and two eggs, a pound of currants (add raisins if you please) a tea-spoonful of allspice, two ounces of candied orange peel cut small, and an ounce of carraway seeds. Roll the dough out several times, and spread over the several ingredients; flour the pan well, and set it on one side the fire to rise; bake an hour and a half. A richer cake may be made by adding more sweetmeats, butter, eggs, and almonds, and so forth. The dough made as bread; when risen, melt the butter in warm milk and put to it with the other ingredients, and put to rise.

Pound Cake
From "The Virginia Housewife", By Mary Randolph, 1836

Wash the salt from a pound of butter, and rub it till it is soft as cream--have ready a pound of flour sifted, one of powdered sugar, and twelve eggs well beaten; put alternately into the butter, sugar, flour, and the froth from the eggs--continuing to beat them together till all the ingredients are in, and the cake quite light: add some grated lemon peel, a nutmeg, and a gill of brandy; butter the pans, and bake them. This cake makes an excellent pudding, if baked in a large mould, and eaten with sugar and wine. It is also excellent when boiled, and served up with melted butter, sugar and wine.

Pumpkin Pie
From "The Great Western Cookbook" By A. M.

Collins, 1851

Stew a rich, sweet pumpkin, pass it through a sieve. Take five eggs, beat them well with two tea-cupsful of sugar, half a pound of butter, a little salt, half a nutmeg, two tea-spoonsful of essence of lemon; beat this well, then thicken it with pumpkin, and bake it on puff-paste.

Rice Pudding
From "The Complete Cook", By J. M. Sanderson, 1864

Take two parts of a pound of rice, put it in a cloth or bag that would hold three times the quantity; put it into boiling water, and let it boil an hour. Take it up, and beat two eggs and add to it; mix and beat with the rice a little sugar, nutmeg, and one ounce of suet, or butter, with or without currants; flour a cloth and tie it tight in it, and let it boil half an hour. Sauce, boiled milk with a little sugar and nutmeg, or wine sauce.

Rice Sponge Cake

From "The Lady's Receipt Book; A Useful Companion for Large and Small Families", By Eliza Leslie, 1847

Put twelve eggs into a scale, and balance them in the other scale with their weight in broken loaf-sugar. Take out four of the eggs, remove the sugar, and balance the remaining eight eggs with an equal quantity of rice-flour. Rub off on some lumps of the sugar, the yellow rind of three fine large ripe lemons. Then powder all the sugar. Break the eggs, one at a time, into a saucer, and put all the whites into a pitcher, and all the yolks into a broad shallow earthen pan. Having poured the whites of egg from the pitcher through a strainer into a rather shallow pan, beat them till so stiff that they stand alone. Then add the powdered sugar, gradually, to the white of egg, and beat it in well. In the other pan, beat the yolks till very smooth and thick. Then mix them, gradually, a little at a time, with the white of egg and sugar. Lastly, stir in, by degrees, the rice-flour, adding it lightly, and stirring it slowly and gently round till the surface is covered with bubbles. Transfer it directly to a butter tin pan; set it immediately into a brisk oven; and bake it an hour and a half or more, according to its thickness. Ice it when cool; flavouring the icing with lemon or rose. This cake will be best the day it is baked.
In every sort of sponge-cake, Naples-biscuit, lady-fingers, and in all cakes made without butter, it is important to know that though the egg and sugar is to be beaten very hard, the flour, which must *always* go in at the last, must be stirred in very slowly and lightly, holding the whisk or stirring-rods

perpendicularly or upright in your hand; and moving it gently round and round on the surface of the batter without allowing it to go down deeply. If the flour is stirred in hard and fast, the cake will certainly be tough, leathery, and unwholesome. Sponge-cake when cut should look coarse-grained and rough.

Suet Paste
From "Directions for Cookery, in its Various Branches" By Eliza Leslie, 1840

Having removed the skirt and stringy fibres from a pound of beef suet, chop it as fine as possible. Sift two quarts of flour into a deep pan, and rub into it one half of the suet. Make, it into a round lump of dough, with cold water, and then knead it a little. Lay the dough on your paste-board, roll it out very thin, and cover it with the remaining half of the suet. Flour it, roll it out thin again, and then roll it into a scroll. Cut it into as many pieces as you want sheets of paste, and roll them out half an inch thick.

Suet paste should always be boiled. It is good for plain puddings that are made of apples, gooseberries, blackberries or other fruit; and for dumplings. If you use it for pot-pie, roll it the last time rather thicker than if wanted for any other purpose. If properly made, it will be light and flaky, and the suet imperceptible. If the suet is minced very fine, and thoroughly incorporated with the flour, not the slightest lump will appear when the paste comes to table. The suet must not be melted before it is used; but merely minced as fine as possible and mixed cold with the flour. If for dumplings to eat with boiled mutton, the dough must be rolled out thick, and cut out of the size you want them, with a tin, or with the edge of a cup or tumbler.

Sweet Potato Pudding
From "The Virginia Housewife", By Mary Randolph, 1836

Boil one pound of sweet potatos very tender, rub them while hot through a colander; add six eggs well beaten, three quarters of a pound of powdered sugar, three quarters of butter, and some grated nutmeg and lemon peel, with a glass of brandy; put a paste in the dish, and when the pudding is done, sprinkle the top with sugar, and cover it with bits of citron. Irish potato pudding is made in the same manner, but is not so good.

Transparent Pudding

From "The Virginia Housewife", By Mary Randolph, 1836

Beat eight eggs very light, add half a pound of pounded sugar, the same of fresh butter melted, and half a nutmeg grated; sit it on a stove, and keep stirring till it is as thick as buttered eggs--put a puff paste in a shallow dish, pour in the ingredients, and bake it half an hour in a moderate oven; sift sugar over it, and serve it up hot.

West Indian Pudding
From "The Book of Household Management", By Isabella Beeton, 1861

1 pint of cream, 1/2 lb. of loaf-sugar, 1/2 lb. of Savoy or sponge-cakes, 8 eggs, 3 oz. of preserved green ginger.
Crumble down the cakes, put them into a basin, and pour over them the cream, which should be previously sweetened and brought to the boiling-point; cover the basin, well beat the eggs, and when the cream is soaked up, stir them in. Butter a mould, arrange the ginger round it, pour in the pudding carefully, and tie it down with a cloth; steam or boil it slowly for 1-1/2 hour, and serve with the syrup from the ginger, which should be warmed, and poured over the pudding.

Ice Cream

"Mrs Scotch Allan sent me ice cream and lady cheek apples from her farm." - Mary Boykin Chesnut, November 30, 1863.

Ice Cream
From "The Great Western Cook Book, or Table Receipts, Adapted to Western Housewifery", By Anna Maria Collins, 1857

To a pound of any preserved fruit, add a quart of good cream; squeeze the juice of two lemons into it, and some sugar; let the whole be passed through a sieve; have the freezing-pot nice and clean, put the cream into it, and cover it; then put it into the tub with ice, broken in small pieces, and some salt; turn the freezer quickly, and as the cream sticks to the sides, scrape it down with an ice-spoon, and so on till it freezes quite hard.
The more the cream is worked to the side with the spoon, the better it is; it makes it smoother and better flavored.
After it is well frozen, take it out and put it in shapes: set it in a tub with ice and salt. When needed, take the shape out, wipe it carefully, for fear of the salt, dip it in luke-warm water. Turn it out on a glass dish, and send it to the table.

Almond Ice Cream

From "The Practical Housekeeper; A Cyclopedia of Domestic Economy", By
Elizabeth Fries Ellet, 1857

Take six ounces of bitter almonds, (sweet ones will not do,) blanch them, and
pound them in a mortar, adding by degrees, a little rose-water. Boil them gently
in a pint of cream till you find that it is highly flavored with them. Then pour
the cream into a bowl, stir in half a pound of powdered loaf-sugar, cover it, and
set it away to cool gradually. "When it is cold, strain it, and then stir it gradually
and hard into three pints of cream. Put it into the freezer, and proceed as
directed. Freeze it twice. It will be found very fine.
Send round always with ice cream, sponge cake: afterwards wine and cordials,
or liquors, as they are now gene rally called.

Coffee Ice Cream

From "The Great Western Cook Book, or Table Receipts, Adapted
to Western Housewifery", By Anna Maria Collins, 1857

Take one quart of cream, five ounces of coffee, and twelve ounces of sugar;
roast the coffee in a stewpan, keeping it constantly stirred, until of a good
brown color; throw it into the custard cream while it is quite hot, and cover it
closely; let it infuse for an hour or two, then strain and freeze.

Lemon Ice Cream

From "Directions for Cookery, in its Various Branches" By Eliza Leslie, 1840

Have ready two quarts of very rich thick cream, and take out a pint. Stir
gradually into the pint, a pound of the best loaf-sugar powdered fine; and the
grated rind and the juice of four ripe lemons of the largest size, or of five or six
smaller ones. If you cannot procure the fruit, you may flavour the cream with
essence or oil of lemon; a tea-spoonful or more, according to its strength. The
strongest and best essence of lemon is the white or whitish; when tinged with
green, it is comparatively weak, having been diluted with water; if quite green,
a large tea-spoonful will not communicate as much flavour as five or six drops
of the white. After you have mixed the pint of cream with the sugar and lemon,
beat it gradually and hard into the remaining cream, that is, the three pints.
Cover it, and let it stand to infuse from half an hour to an hour. Then taste it,
and if you think it necessary, stir in a little more lemon juice or a little more
sugar. Strain it into the freezer through a fine strainer, (a tin one with small
close holes is best,) to get rid of the grated lemon-peel, which if left in would

prevent the cream from being smooth. Cover the freezer, and stand it in the ice cream tub, which should be filled with a mixture, in equal quantities, of coarse salt, and ice broken up as small as possible, that it may lie close and compact round the freezer, and thus add to its coldness. Snow, when it can be procured, is still better than ice to mix with the salt. It should be packed closely into the tub, and pressed down hard. Keep turning the freezer about by the handle till the cream is frozen, which it will generally be in two hours. Occasionally open the lid and scrape down the cream from the sides with a long-handled tin spoon. Take care that no salt gets in, or the cream will be spoiled. When it is entirely frozen, take it out of the freezer and put it into your mould; set it again in the tub, (which must be filled with fresh ice and salt,) and leave it undisturbed till you want it for immediate use. This second freezing, however, should not continue longer than two hours, or the cream will become inconveniently and unpleasantly hard, and have much of the flavour frozen out of it. Place the mould in the ice tub, with the head downwards, and cover the tub with pieces of old carpet while the second freezing is going on. When it has arrived at the proper consistence, and it is time to serve it up, dip a cloth in hot water, and wrap it round the mould for a few moments, to loosen the cream and make it come out easily; setting the mould on a glass or china dish. If a pyramid or obelisk mould, lift it carefully off the top. If the mould or form represents doves, dolphins, lap-dogs, fruit baskets, &c. it will open down the middle, and must be taken off in that manner. Serve it up immediately lest it begin to melt. Send round sponge-cake with it, and wine or cordials immediately after.

If you have no moulds, but intend serving it up in a large bowl or in glasses, it must still be frozen twice over; otherwise it can have no smoothness, delicacy, or consistence, but will be rough and coarse, and feel in the mouth like broken icicles. The second freezing (if you have no mould) must be done in the freezer, which should be washed out, and set again in the tub with fresh ice and salt. Cover it closely, and let the cream stand in it untouched, but not less than two hours. When you put it into glasses, heap it high on the top.

Begin to make ice cream about five or six hours before it is wanted for use. If you commence it too early, it may probably be injured by having to remain too long in the second freezing, as it must not be turned out till a few moments before it is served up.

In damp weather it requires a longer time to freeze.

If cream is scarce, mix with it an equal quantity of rich milk, and then add, for each quart, two table-spoonfuls of powdered arrow-root rubbed smooth in a little cold milk. Orange ice cream is made in the same manner as lemon.

Oyster Cream
From "The Virginia Housewife", By Mary Randolph, 1836

103

Make a rich soup, (see directions for oyster soup,) strain it from the oysters, and freeze it.

Snow Cream
From "A New System of Domestic Cookery", By
Maria Eliza Ketelby Rundell, 1807

Put to a quart of cream the whites of three eggs well beaten, four spoonfuls of sweet wine, sugar to your taste, and a bit of lemon-peel; whip it to a froth, remove the peel, and serve in a dish.

Vanilla Ice Cream
From "Directions for Cookery, in its Various Branches" By Eliza Leslie, 1840

Split up half a vanilla bean, and boil it slowly in half a pint of milk till all the flavour is drawn out, which you may know by tasting it. Then mix into the milk half a pound of powdered loaf-sugar, and stir it very hard into a quart of rich cream. Put it into the freezer, and proceed as directed in the receipt for Lemon Ice Cream; freezing it twice.

7. DRINKS

Soft Drinks

Apple Water
From "Confederate Receipt Book. A Compilation of Over One
Hundred Receipts, Adapted To The Times", By West & Johnston,
1863

Take one tart apple of ordinary size, well baked, let it be well
mashed, pour on it one pint of boiling water, beat them well
together, let it stand to cool, and strain it off for use. It may be
sweetened with sugar if desired.

Chocolate
From "The Great Western Cook Book, or Table Receipts, Adapted
to Western Housewifery", By Anna Maria Collins, 1857

Put the milk and water on to boil, then scrape from one to two squares of
chocolate to a pint of milk and water mixed. When the milk and water boil, take
it off the fire; throw in the chocolate, beat it up well, and serve it up with the
froth. This process will not take ten minutes; you may add sugar to your taste,
either when you add the chocolate, or when poured off.

Clouted or Clotted Cream
From "The Cook's Oracle; and Housekeeper's Manual", By William Kitchiner,
1830

The milk which is put into the pans one morning stands till the next; then set
the pan on a hot hearth, or in a copper tray half full of water; put this over a
stove; in from ten to twenty minutes, according to the quantity of the milk and
the size of the pan, it will be done enough; the sign of which is, that bladders
rise on its surface; this denotes that it is near boiling, which it must by no
means do; and it must be instantly removed from the fire, and placed in the
dairy till the next morning, when the fine cream is thrown up, and is ready for
the table, or for butter, into which it is soon converted by stirring it with the
hand.

English Ginger Beer

From "The Young Housekeeper's Friend", By Mrs. M. H. Cornelius, 1863

4 qts. water, boiling, 1 and 1/2 ounces ginger root, 1 oz. cream of tartar, 1 lb. brown sugar (or white sugar, optional), 2 lemons, sliced thin, 1 cup homemade yeast, or 2 packets or cakes of commercial yeast.

Pour four quarts of boiling water upon an ounce and a half of ginger, an ounce of cream of tartar, a pound of clean brown sugar, and two fresh lemons, sliced thin. It should be wrought [left standing] twenty-four hours, with two gills of good yeast, and then bottled. It improves by keeping several weeks, unless the weather is hot, and it is an excellent beverage. If made with loaf instead of brown sugar, the appearance and flavor are still finer.

Ginger Beer

From "The Practical Housekeeper", By Elizabeth Fries Ellet, 1857

Fourteen gallons water, fourteen pounds loaf sugar, four ounces ginger, well pounded 5 boil one hour, add the whites of eight eggs beat up, and take off the scum; strain the liquor into an earthen pan, let it stand till cold, then put it into your cask with the peel of fourteen lemons cut thin, and their juice strained. Add half a spoonful of ale-yeast on the top. Stop the vessel closely for a fortnight. Then it may be bottled, and in another fortnight will be fit for use.

Harvest Drink

From "The Skillful Housewife's Book; or Complete Domestic Cookery, Taste, Comfort, Economy", By Mrs. L. G. Abell, 1852

Mix with five gallons of good water, half a gallon of molasses, one quart of vinegar, and two ounces of powdered ginger. This will make not only a very pleasant beverage, but one highly invigorating and healthful.

Add half cup of molasses, two cups vinegar, and a dash of ginger to a pan. Bring to a soft boil, when well mixed. When cool, bottle it. To serve, dilute liberally with cool water.

Ice Orangeade

From "Directions for Cookery, in its Various Branches", 1840

Ingredients 1 1/2 pints of orange juice 1/2 pint of clear or filtered water 1/2 pound of powdered loaf-sugar 6 deep-coloured oranges Instructions Take orange juice, and mix it with the water. Stir in powdered loaf-sugar. Pare very thin the yellow rind of the oranges, cut in pieces, and lay it at the bottom of a bowl or tureen. Pour the orange juice and sugar upon it; cover it, and let it infuse an hour. Then strain the liquid into a freezer, and proceed as for ice cream. When it is frozen, put it into a mould, (it will look best in the form of a pine-apple,) and freeze it a second time. Serve it in glass cups, with any sort of very nice sweet cakes. Ice lemonade may be made in the above manner, but with a larger proportion of sugar. The juice of pine-apples, strawberries, raspberries, currants and cherries, may be prepared and frozen according to the above receipts. They will freeze in a shorter time than if mixed with cream, but are very inferior in richness.

Lemonade

From "How to Mix Drinks, or, The Bon Vivant's Companion", By Jerry Thomas, 1864

(Use large bar glass.), The juice of half a lemon, 1 table-spoonful of sugar 2 or three pieces of orange, 1 table-spoonful of raspberry or strawberry syrup. Fill the tumbler one-half full with shaved ice, the balance with water; dash with port wine, and ornament with fruits in season.

"Gen. Jackson mounted his gaunt sorrell and leaving his position, moved to the front. At that moment, someone handed him a lemon-a fruit of which he was specially fond. Immediately a small peice was bitten out of it and slowly and unsparingly he began to extract it's flavor and it's juice. From that moment untill darkness ended the battle that lemon scarcely left his lips except to be used as a baton to emphasize an order. He listened to Yankee shout or Rebel Yell, to the sound of musketry advancing or receeding, to all the signs of promise or aprehension, but he never for an instant lost his interest in that lemon and even spoke of its excellence."- Lt. Henry Kyd Douglas, at Gaines' Mill.

Lemonade

From "The Housekeeper's Encyclopedia of Useful Information for the Housekeeper in All Branches of Cooking and Domestic Economy", By Mrs. E. F. Haskell, 1861

Rub some of the sugar on the peel of the lemon to extract the oil; roll the lemons under the hand on the table, and press out all the juice; add to every lemon two heaping table-spoons of loaf-sugar; mix it thoroughly with the lemon; fill the pitcher one-quarter full of broken ice, and add water.

"Where Jackson got his lemons no fellow could find out, but he was rarely without one. To have lived twelve miles from that fruit would have disturbed him."- General Richard Taylor, son of President Zachary Taylor, writing about General Thomas J. "Stonewall" Jackson's affinity for eating lemons.

Lemonade-To Carry In The Pocket
From "Dr. Chase's Recipes; or, Information for Everybody" By A. W. Chase, MD, Practical Therapeutist, 1864

Loaf sugar 1*[unclear]* lb.; rub it down finely in a mortar, and add citric acid 1/2 oz.; (tartaric acid will do,) and lemon essence 1/2 oz., and continue the trituration until all is intimatcly mixed, and bottle for use. It is best to dry the powders as mentioned in the Persian Sherbet, next following.

Persian Sherbet
"Dr. Chase's Recipes; or, Information for Everybody" By A. W. Chase, MD, Practical Therapeutist, 1864

Pulverized sugar 1 lb.; super-carbonate of soda 4 ozs.; tartaric acid 3 ozs.; put all the articles into the stove oven when moderately warm, being separate, upon paper or plates; let them remain sufficiently long to dry out all dampness absorbed from the air, then rub about 40 drops of lemon oil, (or if preferred any other flavored oil,) thoroughly with the sugar in a mortar--wedge-wood is the best--then add the soda and acid, and continue the rubbing until all are thoroughly mixed.

Bottle and cork tight, for, if any degree of moisture is permitted to reach it, the acid and soda neutralize each other, and the virtue is thus destroyed. A middling sized table-spoon or two tea-spoons of this put into a half pint glass and nearly filled with water and quickly drank, makes an agreeable summer beverage; and if three or four glasses of it are taken within a short time, say an hour or two, it has the effect of a gentle cathartic, hence for those habitually costive it would be found nearly or quite equal to the seidlitz powder, and for children it would be the pleasantest of the two. [The printers have tried it, and can bear testimony to its good qualities.]

A rounding table-spoon can be done up in a paper and carried conveniently in the pocket when persons are going into out-of-the-way places, and added to half pint of cold water, when all the beauties of a lemonade will stand before you waiting to be drank, not costing a penny a glass. This can be made sweeter or more sour, if desired.

Maple Beer

From "The Young Housekeeper's Friend", By Mrs. M. H. Cornelius, 1863

4 gallons water, boiled, 1 qt. maple syrup, 1 tbs. essence of spruce, 1 pint homemade yeast, or 2 packets or cakes commercial yeast.

To four gallons of boiling water, add one quart of maple syrup and a small table-spoonful of essence of spruce. When it is about milk warm, add a pint of yeast; and when fermented, bottle it. In three days it is fit for use.

Molasses Beer

From "Directions for Cookery, in its Various Branches", By Eliza Leslie, 1840

To six quarts of water, add two quarts of West India molasses; half a pint of the best brewer's yeast; two table-spoonfuls of ground ginger; and one table-spoonful of cream of tartar. Stir all together. Let it stand twelve hours, and then bottle it, putting three or four raisins into each bottle. It will be much improved by substituting the juice and grated peel of a large lemon, for one of the spoonfuls of ginger. Molasses beer keeps good but two or three days.

Root Beer

From "Dr. Chase's Recipes; or, Information for Everybody" By A. W. Chase, MD, Practical Therapeutist, 1864

For each gallon of water to be used, take hops, burdock, yellow dock, sarsaparilla, dandelion, and spikenard roots, bruised, of each 1/2 oz.; boil about 20 minutes, and strain while hot, add 8 or 10 drops of oils of spruce and sassafras mixed in equal proportions, when cool enough not to scald your hand, put in 2 or 3 table-spoons of yeast; molasses 2/3 of a pint, or white sugar 1/2 lb. gives it about the right sweetness.

Keep these proportions for as many gallons as you wish to make. You can use more or less of the roots to suit your taste after trying it; it is best to get the dry roots, or dig them and let them get dry, and of course you can add any other root known to possess medicinal properties desired in the beer. After all is mixed, let it stand in a jar with a cloth thrown over it, to work about two hours, then bottle and set in a cool place. This is a nice way to take alternatives, without taking medicine. And families ought to make it every Spring, and drink freely of it for several weeks, and thereby save, perhaps, several dollars in doctors' bills.

Syrup of Vinegar
From "The Virginia Housewife", By Mary Randolph, 1836

Boil two pounds of sugar with four quarts of vinegar, down to a syrup, and bottle it. This makes an excellent beverage when mixed with water, either with or without the addition of brandy. It is nearly equal a flavour to the syrup of lime juice, when made with superior vinegar.

Toast and Water

From "The Cook's Oracle; and Housekeeper's Manual", By William Kitchiner, 1830

Cut a crust of bread off a stale loaf, about twice the thickness toast is usually cut: toast it carefully until it be completely browned all over, but not at all blackened or burnt; pour as much boiling water as you wish to make into drink, into the jug; put the toast into it, and let it stand till it is quite cold: the fresher it is the better.

This is a refreshing summer drink; and when the proportion of the fluids is destroyed by profuse perspiration, may be drunk plentifully. Let a large jug be made early in the day, it will then become warmed by the heat of the air, and may be drunk without danger; which water, cold as it comes from the well, cannot in hot weather. –Or-,

To make it more expeditiously, put the bread into a mug, and just cover it with boiling water; let it stand till cold, then fill it up with cold spring-water, and pour it through a fine sieve.

Obs.-The above is a pleasant and excellent beverage, grateful to the stomach, and deserves a constant place by the bed-side.

To Give A Cool Taste to Water
From "Confederate Receipt Book. A Compilation of Over One Hundred Receipts, Adapted To The Times", By West & Johnston, 1863

A few leaves of sheep mint held in the mouth, or chewed, just before drinking water, will seemingly impart a degree of coolness to the draught.

Alcoholic Drinks

"A soldier will get whiskey at any risk-if anywhere in the neighborhood"-John Brynam to Thomas Morris, March 22, 1862

"Reached St. Louis this morning and while laying at the wharf I obtained permission to go a shore to mail my letters. Got drunk as a fool trying to get the guard drunk." -Pvt. Martin Van Buren Oldham, Company G of the 9th Tennessee Infantry, January 22, 1863, en route to Prison at Camp Douglas. From diary entry.

To Make Cherry Brandy
From "The Book of Household Management", By Isabella Beeton, 1861

Morella cherries, good brandy; to every lb. of cherries allow 3 oz. of pounded sugar.
Have ready some glass bottles, which must be perfectly dry. Ascertain that the cherries are not too ripe and are freshly gathered, and cut off about half of the stalks. Put them into the bottles, with the above proportion of sugar to every lb. of fruit; strew this in between the cherries, and, when the bottles are nearly full, pour in sufficient brandy to reach just below the cork. A few peach or apricot kernels will add much to their flavour, or a few blanched bitter almonds. Put corks or bungs into the bottles, tie over them a piece of bladder, and store away in a dry place. The cherries will be fit to eat in 2 or 3 months, and will remain good for years. They are liable to shrivel and become tough if too much sugar be added to them.

Clarified Lemonade

From "The Lady's Own Cookery Book", 1844

Ingredients 6 lemons 1/2 pound of sugar 1/2 pint of rich white wine 1 quart of boiling water 1/2 pint of boiling milk Instructions Pare the rind of three lemons as thin as you can; put them into a jug, with the juice of six lemons, the sugar, white wine, and boiling water. Let it stand all night. In the morning, add the boiling milk: then run it through a jelly-bag till quite clear.

Ginger Beer
From: "Directions for Cookery, In It's Various Branches", By Eliza Leslie, 1840

0.75 pound of sugar (or about 1.75 cups), 1.5 oz. ginger, 1 gallon water, 1 lemon, grated peel and juice, 1 large tablespoon of yeast (one packet proofed in .25 cup water at 110*)

Prepare the grated items, peeled ginger and lemon peel.

Bring water to a rolling boil. Add sugar, grated ginger, and grated lemon peel to a large bowl. Pour on the boiling water and set aside to cool. Squeeze and strain the lemon juice.

Prepare your ginger beer fermenting bottle. (*I'd recommend a plastic bottle for the fermenting process*).Once the mixture has cooled sufficiently, proof your yeast. Strain the grated bits from your mixture. Add your lemon juice to the strained mixture. Add the proofed yeast to your fermenting bottle. Add the mixture to your fermenting bottle.

Set the fermenting bottle aside to cool thoroughly. Cap the fermenting bottle lightly and place in a shady place overnight.

The next day, it should have a fizz... that is from the fermentation process and means it has a slight alcohol content.

Decant your ginger beer into ginger beer bottles and enjoy!

Lemon Brandy
From "The Book of Household Management", By Isabella Beeton, 1861

1 pint of brandy, the rind of two small lemons, 2 oz. of loaf-sugar, 1/4 pint of water.

Peel the lemons rather thin, taking care to have none of the white pith. Put the rinds into a bottle with the brandy, and let them infuse for 24 hours, when they should be strained. Now boil the sugar with the water for a few minutes, skim it, and, when cold, add it to the brandy. A dessertspoonful of this will be found an excellent flavouring for boiled custards.

Lemon Cordial
From "Directions for Cookery, in its Various Branches" By Eliza Leslie, 1840

Pare off very thin the yellow rind of a dozen large lemons; throw the parings into a gallon of white brandy, and let them steep till next day, or at least twelve hours. Break up four pounds of loaf-sugar into another vessel, and squeeze upon it the juice of the lemons. Let this too stand all night. Next day mix all together, boil two quarts of milk, and pour it boiling hot into the other ingredients. Cover the vessel, and let it stand eight days, stirring it daily. Then strain it through a flannel bag till the liquid is perfectly clear. Let it stand six weeks in a demijohn or glass jar, and then bottle it.

To make it still more clear, you may filter it through a piece of fine muslin pinned down to the bottom of a sieve, or through blotting paper, which must be frequently renewed. It should be white blotting paper.

Mint Cordial
From "The Virginia Housewife", By Mary Randolph, 1836

Pick the mint early in the morning while the dew is on it, and be careful not to bruise it; pour some water over it, and drain it--put two handsful into a pitcher, with a quart of French brandy, cover it, and let it stand till next day; take the mint carefully out, and put in as much more, which must be taken out next day--do this the third time: then put three quarts of water to the brandy, and one pound of loaf sugar powdered; mix it well together--and when perfectly clear, bottle it.

Mint Julep
From "The Lady's Receipt-Book; a Useful Companion for Large or Small Families", By Eliza Leslie, 1847

Put into the bottom of a tumbler, about a dozen sprigs of young and tender mint. Upon them place a large tea-spoonful of fine white sugar; and then pour on peach-brandy, so as to reach nearly one-third the height of the tumbler. Fill up with ice, pounded fine; and lay on the top a thin slice of pine-apple, cut across into four pieces. As an ornament, stick into the centre a handsome cluster of mint-sprigs, so as to rise far above the edge of the tumbler. It will be the better for standing awhile, in a vessel of finely-broken ice.

"The President (Jefferson Davis) was watching me prepare a mint julep for Custis Lee when Colonel McLean came to inform us that a great crowd had gathered and that they were coming to ask the President to speak to them at one o clock." -Mary Boykin Chesnut, October 1, 1864.

"It is a rite that must not be entrusted to a novice, a statistician, nor a Yankee. It is a heritage of the old South, an emblem of hospitality and a vehicle in which noble minds can travel together upon the flower-strewn paths of happy and congenial thought..... When all is ready, assemble your guests on the porch or in the garden, where the aroma of the juleps will rise Heavenward and make the birds sing. Propose a worthy toast, raise the goblet to your lips, bury your nose in the mint, inhale a deep breath of its fragrance and sip the nectar of the

gods."-Simon Bolivar Buckner Jr., March 30, 1937. Letter to Maj. Gen. William D. Connor, regarding the making of Mint Julep.

Molasses Beer
From "The Virginia Housewife", By Mary Randolph, 1836

Put five quarts of hops, and five of wheat bran, into fifteen gallons of water; boil it three or four hours, strain it, and pour it into a cask with one head taken out; put in five quarts of molasses, stir it till well mixed, throw a cloth over the barrel; when moderately warm, add a quart of good yeast, which must be stirred in; then stop it close with a cloth and board. When it has fermented and become quite clear, bottle it--the corks should be soaked in boiling water an hour or two, and the bottles perfectly clean, and well drained.

Mulled Cider
From "Directions for Cookery, in its Various Branches" By Eliza Leslie, 1840

Allow six eggs to a quart of cider. Put a handful of whole cloves into the cider, and boil it. While it is boiling, beat the eggs in a large pitcher; adding to them as much sugar as will make the cider very sweet. By the time the cider boils, the eggs will be sufficiently light. Pour the boiling liquor on the beaten egg, and continue to pour the mixture backwards and forwards from one pitcher to another, till it has a fine froth on it. Then pour it warm into your glasses, and grate some nutmeg over each.
Port wine may be mulled in the same manner.

To Mull Wine
From "The Practical Housekeeper", By Elizabeth Fries Ellet, 1857

Boil the spices (cinnamon, nutmeg grated, cloves, and mace) in any quantity approved, in half a gill of water; put to this a full pint of port, with sugar to taste. Mix it well, and serve hot with thin slips of toast or rusks. Lemon or orange juice may be added, and the water may be strained off from the spices. *Ale or Porter may be mulled* as above, and have toast or biscuits put to them. Formerly the yolks of eggs were mixed with mulled wine, as in making custard or egg-caudle, and many flavoring ingredients were employed which are now disused.

Punch
From "Directions for Cookery, in its Various Branches" By Eliza Leslie, 1840

Roll twelve fine lemons under your hand on the table; then pare off the yellow rind very thin, and boil it in a gallon of water till all the flavour is drawn out. Break up into a large bowl, two pounds of loaf-sugar, and squeeze the lemons over it. When the water has boiled sufficiently, strain it from the lemon-peel, and mix it with the lemon juice and sugar. Stir in a quart of rum or of the best whiskey.

Two scruples of flowers of benjamin, steeped in a quart of rum, will make an infusion which much resembles the arrack of the East Indies. It should be kept in a bottle, and a little of it will be found to impart a very fine and fragrant flavour to punch made in the usual manner.

Rose Brandy
From "The Virginia Housewife", By Mary Randolph, 1836

Gather leaves from fragrant roses without bruising, fill a pitcher with them, and cover them with French brandy; next day, pour off the brandy, take out the leaves, and fill the pitcher with fresh ones, and return the brandy; do this till it is strongly impregnated, then bottle it; keep the pitcher closely covered during the process. It is better than distilled rose water for cakes, &c.

Rose Cordial
From "Directions for Cookery, in its Various Branches" By Eliza Leslie, 1840

Put a pound of fresh rose leaves into a tureen, with a quart of lukewarm water. Cover the vessel, and let them infuse for twenty-four hours. Then squeeze them through a linen bag till all the liquid is pressed out. Put a fresh pound of rose leaves into the tureen, pour the liquid back into it, and let it infuse again for two days. You may repeat this till you obtain a very strong infusion. Then to a pint of the infusion add half a pound of loaf-sugar, half a pint of white brandy, an ounce of broken cinnamon, and an ounce of coriander seeds. Put it into a glass jar, cover it well, and let it stand for two weeks. Then filter it through a fine muslin or a blotting paper (which must be white) pinned on the bottom of a sieve; and bottle it for use.

Spruce Beer
From "The Virginia Housewife", By Mary Randolph, 1836

Boil a handful of hops, and twice as much of the chippings of sassafras root, in ten gallons of water; strain it, and pour in, while hot, one gallon of molasses, two spoonsful of the essence of spruce, two spoonsful of powdered ginger, and one of pounded allspice; put it in a cask--when sufficiently cold, add half a pint of good yeast; stir it well, stop it close, and when fermented and clear, bottle and cork it tight.

To Make Syllabub
From "The Book of Household Management", By Isabella Beeton, 1861

1 pint of sherry or white wine, 1/2 grated nutmeg, sugar to taste, 1-1/2 pint of milk.
Put the wine into a bowl, with the grated nutmeg and plenty of pounded sugar, and milk into it the above proportion of milk frothed up. Clouted cream may be laid on the top, with pounded cinnamon or nutmeg and sugar; and a little brandy may be added to the wine before the milk is put in. In some counties, cider is substituted for the wine: when this is used, brandy must always be added. Warm milk may be poured on from a spouted jug or teapot; but it must be held very high.

Coffee and Tea

"The infusion, or decoction of coffee, forms a well known favorite beverage. Like tea, it diminishes the disposition to sleep, and hence it is often resorted to by those who desire nocturnal study. It may also be used to counteract the stupor induced by opium, alcoholic drinks, and other narcotics. In some constitutions it acts as a mild laxative, yet it is usually described as producing constipation. The immoderate use of coffee produces various nervous diseases, such as anxiety, tremor, disordered vision, palpitation, and feverishness."- Catharine Esther Beecher, 1850

Black Tea
From "The Great Western Cook Book, or Table Receipts, Adapted to Western Housewifery", By Anna Maria Collins, 1857

It is best boiled a minute; it is not so powerful as green, and therefore requires at least a tablespoonful to a quart of water. It is made as green tea.

"They had champagne and Russian tea, the latter from a samovar made in Russia." -Mary Boykin Chesnut, June 25, 1862, describing a visit from Wade Hampton.

Coffee
From "The Great Western Cook Book, or Table Receipts, Adapted to Western Housewifery", By Anna Maria Collins, 1857

IT requires a table-spoonful of ground coffee, to every cup of tincture. Take six tea-spoonsful of ground coffee, add the white of an egg, mix it well together with a small quantity of cold water, pour on it six or seven tea-cupsful of boiling water; stir it well, let it boil ten minutes; then let it stand by the fire, without boiling, ten minutes. It will then be ready to pour off.

Coffee should never be roasted too much; a light brown is sufficient; when it is suffered to become black, it looses its flavor, and is bitter and disagreeable.

Compound Camomile Tea
From "The Practical Housekeeper; A Cyclopedia of Domestic Economy", By Elizabeth Fries Ellet, 1857

Twenty camomile flowers, half the thin peel of a lemon, four cloves: pour on them a coffee cup of boiling water, cover and let them stand all night. Strain the liquor in the morning. A wine glass full may be taken a little before breakfast. Dr. Maton always recommended this, with a teaspoonful of salvolatile for indigestion.

Dandelion Tea
From "A Plain Cookery Book for the Working Classes", By Charles Elme Francatelli, 1852

Infuse one ounce of dandelion in a jug with a pint of boiling water for fifteen minutes; sweeten with brown sugar or honey, and drink several tea-cupfuls during the day. The use of this tea is recommended as a safe remedy in all bilious affections; it is also an excellent beverage for persons afflicted with dropsy.

Dandelion and Parsley Tea

From "The Practical Housekeeper; A Cyclopedia of Domestic Economy", By
Elizabeth Fries Ellet, 1857

Wash and scrape six dandelion roots and six of parsley; pour on them a pint of
boiling water; let it infuse three hours before the fire. A little salt or saltpetre
may be added. (Lady Cush prescribes this in dropsy; it acts on the kidneys.)
The flowers of any plant should be dried in every case.

Elder Flower Tea

From "The Practical Housekeeper; A Cyclopedia of Domestic Economy", By
Elizabeth Fries Ellet, 1857

Infuse the dried flowers as common tea is made. A little acid with sugar will
make the taste pleasant. (To promote perspiration.)

To Make Green Tea

From "The Great Western Cook Book, or Table Receipts, Adapted
to Western Housewifery", By Anna Maria Collins, 1857

Scald your tea-pot, put in two tea-spoonsful of tea to a quart of water, let it
stand a few minutes in the hot tea-pot before you fill up. This is considered a
good way; or, you can pour on a tea-cup of boiling water, and let it steep; this
an old fashion, and the one I have always followed in making tea. Tea is never
better for standing over fifteen minutes.

Substitute for Coffee

From "Confederate Receipt Book. A Compilation of Over One Hundred
Receipts, Adapted To The Times", By West & Johnston, 1863

Take sound ripe acorns, wash them while in the shell, dry them, and parch until they open, take the shell off, roast with a little bacon fat, and you will have a splendid cup of coffee.

"The snow is very deep and as cold as thunder. We marched eight miles without resting. We then fixed our bed in the snow and stole fodder for a bed and rails to make fire. We took snow, put it in our kettles, and made coffee. When I say coffee, I mean Confederate coffee - parched corn - that is our coffee. Ate our corn bread and bacon..."- Pvt. Louis Leon, Company C, First North Carolina Regiment, February 4, 1863, from his diary.

Substitute for Cream in Tea or Coffee
From "Confederate Receipt Book. A Compilation of Over One Hundred Receipts, Adapted To The Times", By West & Johnston, 1863

Beat the white of an egg to a froth, put to it a very small lump of butter, and mix well, then turn the coffee to it gradually, so that it may not curdle. If perfectly done it will be an excellent substitute for cream. For tea omit the butter, using only the egg.

8. KETCHUPS, SALAD DRESSINGS, VINEGARS AND SAUCES

Ketchups/Catsups

Celery Catsup

From "The Housekeeper's Encyclopedia of Useful Information for the Housekeeper in All Branches of Cooking and Domestic Economy", By Mrs. E. F. Haskell, 1861

1 oz celery seed, 1 tsp. white pepper, ground, 6 oysters, 1 tsp. salt, 1 qt vinegar (strong--10 percent acid if available).
Mix an ounce of celery seed ground, with a teaspoon of ground white pepper; bruise half a dozen oysters with a teaspoon of salt; mix and pass the whole through a sieve; pour over the mixture one quart of the best white vinegar; bottle and seal tight.

Cucumber Catsup

From "The Housekeeper's Encyclopedia of Useful Information for the Housekeeper in All Branches of Cooking and Domestic Economy", By Mrs. E. F. Haskell, 1861

Cucumbers, Vinegar, Salt.
Grate large cucumbers before they begin to turn yellow; drain out the juice and put the pulp through a sieve to remove the large seeds; fill a bottle half-full of the pulp, discarding the juice, and add the same quantity of ten per cent. vinegar; cork tightly; when used, add pepper and salt.

Grape Catsup

From "The Housekeeper's Encyclopedia of Useful Information for the Housekeeper in All Branches of Cooking and Domestic Economy", By Mrs. E. F. Haskell, 1861

Grapes, 1 tsp. cinnamon, broken, 1 tsp. mace, 1/2 tsp. cloves, Wine or vinegar. Boil grapes over water; to each quart allow a teaspoon of broken cinnamon, one of mace, one half-teaspoon of cloves; simmer over water one hour; strain, and add to every quart one pound of sugar; reduce nearly to jelly, and add wine or vinegar to thin it to the proper consistency.

Ketchup

From "The Lady's Own Cookery Book", By Charlotte Campbell Bury, 1844

Put a pint of the best white wine vinegar into a wide-mouthed quart bottle; add twelve cloves of shalots, peeled and bruised; take a quarter of a pint of the strongest red wine and boil it a little; wash and bone about a dozen anchovies, let them dissolve in the wine, and, when cold, put them into the vinegar bottle, stopping it close with a cork, and shaking it well. Into the same quantity of wine put a spoonful of pepper bruised, a few races of split ginger, half a spoonful of cloves bruised, and a few blades of large mace, and boil them till the strength of the spice is extracted. When the liquor is almost cold, cut in slices two large nutmegs, and when quite cold put into it some lemon-peel. Put that into the bottle, and scrape thin a large, sound horseradish root, and put that also into the bottle; stop it down close; shake it well together every day for a fortnight, and you may then use it.

Mushroom Catsup

From "The Cook's Oracle", By Dr. William Kitchiner, 1832

1 quart mushrooms, Salt, 1 and 1/2 oz. black peppercorns, whole, 1/2 oz. allspice, whole Brandy.
Take care they are the right sort, and fresh gathered. Full-grown flaps are to be preferred: put a layer of these at the bottom of a deep earthen pan, and sprinkle them with salt; then another layer of mushrooms, and some more salt on them; and so on alternately, salt and mushrooms: let them remain two or three hours, by which time the salt will have penetrated the mushrooms, and rendered them easy to break; then pound them in a mortar, or mash them well with your hands, and let them remain a couple of days, not longer, stirring them up and

mashing them well each day; then pour them into a stone jar, and to each quart add an ounce and a half of whole black pepper, and half an ounce of allspice; stop the jar very close, and set it in a stew-pan of boiling water, and keep it boiling for two hours at least.

Take out the jar, and pour the juice clear from the settlings through a hair-sieve (without squeezing the mushrooms) into a clean stew-pan; let it boil very gently for half an hour: those who are for superlative catchup, will continue the boiling till the mushroom-juice is reduced to half the quantity; it may then be called double cat-sup or dog-sup.

There are several advantages attending this concentration; it will keep much better, and only half the quantity be required; so you can flavour sauce, &c., without thinning it....

Skim it well and pour it into a clean dry jar, or jug; cover it close, and let it stand in a cool place till next day; then pour it off as gently as possible (so as not to disturb the settlings at the bottom of the jug.) through a tamis, or thick flannel bag, till it is perfectly clear; add a table-spoonful of good brandy to each pint of catchup, and let it stand as before; a fresh sediment will be deposited, from which the catchup is to be quietly poured off, and bottled in pints or half pints (which have been washed with brandy or spirit): it is best to keep it in such quantities as are soon used. Take especial care that it is closely corked, and sealed down, or dipped in bottle cement.

Mushroom Catsup
From "The Virginia Housewife", By Mary Randolph, 1836

Take the flaps of the proper mushrooms from the stems--wash them, add some salt, and crush them; then boil them some time, strain them through a cloth, put them on the fire again with salt to your taste, a few cloves of garlic, and a quarter of an ounce of cloves pounded, to a peck of mushrooms; boil it till reduced to less than half the original quantity--bottle and cork it well.

Oyster Catchup
From "The Cook's Oracle; and Housekeeper's Manual", By William Kitchiner, 1830

Take fine fresh Milton oysters; wash them in their own liquor; skim it; pound them in a marble mortar; to a pint of oysters add a pint of sherry; boil them up, and add an ounce of salt, two drachms of pounded mace, and one of Cayenne; let it just boil up again; skim it, and rub it through a sieve, and when cold, bottle it, cork it well, and seal it down.

Peach Catsup

From "The Housekeeper's Encyclopedia of Useful Information for the Housekeeper in All Branches of Cooking and Domestic Economy", By Mrs. E. F. Haskell, 1861

Peaches, Sugar, (Per quart of resulting juice:), 1 tsp. mace, broken not ground, 2 tsp. cinnamon, 1/2 tsp. cloves, 1 tsp. black peppercorns, whole, Strong vinegar.
Boil ripe peaches over steam with the pits; press out all the juice; to every quart allow a pound of loaf-sugar; boil without the sugar until it is reduced one-third; add to each quart of juice before boiling a teaspoon of broken, not ground, mace, two of cinnamon, half a teaspoon of cloves, and one of peppercorns; boil all together; when half reduced remove the spices, add the sugar, boil until quite thick, and reduce to a convenient consistency for bottling with strong vinegar.

Plum Catsup

From "The Housekeeper's Encyclopedia of Useful Information for the Housekeeper in All Branches of Cooking and Domestic Economy", By Mrs. E. F. Haskell, 1861

Whole plums, Per quart of resulting juice: 1 tsp. cinnamon sticks, broken, 1 tsp. mace, 1/2 tsp cloves, 1/2 tsp pepper (black or red not specified), 2 lbs. sugar, 1 qt. strong vinegar.
Boil whole plums over steam; press out the juice; pass the pulp through the sieve; boil in a quart of the juice a teaspoon of broken cinnamon, one of mace, and half as much of cloves and pepper until reduced half; add this to the pulp, with two pounds of loaf sugar, and heat it, stirring constantly; when the sugar is dissolved, reduce the catsup with one quart of ten per cent vinegar.

Sweet Catsup

From "The Great Western Cook Book, or Table Receipts, Adapted to Western Housewifery", By Anna Maria Collins, 1857

Mix a glass of wine, a half glass of vinegar, three tea-spoonsful of thyme, a lump of sugar, one sliced onion, a little cinnamon, and three cloves; boil them a quarter of an hour.

Tomato Catsup
From "The Virginia Housewife", By Mary Randolph, 1836

Gather a peck of tomatos, pick out the stems, and wash them; put them on the fire without water, sprinkle on a few spoonsful of salt, let them boil steadily an hour, stirring them frequently; strain them through a colander, and then through a sieve; put the liquid on the fire with half a pint of chopped onions, half a quarter of an ounce of mace broke into small pieces; and if not sufficiently salt, add a little more—one table-spoonful of whole black pepper; boil all together until just enough to fill two bottles; cork it tight. Make it in August, in dry weather.

Tomato Catsup
From "Miss Beecher's Domestic Receipt Book", By Catharine Esther Beecher, 1850

Pour boiling water on the tomatoes, let them stand until you can rub off the skin, then cover them with salt, and let them stand twenty-four hours. Then strain them, and to two quarts put three ounces of cloves, two ounces of pepper, two nutmegs. Boil half an hour, then add a pint of wine.

Walnut Ketchup
From "The Practical Housekeeper; A Cyclopedia of Domestic Economy", By Elizabeth Fries Ellet, 1857

Take six half-sieves of green walnut-shells, put them into a tub, mix them up well with common salt, (from two to three pounds,) let them stand for six days, frequently beating and mashing them; by this time the shells become soft and pulpy. Then by banking it up on one side of the tub, and at the same time by raising the tub on that side, the liquor will drain clear off to the other; then take that liquor out; the mashing and banking up may be repeated as often as liquor is found. The quantity will be about six quarts. When done let it be simmered in an iron boiler as long as any scum arises; then bruise a quarter of a pound of ginger, a quarter of a pound of allspice, two ounces of long pepper, two ounces of cloves, with the above ingredients; let it slowly boil for half an hour. When boiled, let an equal quantity of the spice go into each bottle; when corked, let the bottle be filled quite up; cork them tight, seal them over, and put them into a cool and dry place for one year before they are used.

Salad Dressings and Vinegars

Basil Vinegar or Wine
From "The Complete Cook", By J. M. Sanderson, 1864

Sweet basil is in perfection about the middle of August; gather the fresh green leaves, quite free from stalk, and before it flowers; fill a wide-mouthed bottle with them, fill it with vinegar or wine, and steep them ten days; if you want a very strong essence, strain the liquor, put it on some fresh leaves, and let them steep fourteen days more; strain it and bottle, cork it close; it is a very agreeable addition to cold meat, soups, sauces, and to the mixture generally made for salads. A table-spoonful, when the soup is ready, impregnates a tureen-full with the basil and acid flavours at a very little expense, when fresh basil and lemons are very dear.
The flavour of other sweet or savoury herbs may be preserved in the same manner, by infusing them in wine or vinegar.

Camp Vinegar
From "A New System of Domestic Cookery", By
Maria Eliza Ketelby Rundell, 1807

Slice a large head of garlic; and put it into a wide-mouthed bottle, with half an ounce of Cayenne, two tea-spoonfuls of real soy, two of walnut-ketchup, four anchovies chopped, a pint of vinegar, and enough cochineal to give it the colour of lavender-drops. Let it stand six weeks; then strain off quite clear, and keep in small bottles sealed up.

Cayenne Vinegar, or Essence of Cayenne
From "The Book of Household Management", By Isabella Beeton, 1861

1/2 ounces of cayenne pepper 1/2 pint of strong spirit, or 1 pint of vinegar. Instructions Put the vinegar, or spirit, into a bottle, with the above proportion of cayenne, and let it steep for a month, when strain off and bottle for use. This is excellent seasoning for soups or sauces, but must be used very sparingly.

Celery Vinegar
From "Miss Beecher's Domestic Receipt Book", By
Catharine Esther Beecher, 1850

This is fine to keep in the castor stand. Pound two gills of celery seed, and add sharp vinegar. Shake every day for a week or two. The flavor of sweet herbs and sage can be obtained by pouring vinegar on to them, and for three successive days taking them out, and putting in a fresh supply of herbs. It must be kept corked and sealed.

Chilli Vinegar (Hot Sauce)
From: "Directions for Cookery, In It's Various Branches", By Eliza Leslie, 1840

Ingredients 100 red chillies or capsicums, fresh gathered 1 quart of the best vinegar.
Instructions Take red chillies or capsicums, cut them into small pieces and infuse them for a fortnight in the vinegar, shaking the bottle every day. Then strain it.

Chili Vinegar
From "The Book of Household Management", By Isabella Beeton, 1861

Ingredients 50 fresh red English chilies 1 pint of vinegar.
Instructions Pound or cut the chilies in half, and infuse them in the vinegar for a fortnight, when it will be fit for use. This will be found an agreeable relish to fish, as many people cannot eat it without the addition of an acid and cayenne pepper.

Cider Vinegar
From "The Practical Housekeeper; A Cyclopedia of Domestic Economy", By
Elizabeth Fries Ellet, 1857

Put a pound of white sugar to a gallon of cider and shaking them well together, let them ferment for four months; a strong and well--colored vinegar--will be the result.

Cucumber Vinegar (a Very Nice Addition to Salads)

From "The Book of Household Management", By Isabella Beeton, 1861

Ingredients 10 large cucumbers, or 12 smaller ones, 1 quart of vinegar, 2 onions, 2 shalots, 1 tablespoonful of salt, 2 tablespoonfuls of pepper, 1/4 teaspoonful of cayenne.
Pare and slice the cucumbers, put them in a stone jar or wide-mouthed bottle, with the vinegar; slice the onions and shalots, and add them, with all the other ingredients, to the cucumbers. Let it stand 4 or 5 days, boil it all up, and when cold, strain the liquor through a piece of muslin, and store it away in small bottles well sealed. This vinegar is a very nice addition to gravies, hashes, etc., as well as a great improvement to salads, or to eat with cold meat.

Garlic Vinegar

From "The Cook's Oracle; and Housekeeper's Manual", By William Kitchiner, 1830

Garlic is ready for this purpose from midsummer to Michaelmas.
Peel and chop two ounces of garlic, pour on them a quart of white wine vinegar, stop the jar close, and let it steep ten days, shaking it well every day; then pour off the clear liquor into small bottles.

Gooseberry Vinegar

From "A New System of Domestic Cookery", By
Maria Eliza Ketelby Rundell, 1807

Boil spring water; and when cola, put to every three quarts, a quart of bruised gooseberries in a large tub.
Let them remain sixty hours, stirring often; then strain through a hair bag, and to each gallon of liquor add a pound of the coarsest sugar. Put it into a barrel, and a toast and yeast; cover the bung-hole with a bit of slate, &c. as above. The greater quantity of sugar and fruit, the stronger the vinegar.

Gooseberry Vinegar

From "The Practical Housekeeper; A Cyclopedia of Domestic Economy", By Elizabeth Fries Ellet, 1857

Boil water, and when cold put to every three quarts one quart of bruised gooseberries in a large tub. Let them remain sixty hours, stirring often; then strain through a hair bag, and to each gallon of liquor add one pound of the coarsest sugar. Put it into a barrel, and a toast and yeast; cover the bung-hole with a bit of slate. Set the barrel in the sun, observing that the cask be well painted, and the iron hoops all firm. The greater the quantity of sugar and fruit, the stronger the vinegar; and as this is particularly useful for pickles, it might be well to make it of double the strength for that purpose.

Mint Vinegar

From "The Book of Household Management", By Isabella Beeton, 1861

Vinegar, mint.
Procure some nice fresh mint, pick the leaves from the stalks, and fill a bottle or jar with them. Add vinegar to them until the bottle is full; cover closely to exclude the air, and let it infuse for a fortnight. Then strain the liquor, and put it into small bottles for use, of which the corks should be sealed.

Raspberry Vinegar Syrup

From: "The Lady's Receipt Book, A Useful Companion for Large and Small Families", By Eliza Leslie, 1847

Take a sufficiency of fine ripe raspberries. Put them into a deep pan, and mash them with a wooden beetle. Then pour them, with all their juice, into a large linen bag, and squeeze and press out the liquid into a vessel beneath. Measure it; and to each quart of the raspberry-juice allow a pound of powdered white sugar, and a pint of the best cider vinegar. First mix together the juice and the vinegar, and give them a boil in a preserving-kettle. When they have boiled well, add gradually the sugar, with a beaten white of egg to every two pounds; and boil and skim it till the scum ceases to rise. When done, put it into clean bottles, and cork them tightly. It is a very pleasant and cooling beverage in warm weather, and for invalids who are feverish. To use it, pour out half a tumbler of raspberry vinegar, and fill it up with ice-water.
It is a good palliative for a cold, mixed with hot water, and taken as hot as

possible immediately on going to bed, so as to produce perspiration.

Ravigotte, a French Salad Sauce
From "The Book of Household Management", By Isabella Beeton, 1861

1 teaspoonful of mushroom ketchup, 1 teaspoonful of cavice, 1 teaspoonful of Chili vinegar, 1 teaspoonful of Reading sauce, a piece of butter the size of an egg, 3 tablespoonfuls of thick Béchamel, No. 367, 1 tablespoonful of minced parsley, 3 tablespoonfuls of cream; salt and pepper to taste.
Scald the parsley, mince the leaves very fine, and add it to all the other ingredients; after mixing the whole together thoroughly, the sauce will be ready for use.

Salad Dressing (Excellent)
From "The Book of Household Management", By Isabella Beeton, 1861

1 teaspoonful of mixed mustard, 1 teaspoonful of pounded sugar, 2 tablespoonfuls of salad oil, 4 tablespoonfuls of milk, 2 tablespoonfuls of vinegar, cayenne and salt to taste.
Put the mixed mustard into a salad-bowl with the sugar, and add the oil drop by drop, carefully stirring and mixing all these ingredients well together. Proceed in this manner with the milk and vinegar, which must be added very gradually, or the sauce will curdle.
Put in the seasoning, when the mixture will be ready for use. If this dressing is properly made, it will have a soft creamy appearance, and will be found very delicious with crab, or cold fried fish (the latter cut into dice), as well as with salads. In mixing salad dressings, the ingredients cannot be added too gradually, or stirred too much.

Salad Dressing for Lettuce
From "The Practical Housekeeper; A Cyclopedia of Domestic Economy", By Elizabeth Fries Ellet, 1857

Two hard-boiled eggs, the yolks mashed with four teaspoonfuls of sweet oil, a saltspoon of salt, and a teaspoonful of mustard, with two table-spoonfuls of vinegar. Add the lettuce cut up fine, and mince the white of egg to throw over it.

Salad Mixture

From "The Great Western Cook Book, or Table Receipts, Adapted
to Western Housewifery", By Anna Maria Collins, 1857

Boil a couple of eggs fifteen minutes, and put them in a basin of water a few
minutes. The yolks must be quite cold and hard. Rub them through a sieve
with a wooden spoon, and mix them with a table-spoonful of water or rich
cream. Then add two table-spoonsful of oil or melted butter. When these are
well mixed, add by degrees a tea-spoonful of salt, or powdered loaf-sugar, the
same of mustard, and, when these are smoothly united, add, very gradually,
three table-spoonsful of vinegar, and rub it with the other ingredients till it is
thoroughly incorporated with them; cut up the white of the egg, and garnish the
top with it. This is a good sauce for any kind of salad, and is delicious when
mixed with minced turkey or chicken, and celery.
Let the sauce remain in the bottom of the bowl, and do not stir the salad in it
till it is to be eaten.

Strawberry Vinegar
From "Miss Beecher's Domestic Receipt Book", By
Catharine Esther Beecher, 1850

Put four pounds very ripe strawberries, nicely dressed, to three quarts of the
best vinegar, and let them stand three, or four days. Then drain the vinegar
through a jelly-bag, and pour it on to the same quantity of fruit. Repeat the
process in three days a third time.Finally, to each pound of the liquor thus
obtained, add one pound of fine sugar. Bottle it and let it stand covered, but not
tight corked, a week; then cork it tight, and set it in a dry and cool place, where
it will not freeze.
Raspberry vinegar can be made in the same way.
Author's Note: This can also be used as a drink!

Sydney Smith's Salad Dressing
From "The Lady's Receipt-Book; a Useful Companion for Large or Small
Families", By Eliza Leslie, 1847

Have ready two well-boiled potatoes, peeled and rubbed through a sieve; they
will give peculiar smoothness to the mixture. Also, a very small portion of raw
onion, not more than a *quarter* of a tea-spoonful, (as the presence of the onion
is to be scarcely hinted,) and the pounded yolks of two hard-boiled eggs. Mix
these ingredients on a deep plate with two small tea-spoonfuls of salt; one of
made mustard; three table-spoonfuls of olive oil; and one table-spoonful of

vinegar. Add, lastly, a tea-spoonful of essence of anchovy; mash, and mix the whole together (using a boxwood spoon) and see that all the articles are thoroughly amalgamated. Having cut up a sufficiency of lettuce, (that has been well washed in cold water, and drained,) add to it the dressing immediately before dinner, mixing the lettuce through it with a boxwood fork.

This salad dressing was invented by the Rev. Sydney Smith, whose genius as a writer and a wit is well-known on both sides the Atlantic. If *exactly* followed, it will be found very fine on trial; no peculiar flavour predominating, but excellent as a whole. The above directions are taken from a manuscript receipt given by Mr. Smith to an American gentleman then in London.

In preparing this, or any other salad-dressing, take care not to use that excessively pungent and deleterious combination of drugs which is now so frequently imposed upon the public, as *the best white wine vinegar*. In reality, it has no vinous material about it, and it may be known by its violent and disagreeable sharpness, which overpowers and destroys the taste (and also the substance) of whatever it is mixed with. And it is also very unwholesome. Its colour is always very pale, and it is nearly as clear as water. No one should buy or use it. The first quality of *real* cider vinegar is good for all purposes.

The above receipt may be tried for lobster-dressing.

Vinegar for Salads
From "The Complete Cook", By J. M. Sanderson, 1864

Take three ounces each of tarragon, chives, eschalots, savoury, a handful of the tops of balm and mint, all dry and pounded; put these into a wide-mouthed bottle, with a gallon of the best vinegar, cork it close and set it in the sun, and in a fortnight strain it off, and press the herbs to get out all the juice; let it stand a day to settle, and then strain it through a filtering bag.

Sauces

Anchovy Sauce

From "Directions for Cookery, in its Various Branches" By Eliza
Leslie, 1840

Soak eight anchovies for three or four hours, changing the water
every hour. Then put them into a sauce-pan with a quart of cold
water. Set them on hot coals and simmer them till they are entirely
dissolved, and till the liquid is diminished two-thirds. Then strain it,
stir two glasses of red wine, and add to it about half a pint of melted
butter.
Heat it over again, and send it to table with salmon or fresh cod.

Apple Sauce

From "The Great Western Cook Book, or Table Receipts, Adapted
to Western Housewifery", By Anna Maria Collins, 1857

Pare and core three good sized baking apples, put them into a saucepan with
two table-spoonsful of cold water. Cover the saucepan close, and set it on a
trivet, over a slow fire for two hours, more or less, as some apples are much
more easily cooked than others. When the apples are done enough, pour off the
water and let them stand a few minutes to get dry, then put in a small piece of
butter and a tea-spoonful of powdered sugar. Some add grated lemon peel.

Asparagus Sauce

From "The Kentucky Housewife: Containing Nearly Thirteen Hundred Full
Receipts", By Lettice Bryan, 1839

Take the white tender stalks of asparagus, wash and scrape them neatly, tie
them in little bundles, and boil them in water, with a little salt, till they are
tender; then chop them small, season them with pepper, and put them into a
sauce-pan, with equal portions of butter and cream; add a very little flour, boil it
up, and serve it in a boat. There should be plenty of butter and cream, to make
the sauce sufficiently liquid; a small handful of asparagus to a pint of the butter
and cream, will be well proportioned. This is a delicious sauce for poultry and
game.

Bechamel, or French White Sauce

From "The Book of Household Management", By Isabella Beeton, 1861

1 small bunch of parsley, 2 cloves, 1/2 bay-leaf, 1 small faggot of savoury herbs, salt to taste; 3 or 4 mushrooms, when obtainable; 2 pints of white stock, 1 pint of cream, 1 tablespoonful of arrowroot.

Put the stock into a stewpan, with the parsley, cloves, bay-leaf, herbs, and mushrooms; add a seasoning of salt, but no pepper, as that would give the sauce a dusty appearance, and should be avoided. When it has boiled long enough to extract the flavour of the herbs, etc., strain it, and boil it up quickly again, until it is nearly half-reduced. Now mix the arrowroot smoothly with the cream, and let it simmer very gently for 5 minutes over a slow fire; pour to it the reduced stock, and continue to simmer slowly for 10 minutes, if the sauce be thick. If, on the contrary, it be too thin, it must be stirred over a sharp fire till it thickens. This is the foundation of many kinds of sauces, especially white sauces. Always make it thick, as you can easily thin it with cream, milk, or white stock.

Time-Altogether, 2 hours.

Beef Gravy

From "The Cook's Oracle; and Housekeeper's Manual", By William Kitchiner, 1830

Cover the bottom of a stew-pan that is well tinned and quite clean, with a slice of good ham, or lean bacon, four or five pounds of gravy beef cut into half-pound pieces, a carrot, an onion with two cloves stuck in it, and a head of celery; put a pint of broth or water to it, cover it close, and set it over a moderate fire till the water is reduced to as little as will just save the ingredients from burning; then turn it all about, and let it brown slightly and equally all over; then put in three quarts of boiling water; when it boils up, skim it carefully, and wipe off with a clean cloth what sticks round the edge and inside of the stew-pan, that your gravy may be delicately clean and clear. Set it by the side of a fire, where it will stew gently (to keep it clear, and that it may not be reduced too much) for about four hours: if it has not boiled too fast, there should be two quarts of good gravy; strain through a silk, or tamis-sieve; take very particular care to skim it well, and set it in a cold place.

Egg Sauce

From: "Directions for Cookery, In It's Various Branches", By Eliza Leslie, 1840

Boil four eggs a quarter of an hour. Dip them into cold water to prevent their looking blue. Peel off the shell. Chop the yolks of all, and the whites of two, and stir them into melted butter. Serve this sauce with boiled poultry or fish.

Fish Sauce

From "The Great Western Cook Book, or Table Receipts, Adapted to Western Housewifery", By Anna Maria Collins, 1857

Take walnuts when they are old enough to pickle, slice them, and between every layer of walnuts, throw a handful of salt. Stir it every day for two weeks. Then strain the liquor, let it settle, pour off the clear and boil it with a pound of anchovies to each pint; skim it, and when it is cool boil it again; add a pint of Port wine, one of good vinegar, to each pint of the liquor, also half an ounce each of mace and cloves, some sliced horse-radish, and a head of garlic, to a quart of the liquor, and some grains of black pepper. Cork it up tight in bottles.

Gravy for Roast Meat

From "The Great Western Cook Book, or Table Receipts, Adapted to Western Housewifery", By Anna Maria Collins, 1857

Most joints will afford sufficient trimmings to make half a pint of plain gravy, which you may color with a little burnt sugar.
For those that do not, about half an hour before you think the meat will be done, mix half a tea-spoonful of salt in a quarter of a pint of boiling water. Drop this by degrees on the brown part of the meat, set a dish under to catch it, and set it by. Let it cool, and remove the fat from the top, and when the meat is ready, warm it, and pour it into the dish.

Harvey's Sauce

From "Directions for Cookery, in its Various Branches" By Eliza Leslie, 1840

Dissolve six anchovies in a pint of strong vinegar, and then add to them three table-spoonfuls of India soy, and three table-spoonfuls of mushroom catchup, two heads of garlic bruised small, and a quarter of an ounce of cayenne. Add sufficient cochineal powder to colour the mixture red. Let all these ingredients infuse in the vinegar for a fortnight, shaking it every day, and then strain and bottle it for use. Let the bottles be small, and cover the corks with leather.

Horseradish Sauce, to Serve with Roast Beef

From "The Book of Household Management", By Isabella Beeton, 1861

4 tablespoonfuls of grated horseradish, 1 teaspoonful of pounded sugar, 1 teaspoonful of salt, 1/2 teaspoonful of pepper, 2 teaspoonfuls of made mustard vinegar.

Grate the horseradish, and mix it well with the sugar, salt, pepper, and mustard; moisten it with sufficient vinegar to give it the consistency of cream, and serve in a tureen: 3 or 4 tablespoonfuls of cream added to the above, very much improve the appearance and flavour of this sauce. To heat it to serve with hot roast beef, put it in a bain marie or a jar, which place in a saucepan of boiling water; make it hot, but do not allow it to boil, or it will curdle. Note: This sauce is a great improvement on the old-fashioned way of serving cold-scraped horseradish with hot roast beef. The mixing of the cold vinegar with the warm gravy cools and spoils everything on the plate. Of course, with cold meat, the sauce should be served cold.

Mayonnaise, a Sauce or Salad-Dressing for Cold Chicken, Meat, and Other Cold Dishes

From "The Book of Household Management", By Isabella Beeton, 1861

The yolks of 2 eggs, 6 tablespoonfuls of salad-oil, 4 tablespoonfuls of vinegar, salt and white pepper to taste, 1 tablespoonful of white stock No. 107 (see recipe for "White Stock"), 2 tablespoonfuls of cream.

Put the yolks of the eggs into a basin, with a seasoning of pepper and salt; have ready the above quantities of oil and vinegar, in separate vessels; add them very gradually to the eggs; continue stirring and rubbing the mixture with a wooden spoon, as herein consists the secret of having a nice smooth sauce. It cannot be stirred too frequently, and it should be made in a very cool place, or, if ice is at hand, it should be mixed over it. When the vinegar and oil are well incorporated with the eggs, add the stock and cream, stirring all the time, and it will then be ready for use.

For a fish Mayonnaise, this sauce may be coloured with lobster-spawn, pounded; and for poultry or meat, where variety is desired, a little parsley-juice may be used to add to its appearance. Cucumber, Tarragon, or any other flavoured vinegar, may be substituted for plain, where they are liked.

Melted Butter (the French Sauce Blanche)

From "The Book of Household Management", By Isabella Beeton, 1861

1/4 lb. of fresh butter, 1 tablespoonful of flour, salt to taste, 1/2 gill of water, 1/2 spoonful of white vinegar, a very little grated nutmeg.

Mix the flour and water to a smooth batter, carefully rubbing down with the back of a spoon any lumps that may appear. Put it in a saucepan with all the other ingredients, and let it thicken on the fire, but do not allow it to boil, lest it should taste of the flour.

Time-1 minute to simmer.

Common Mustard
From "Directions for Cookery, in its Various Branches" By Eliza Leslie, 1840

Is best when fresh made. Take good flour of mustard; put it in a plate, add to it a little salt, and mix it by degrees with boiling water to the usual consistence, rubbing it for a long time with a broad-bladed knife or a wooden spoon. It should be perfectly smooth. The less that is made at a time the better it will be. If you wish it very mild, use sugar instead of salt, and boiling milk instead of water.

Peach Sauce
From: "The New England Economical Housekeeper", By Esther Allen Howland, 1845

Peel the peaches and cut into small cubes.

Add the peaches to a saucepan with a cup of brown sugar and enough water to cover.

Bring to a boil. Reduce heat and boil on low for 30 minutes.

Sauce Robart, for Rumps or Steaks
From "A New System of Domestic Cookery", By Maria Eliza Ketelby Rundell, 1807

Put a piece of butter, the size of an egg, into a saucepan, set it over the fire, and when browning, throw in a handful of sliced onions cut small; fry them brown, but don't let them burn; add half a spoonful of flour, shake the onions in it, and give it another fry: then put four spoonfuls of gravy, and some pepper and salt, and boil it gently ten minutes; skim off the fat; add a tea-spoonful of made mustard, a spoonful of vinegar, and the juice of half a lemon; boil it all, and pour it round the steaks. They should be of a fine yellow brown, and garnished with fried parsley and lemon.

Tomata Honey

From "Directions for Cookery, in its Various Branches" By Eliza Leslie, 1840

To each pound of tomatas, allow the grated peel of a lemon and six fresh peach-leaves. Boil them slowly till they are all to pieces; then squeeze and strain them through a bag. To each pint of liquid allow a pound of loaf-sugar, and the juice of one lemon. Boil them together half an hour, or till they become a thick jelly. Then put it into glasses, and lay double tissue paper closely over the top. It will be scarcely distinguishable from real honey.

Turtle Sauce

From "The Great Western Cook Book, or Table Receipts, Adapted to Western Housewifery", By Anna Maria Collins, 1857

Put into the stewpan a pint of beef gravy, thickened; add to this a wine-glassful of Madeira, the juice and peel of half a lemon, an eschallot quartered, a few grains of cayenne pepper, and let them simmer together five minutes, and then strain them through a fine, hair sieve.

9. PICKLED DISHES

An Excellent Pickle

From "The Book of Household Management" By Isabella Beeton, 1861

Equal quantities of medium-sized onions, cucumbers, and sauce-apples; 1-1/2 teaspoonful of salt, 3/4 teaspoonful of cayenne, 1 wineglassful of soy, 1 wineglassful of sherry; vinegar.

Slice sufficient cucumbers, onions, and apples to fill a pint stone jar, taking care to cut the slices very thin; arrange them in alternate layers, shaking in as you proceed salt and cayenne in the above proportion; pour in the soy and wine, and fill up with vinegar. It will be fit for use the day it is made.

Pickling Apples

From "Dr. Chase's Recipes; or, Information for Everybody", By Dr. Alvin Wood Chase, 1864

Best vinegar 1 gal.; sugar 4 lbs.; apples all it will cover handsomely; cinnamon and cloves, ground, of each 1 tablespoon.

Pare and core the apples, tying up the cinnamon and cloves in a cloth and putting with the apples, into the vinegar and sugar and cooking until done, only. Keep in jars. They are nicer than preserves, and more healthy, and keep a long time; not being too sour, nor too sweet, but an agreeable mixture of the two. It will be seen below that the different fruits require different quantities of sugar and vinegar, the reason for it is the difference in the fruit.

Beet Roots

From "The Cook's Oracle; and Housekeeper's Manual", By William Kitchiner, 1830

Boil gently till they are full three parts done (this will take from an hour and a half to two and a half); then take them out, and when a little cooled, peel them, and cut them in slices about half an inch thick. Have ready a pickle for it, made by adding to each a quart of vinegar an ounce of ground black pepper, half an ounce of ginger pounded, same of salt, and of horseradish cut in thin slices; and you may warm it, if you like, with a few capsicums, or a little Cayenne; put these ingredients into a jar; stop it close, and let them steep three days on a trivet by the side of the fire; then, when cold, pour the clear liquor on the beet-root, which have previously arranged in a jar.

To Pickle Cauliflowers

From "Directions for Cookery, in its Various Branches" By Eliza Leslie, 1840

Take the whitest and closest full-grown cauliflowers; cut off the thick stalk, and split the blossom or flower part into eight or ten pieces. Spread them oh a large dish, sprinkle them with salt, and let them stand twenty-four hours. Then wash off the salt, drain them, put them into a broad flat jar or pan, scald them with salt and water, (allowing a quarter of a pound of salt to a quart of water,) cover them closely and let them stand in the brine till next day. Afterwards drain them in a hair sieve, and spread them on a cloth in a warm place to dry for a day and a night. Then put them carefully, piece by piece, into clean broad jars and pour over them a pickle which has been prepared as follows:--Mix together three ounces of coriander seed, three ounces of turmeric, one ounce of mustard seed, and one ounce of ginger. Pound the whole in a mortar to a fine powder. Put it into three quarts of the best white wine vinegar, set it by the side of the fire in a stone jar, and let it infuse three days. These are the proportions, but the quantity of the whole pickle must depend on the quantity of cauliflower, which must he kept well covered by the liquid. Pour it over the cauliflower, and secure the jars closely from the air.
You may pickle brocoli in the same manner. Also the green tops of asparagus.

To Pickle Cucumbers

From "The Virginia Housewife", By Mary Randolph, 1836

Gather them full grown, but quite young--take off the green rind, and slice them tolerably thick; put a layer in a deep dish, strew over it some chopped onion and salt; do this until they are all in; sprinkle salt on the top, let them stand six hours, put them in a colander—when all the liquor has run off, put them in a pot; strew a little cayenne pepper over each layer, and cover them with strong cold vinegar; when the pot is full, pour on some sweet oil, and tie it, up close; at the end of a fortnight, pour off the first vinegar, and put on fresh.

To Pickle Cucumbers
From "Miss Beecher's Domestic Receipt Book", By
Catharine Esther Beecher, 1850

Wash the cucumbers in cold water, being careful not to bruise, or break them. Make a brine of rock, or blown salt (rock is the best), strong enough to bear up an egg, or potato, and of sufficient quantity to cover the cucumbers.
Put them into an oaken tub, or stone-ware jar, and pour the brine over them. In twenty-four hours, they should be stirred up from the bottom with the hand. The third day pour off the brine, scald it, and pour it over the cucumbers. Let them stand in the brine nine days, scalding it every third day, as described above. Then take the cucumbers into a tub, rinse them in cold water, and if they are too salt, let them stand in it a few hours. Drain them from the water, put them back into the tub or jar, which must be washed clean from the brine. Scald vinegar sufficient to cover them, and pour it upon them. Cover them tight, and in a week they will be ready for use. If spice is wanted, it may be tied in a linen cloth, and put into the jar with the pickles, or scalded with the vinegar, and the bag thrown into the pickle jar. If a white scum rises, take it off and scald the vinegar, and pour it back. A small lump of alum added to the vinegar, improves the hardness of the cucumbers.

Pickled Eggs
From "Directions for Cookery, in its Various Branches" By Eliza Leslie, 1840

Boil twelve eggs quite hard, and lay them in cold water; having peeled off the shells. Then put them whole into a stone jar, with a quarter of an ounce of whole mace, and the same quantity of cloves; a sliced nutmeg; a table-spoonful of whole pepper; a small bit of ginger; and a peach leaf. Fill up the jar with boiling vinegar; cover it closely that the eggs may cool slowly. When they are cold, tie up the jar; covering the cork with leather. After it has stood three days pour off the pickle, boil it up again, and return it boiling hot to the eggs and spice. They will be fit for use in a fortnight.

To Pickle Eggs

From "The Book of Household Management" by Isabella Beeton, 1861

16 eggs, 1 quart of vinegar, 1/2 oz. of Black pepper, 1/2 oz. of Jamaica pepper, 1/2 oz. of ginger.
Boil the eggs for 12 minutes, then dip them into cold water, and take off the shells. Put the vinegar, with the pepper and ginger, into a stewpan, and let it simmer for 10 minutes. Now place the eggs in a jar, pour over them the vinegar, &c., boiling hot, and, when cold, tie them down with bladder to exclude the air. This pickle will be ready for use in a month.

Pickled Gherkins
From "The Book of Household Management", By Isabella Beeton, 1861

Salt and water, 1 oz. of bruised ginger, 1/2 oz. of whole black pepper, 1/4 oz. of whole allspice, 4 cloves, 2 blades of mace, a little horseradish. This proportion of pepper, spices, &c., for 1 quart of vinegar.
Let the gherkins remain in salt and water for 3 or 4 days, when take them out, wipe perfectly dry, and put them into a stone jar. Boil sufficient vinegar to cover them, with spices and pepper, &c., in the above proportion, for 10 minutes; pour it, quite boiling, over the gherkins, cover the jar with vine-leaves, and put over them a plate, setting them near the fire, where they must remain all night. Next day drain off the vinegar, boil it up again, and pour it hot over them. Cover up with fresh leaves, and let the whole remain till quite cold. Now tie down closely with bladder to exclude the air, and in a month or two, they will be fit for use.

Pickled Large, Green Peppers
"The Great Western Cook Book, or Table Receipts,
Adapted to Western Housewifery", By Anna Maria
Collins, 1857

Cut out the part that holds the stem, be very particular to cut them even, scrape them out, and lay them in salt and water two or three days; then wash them well in cold water, then lay them to drain. If you have a peck of peppers, prepare a large cabbage head thus: cut it up as you do for cold-slaw, very fine; use none but the whole part of the cabbage; a dozen large onions minced very fine, four or five young cucumbers cut in very small pieces, mix them together; add an ounce of allspice, ginger, a half ounce of cloves, cinnamon one ounce, and two ounces of white or black mustard-seed; scald these all well in barely as much vinegar as will cover them, then pour it in a stone vessel and let it cool, then take your peppers and fill them as full as possible, then sew on the stem, or the pieces you have cut out; put them in a jar and fill with cold, strong vinegar.

Fine Lemon Pickle
From "The Lady's Receipt-Book; a Useful Companion for Large or Small Families", By Eliza Leslie, 1847

Take some fresh ripe lemons, and (having first rolled each one under your hand upon the table) cut them into quarters, and remove all the seeds. Put the pieces of lemon, with all the juice, into a stone jar. Have ready a sufficient quantity of excellent vinegar to cover the lemon well: the vinegar being boiled with a clove or two of garlic; some blades of mace; a broken up nutmeg; whole pepper, (the white or peeled pepper-corns will be best;) some cayenne or bird-pepper: and a very little salt. The proportion of these ingredients may be according to your taste, but the seasoning should be high, yet not so as to overpower the lemon-flavour. Having boiled the vinegar, with all these articles, about ten minutes, pour the whole boiling hot upon the lemon in the jar, and immediately cover it closely. Let the jar stand three weeks in the chimney-corner, stirring it frequently, and setting it occasionally in the oven after the baking is done. Then roll a sheet of blotting paper into a cone, pinning up the side, and folding the cone so as to close up the pointed end. Have ready some small clean black bottles. Set the paper cone into the mouth of the bottle, and through it filter the liquid. Seal the corks. This will be found an excellent sauce for fish, or any sort of white meat; and will keep for years.

Mangoes
From "The Great Western Cook Book, or Table Receipts, Adapted to Western Housewifery", By Anna Maria Collins, 1857

Take small muskmelons of a late growth, and cut a small piece out of the side of each. Scrape out the inside, and wipe all the furze from the outside; put them in salt and water nine days, and prepare them for the vinegar in the same way you do cucumbers. When they are ready, fill them with small pieces of horseradish, ginger, mace, cloves, black pepper, nasturtion-seed, nutmeg, very small onions, or garlic, and white mustard-seed. Sew in the piece that was cut out. Boil good vinegar a few minutes and pour it on them. If they are not sufficiently green, put a tablespoonful of alum to every three quarts of vinegar. This adds to the consistence, as well as to the color of green pickles. If you use a copper, brass, or bell-metal vessel, be sure not to let the vinegar cool in them, as it would be rendered poisonous. Common earthen ware should not be used for pickles.

Pickled Mushrooms

From "The Book of Household Management", By Isabella Beeton, 1861

Sufficient vinegar to cover the mushrooms; to each quart of mushrooms, 2 blades of pounded mace, 1 oz. of ground pepper, salt to taste.
Choose some nice young button mushrooms for pickling, and rub off the skin with a piece of flannel and salt, and cut off the stalks; if very large, take out the red inside, and reject the black ones, as they are too old. Put them in a stewpan, sprinkle salt over them, with pounded mace and pepper in the above proportion; shake them well over a clear fire until the liquor flows, and keep them there until it is all dried up again; then add as much vinegar as will cover them; just let it simmer for 1 minute, and store it away in stone jars for use. When cold, tie down with bladder and keep in a dry place; they will remain good for a length of time, and are generally considered delicious.

To Pickle Onions
From "The Virginia Housewife", By Mary Randolph, 1836

Get white onions that are not too large, cut the stem close to the root with a sharp knife, put them in a pot, pour on boiling salt and water to cover them, stop the pot closely, let them stand a fortnight, changing the salt and water every three days; they must be stirred daily, or those that float will become soft; at the end of this time, take off the skin and outer shell, put them in plain cold vinegar with a little turmeric. If the vinegar be not very pale, the onion will not be of a good colour.

Onions Pickled White
From "Directions for Cookery, in its Various Branches" By Eliza Leslie, 1840

Peel some very small white onions, and lay them for three days in salt and water changing the water every day. Then wipe them, and put them into a porcelain kettle with equal quantities of milk and water, sufficient to cover them well. Simmer them over a slow fire, but when just ready to boil take them off, and drain and dry them, and put them into wide-mouthed glass bottles; interspersing them with blades of mace. Boil a sufficient quantity of distilled white wine vinegar to cover them and fill up the bottles, adding to it a little salt; and when it is cold, pour it into the bottles of onions. At the top of each bottle put a spoonful of sweet oil. Set them away closely corked.

Peach Pickles

From "The Lady's Receipt-Book; a Useful Companion for Large or Small Families", By Eliza Leslie, 1847

Stir two pounds of white sugar into two quarts of the best cider vinegar. Boil it ten minutes, skimming it well. Have ready some large fully-ripe peaches; rub them with a clean flannel to take off the down, and stick four cloves into each. Put them into glass or white-ware jars, (rather more than half-full,) and pour on them the vinegar boiling hot. Cover them closely, set them in a cool place, and let them rest for a week. Then pour off the liquid, and give it another boiling. Afterwards pour it again on the peaches; cover them closely, corking the jars, and tying leather over each, and put them away till wanted for use.

Instead of cloves you may stick the peaches with blades of mace, six blades to each peach.

Apricots may be pickled as above.

Morella cherries also, using mace instead of cloves.

If you find a coat of mould on the top of a jar of pickles, remove it carefully, and do not throw away the pickles, as they may still be quite good beneath.

To Pickle Peppers
From "The Virginia Housewife", By Mary Randolph, 1836

Gather the large bell pepper when quite young, leave the seeds in and the stem on, cut a slit in one side between the large veins, to let the water in; pour boiling salt and waler on, changing it every day for three weeks--you must keep them closely stopped; if at the end of this time, they be a good green, put them in pots, and cover them with cold vinegar and a little turmeric; those that are not sufficiently green, must be continued under the same process till they are so. Be careful not to cut through the large veins, as the heat will instantly diffuse itself through the pod.

To Pickle Peppers
From "Miss Beecher's Domestic Receipt Book", By Catharine Esther Beecher, 1850

Take green peppers, take the seeds out carefully, so as not to mangle them, soak them nine days in salt and water, changing it every day, and keep them in a warm place. Stuff them with chopped cabbage, seasoned with cloves, cinnamon, and mace; put them in cold spiced vinegar.

Radish Pods

From "Directions for Cookery, in its Various Branches" By Eliza Leslie, 1840

Gather sprigs or bunches of radish pods while they are young and tender, but let the pods remain on the sprigs; it not being the custom to pick them off. Put them into strong salt and water, and let them stand two days. Then drain and wipe them and put them into a clean stone jar. Boil an equal quantity of vinegar and water. Pour it over the radish pods while hot, and cover them closely to keep in the steam. Repeat this frequently through the day till they are very green. Then pour off the vinegar and water, and boil for five minutes some very strong vinegar, with a little bit of alum, and pour it over them. Put them into a stone jar, (and having added some whole mace, whole pepper, a little turmeric and a little sweet oil,) cork it closely, and tie over it a leather or oil-cloth.

To Pickle Tomatoes

From "The Great Western Cook Book, or Table Receipts, Adapted
to Western Housewifery", By Anna Maria Collins, 1857

Wash a peck of very green tomatoes, wipe them with a coarse napkin, then slice them as fine as it is possible for a knife to cut, sprinkle them with salt, and lay them in a sieve to drain. Slice a half peck of onions, and scald them in salt and water; have ready allspice, white mustard-seed, black pepper, six red pepper-pods, cinnamon, cloves, horseradish, ginger. Take a large stone jar, put in a layer of tomatoes, then lay on some of each spice and horseradish, then layer of onions, then another of tomatoes, let the last layer be spiced well, and then fill it up with strong cider vinegar. An ounce of each kind of spice and a pint of cramped horseradish is sufficient to a peck of tomatoes. Try and have the jar air-tight.

Pickled Walnuts

From "Miss Beecher's Domestic Receipt Book", By
Catharine Esther Beecher, 1850

Take a hundred nuts, an ounce of cloves, an ounce of allspice, an ounce of nutmeg, an ounce of whole pepper, an ounce of race ginger, an ounce of horseradish, half pint of mustard seed, tied in a bag, and four cloves of garlic. Wipe the nuts, prick with a pin, and put them in a pot, sprinkling the spice as you lay them in; then add two tablespoonfuls of salt; boil sufficient vinegar to fill the pot, and pour it over the nuts and spice. Cover the jar close, and keep it for a year, when the pickles will be ready for use.
Butternuts may be made in the same manner, if they are taken when green, and soft enough to be stuck through with the head of a pin. Put them for a week or two in weak brine, changing it occasionally. Before putting in the brine, rub them about with a broom in brine to cleanse the skins. Then proceed as for the walnuts.

The vinegar makes an excellent catsup.

10. HOLIDAYS

Christmas

The wife of Confederate President Jefferson Davis wrote an article detailing the Davis family Christmas of 1864 at the Confederate White House. In the article, she mentions the following goodies of Egg Nog, Molasses Candy, Blanc Mange and Mince Pie as being served:

"Then the coveted eggnog was passed around in tiny glass cups and pronounced good."…. "At last quiet settled on the household and the older members of the family began to stuff stockings with molasses candy…."….. "For me there were six cakes of delicious soap, made from the grease of ham boiled for a family at Farmville…." "Our chef did wonders with the turkey and roast beef, and drove the children quite out of their propriety by a spun sugar hen, life-size, on a nest full of blanc mange eggs. The mince pie and plum pudding made them feel, as one of the gentlemen laughingly remarked, "like their jackets were buttoned," a strong description of repletion which I have never forgotten."

Egg Nog
From "Directions for Cookery, in its Various Branches" By Eliza Leslie, 1840

Beat separately the yolks and whites of six eggs. Stir the yolks into a quart of rich milk, or thin cream, and add half a pound of sugar. Then mix in half a pint of rum or brandy. Flavour it with a grated nutmeg. Lastly, stir in gently the beaten white of an egg.

It should be mixed in a china bowl.

Molasses Candy

From "Directions for Cookery, in its Various Branches" By Eliza Leslie, 1840

Mix a pound of the best brown sugar with two quarts of West India molasses, (which must be perfectly sweet,) and boil it in a preserving kettle over a moderate fire for three hours, skimming it well, and stirring it frequently after the scum has ceased to rise; taking care that it does not burn. Have ready the grated rind and the juice of three lemons, and stir them into the molasses after it has boiled about two hours and a half; or you may substitute a large tea-spoonful of strong essence of lemon. The flavour of the lemon will all be boiled out if it is put in too soon. The mixture should boil at least three hours, that it may be crisp and brittle when cold. If it is taken off the fire too soon, or before it has boiled sufficiently, it will not congeal, but will be tough and ropy, and must be boiled over again. It will cease boiling of itself when it is thoroughly done. Then take it off the fire; have ready a square tin pan; put the mixture into it, and set it away to cool.

You may make molasses candy with almonds blanched and slit into pieces; stir them in by degrees after the mixture has boiled two hours and a half. Or you may blanch a quart of ground-nuts and put them in instead of the almonds.

Blanc Mange

From "The Great Western Cook Book, or Table Receipts, Adapted
to Western Housewifery", By Anna Maria Collins, 1851
Take two ounces of Russia isinglass (Russian Sturgeon
Isinglass is from dried sturgeon bladders of the highest
quality), one quart of new milk, half a pound of sugar, flavor
it with rose, or peach-water. Boil it five minutes, let it cool till
it is about milk-warm, then put it in moulds.

To Make A Hen's Nest
From "The Virginia Housewife", By Mary Randolph, 1836

Get five small eggs, make a hole at one end, and empty the shells—fill them with blanc mange: when stiff and cold, take off the shells, pare the yellow rind very thin from six lemons, boil them in water till tender, then cut them in thin strips to resemble straw, and preserve them with sugar; fill a small deep dish half full of nice jelly--when it is set, put the straw on in form of a nest, and lay the eggs in it. It is a beautiful dish for a dessert or supper.

Mince Pie
From "The Great Western Cook Book", By Anna Maria Collins, 1851

Two pounds of beef-suet, chopped fine; two pounds of apples, cored, pared, and chopped fine; three pounds of currants, washed and picked; one pound of raisins, stoned and chopped fine; one pound of good brown sugar; half a pound of citron, cut into thin slices; two pounds of ready-dressed roast beef, free from skin and gristle, chopped fine; two nutmegs, grated; one ounce of salt; half an ounce of allspice, half an ounce of cloves, all ground fine; the juice of six lemons, with their rinds grated; half a pint of brandy, a pint of sweet wine, a quart of good cider. Mix the suet, apple, currants, meat, plums, and sweetmeats, well together, in a large pan, and strew in the spice by degrees; mix the sugar, lemon-juice, wine, brandy, and cider, and pour it into the other ingredients, and stir them well together. Cover it closely, and set it away in a cold place; when wanted, stir up the meat from the bottom, and add some brandy to the quantity you use.

Mulled Wine
From "Directions for Cookery, in its Various Branches" By Eliza Leslie, 1840

Boil together in a pint of water two beaten nutmegs, a handful of broken cinnamon, and a handful of cloves slightly pounded. When the liquid is reduced to one half, strain it into a quart of port wine, which must be set on hot coals, and taken off as soon as it comes to a boil. Serve it up hot in a pitcher with little glass cups round it, and a plate of fresh rusk.

Valentine's Day

Valentine's Day was a well-established holiday by the 1860's. Handmade cards and tokens were carefully and lovingly fashioned for sweethearts. Such cards were cherished during the Civil War as husbands and wives, and young lovers were separated not only by distance, but by the fear they would never be reunited as a result of disease or death on the battlefield. In 1862, Confederate soldier Robert King made a basket weave folded card for his wife from scrounged paper. Once opened, it showed two crying lovers. This was a sad foretelling of his death. Soldiers also made such folded cards like a "Puzzle Purse" by folding in the corners to make a paper pouch in which they would insert a trinket or lock of hair for their loved ones (for directions, visit http://www.origami-resource-center.com/valentine-puzzle-purses.html). As the war raged on and intensified, the Union blockade increased the scarcity of paper in the Confederate States and made mail delivery dangerous and difficult. Valentines and letters thus became ever more precious communications. Unlike modern Valentines, Civil War Valentines often combined the sentiments of love, patriotism, duty, and loss. The fact that they were handmade reinforced the recipient's feeling of a personal connection to the card or token, knowing that their loved one put forth their own personal affection in it's construction.

"Isabella says that war leads to love making. She says these soldiers do more courting here in a day than they would do at home, without a war, in ten years." -Mary Boykin Chesnut, February 12, 1864.

Kisses

From "The Practical Housekeeper; A Cyclopedia of Domestic Economy" By Elizabeth Fries Ellet, 1857

Beat the whites of four eggs till they stand alone. Then beat in, gradually, a pound of finely-powdered sugar, a tea-spoonful at a time. Add eight drops of the essence of lemon, and beat the whole very hard.

Lay a wet sheet of paper on the bottom of a square tin pan. Drop on it, at equal distance, small teaspoonfuls of stiff currant jelly. Put a little of the beaten egg and sugar at first, under the currant jelly. With a large spoon, pile some of the beaten white of egg and sugar, on each lump of jelly, so as to cover it entirely. Drop on the mixture as evenly as possible, so as to make the kisses of a round, smooth shape.

Set them in a cool oven, and as soon as they are colored, they are done. Then take them out, and place the two bottoms together. Lay them lightly on a sieve, and dry them in a cool oven, till the two bottoms stick fast together so as to form one ball or oval.

Bola D' Amour-Love Cakes

From "The Practical Housekeeper; A Cyclopedia of Domestic Economy" By Elizabeth Fries Ellet, 1857

Take the yolks of eggs, as many as are required for the dish (about twelve), and beat them up in a pan with an equal weight of sugar, the same as sponge cake, using any kind of liquor or essence for flavoring. "When the mixture is beaten up light and thick, have ready some clarified butter in a stewpan, made hot enough for frying. Pour the mixture into a funnel having a small bore or pipe, and let it run into the hot butter, turning the hand while it is running, so that it may be formed into threads all over the surface of the pan. In about two minutes it will be done, when it should be taken out with a skimmer, and be placed on a dish for serving, garnishing it with any kind of preserve, and serve cold.

Another way is, to beat up the eggs with some liquor, and run it into some boiling syrup at the blow.

Easter

Roast Ham

From "The Practical Housekeeper; A Cyclopedia of Domestic Economy" By Elizabeth Fries Ellet, 1857

Take a very fine ham (a Westphalia, if you can procure it), soak it in lukewarm water for a day or two, changing the water frequently. The day before you intend to cook it, take the ham out of the water, and, having removed the skin, trim it nicely, and pour over it a bottle of an inferior white wine; let it steep till next morning, frequently during the day washing the wine over it; put it in a cradle-spit in time to allow at least six hours for slowly roasting it; baste with hot water continually. When done, dredge it with fine bread raspings, and brown before the fire.

Thanksgiving

In 1862, Confederate President Jefferson Davis proclaimed "a day of fasting, humiliation and prayer". In his Proclamation, Davis writes: "It is my privilege to invite you once more to His footstool, not now in the garb of fasting and sorrow, but with joy and gladness, to render thanks for the great mercies received at His hand. A few months since, and our enemies poured forth their invading legions upon our soil. They laid waste our fields, polluted our altars and violated the sanctity of our homes....The brave troops which rallied to its defense have extinguished these vain hopes, and, under the guidance of the same almighty hand, have scattered our enemies and driven them back in dismay....In such circumstances, it is meet and right that, as a people, we should bow down in adoring thankfulness to that gracious God who has been our bulwark and defense, and to offer unto him the tribute of thanksgiving and praise. In his hand is the issue of all events, and to him should we, in an especial manner, ascribe the honor of this great deliverance.
Now, therefore, I, Jefferson Davis, President of the Confederate States, do issue this, my proclamation, setting apart Thursday, the 18th day of September inst., as a day of prayer and thanksgiving to Almighty God for the great mercies vouchsafed to our people, and more especially for the triumph of our arms at Richmond and Manassas; and I do hereby invite the people of the Confederate States to meet on that day at their respective places of public worship, and to unite in rendering thanks and praise to God for these great mercies, and to implore Him to conduct our country safely through the perils which surround us, to the final attainment of the blessings of peace and security."

Turkey Roast
From: "The Practical Housekeeper; A Cyclopedia of Domestic Economy"
By Elizabeth Fries, 1857

It is stuffed with either sausage meat or fillet of veal stuffing, or crumbs of bread and veal. While roasting, a piece of paper should be placed over the part stuffed, as being bulky it will catch, the fire and become scorched; but keep the heat well to the breast, in order that it may be as well done as the rest of the bird. Baste well, and froth it up. Serve with gravy in the dish, and bread sauce in a tureen. To the sausage meat, if used, add a few bread-crumbs and a beaten egg. Turkey is sometimes stuffed with truffles; they are prepared thus: they must be peeled, and chopped, and pounded in a mortar, in quantities of a pound and a half will be found sufficient: rasp the same weight of fat of bacon, and mix it with the truffles. Stuff the tur-key with it; this stuffing is usually placed in the turkey two days previous to cooking: it is supposed to impart a flavor to the flesh of the fowl. Cut thin slices of fat bacon and place over the breast of the turkey. Secure it with half a sheet of clean white paper, and roast. Chestnuts dressed in the same fashion are found an excellent substitute for truffles. Two hours will roast it. If you wish to make plain stuffing, pound a cracker, or crumble some bread very fine, chop some raw salt pork very fine, or use butter; sift some sage, (and summer-savory, or sweet mar-joram, if you have them in the house, and fancy them), and mould them all together, season with a little pepper. An egg worked in makes the stuffing cut Letter.

Chestnut Sauce
From: "The Practical Housekeeper; A Cyclopedia of Domestic Economy"
By Elizabeth Fries, 1857

Scald a score of chestnuts in hot water for ten minutes; skin them; let them stew gently for about half an hour in some good gravy seasoned with a glass of white wine, a little white pepper, salt, and mace or nutmeg; and when quite soft, serve them in the dish.

Or:--Pulp them through a colander to thicken the gravy, making it either brown or white, by using in the former beef-gravy, and in the latter veal-broth, with pounded almonds, and without pepper.

Either of these is equally fit for sauce to guinea-bird or turkey, as well as for stuffing the body of the bird.

11. DISHES THE SOLDIERS ATE

"Our fare is tolerable good yet. We get flour, bacon, lard, and some fresh beef besides potatoes and sugar. We get no molasses owing to the scarcity of them." – Pvt. Jesse T. Jordan, Co. A, 17th South Carolina Infantry, James Island, South Carolina, March 15, 1862. Letter to his wife. He died on James Island on 2 May 1862.

"And I want you to bring some red pepper for I want you to bake me one loaf of tight bread. I want one more good bottle of brew from home for we can't cook good here and the beef that we draw they have to lean it up against a tree to shoot it or prop it with rocks. It is one pound of beef and ten pounds of bones." - James Andrew James, T. B. Ferguson's (South Carolina) Battery Camp near Dalton, Georgia, January 18, 1864. Letter to his father

Food for both Union and Confederate soldiers was provided by their Commissary Departments, this food, however, was issued uncooked. For many men, this was their first time cooking their own food. Without a female to prepare their food, as they were accustomed to at home, they had to learn in a hurry, as well as learn by trial and error. Captain Sanderson understood and echoed the ignorance of cooking by the men when he writes "In making up the following receipts, the author has been actuated by a desire to aid the efforts of those of his countrymen who, with best intentions, lack the knowledge to utilize them..." Soldiers then gathered in small groups to cook their food. They called these groups "messes" and referred to others in the group as "messmates". Messmates took turns preparing and cooking meals and in carrying the mess' equipment, such as a frying pan that were privately purchased or came from home. Jokingly, some mess mates named their groups "Pan Companies". Since there were no big kitchens in the war, each soldier was given his rations and it was his responsibility to cook it. As a result, different ways of cooking and preparing the rations emerged throughout the war. The soldiers carried their food in a haversack along with their pan (if they had one), plate and cup.

To add to their rations, some blessed soldiers would occasionally receive packages from home. These might contain items like coffee, apples, apple butter, fresh pork, dried fruit, milk, eggs, risen bread, cakes, preserves or jelly, pickles, egg-nog, sugar, bicarbonate of soda, salt, fresh butter, roast beef, ham and turkey. These parcels of food not only sustained men physically, but it was a morale boost to receive a package from home. Additionally, such packages, provided a way to make extra money by selling the goodies. Soldiers with money had the opportunity to buy food along the way. Seedy entrepreneurs known as "Sutlers" often followed the armies on their marches. Soldiers with money could afford the luxury foods the sutlers sold, as it would take most of their monthly pay to buy just a few items.

As to the kitchens in the Federal Army (when and where kitchens were practical), for every 100-man company, a skilled cook would be appointed two privates; one position would be permanent and the other would rotate among the men of the company. The skilled cook would be given the rank of "Cook Major" and receive a monthly salary of $50. It would be the Cook Major's responsibility to prepare the food, ration it, and delegate tasks to the company cooks.

While garrisoned at Ft. Pillow, Tennessee for training in June of 1861, the officers' kitchen for Bankhead's Battery (Confederate) was placed ten feet behind the Captains tent. Two other kitchens for the enlisted men were established on either side of the area between the Lieutenant's tents and the tents of the men. Each man was then issued his tin plate, cup, spoon, knife and fork. Eight men were assigned to each "mess", and each mess was issued an iron kettle, an oven, a wash pan, a tin bucket, a wooden bucket and a coffee pot. Rations would be issued at 10:00am daily.

"I wish you could see the things they give us all. I got a frying pan & a pan as big as you ever saw & a half a bucket with a lid & a brass handle & a stool that is worth $5.00 and a halter worth $10 & one fine calico comfort." -Pleasant H.

Bryan, Co. I., 7th Georgia Infantry, April 29, 1861, Camp Pembroke (near Savannah, Georgia). Letter to his wife, Nancy.

"Our rations were cooked up by a special detail ten miles in the rear, and were sent to us every three days, and then those three days' rations were generally eaten up at one meal, and the private soldier had to starve the other two days and a half.....The men looked sick, hollow-eyed, and heart-broken, living principally upon parched corn, which had been picked out of the mud and dirt under the feet of officers' horses. We thought of nothing but starvation."- Pvt. Sam Watkins, on Lookout Mountain, Co, H, 1st Tennessee Infantry

"....we have just got orders to cook four days rations & we don't know whether we will go north or south." -Pvt. James F. Currie (from Lauderdale County, Tennessee) of Co. M, 7th Tennessee (Confederate) Cavalry ("Duckworth's Cavalry"), Abbeville, Mississippi, June 2, 1864. Letter to his wife, Kate.

In 1862, Federal Capt. James M. Sanderson wrote the first cookbook to be distributed to the Federal soldiers. The book was titled: "Camp Fires and Camp Cooking; or Culinary Hints for the Soldier: Including Receipt for Making Bread in the "Portable Field Oven" Furnished by the Subsistence Department". In this book, Sanderson described several techniques, such as suspending pots over a campfire, making cooking slightly more convenient. Given the important contribution of Sanderson's book to the culinary education and health of the army, the majority of the recipes in this chapter are from his work.

Below is a brief description (from the aforementioned book by Capt. Sanderson) of kitchen utensils, as well as a description of a proper fire pit for the camp kitchen. Also included from the same book is a recipe for Boiled Pork and Bean Soup (NOTE: as with all other recipes containing dry beans, the beans would have to be soaked over-night. Soaking them could be hindered due to the time constraints of marches, campaigns and battle, so they were most likely not consumed by non-garrisoned troops or troops on active campaign on a regular basis).

Camp Cooking and Camp Kettles

"The utensils and means furnished by government to the soldier for preparing his food are of the most primitive character. The former consist of camp kettles, made of iron, with a handle, and varying in size from four to seven gallons, (they should be made so as to have one slide into the other, in nests of four,) and mess pans, also of iron, about 12 inches in diameter, and sloping to the bottom. The latter consist of a certain amount of wood per diem, which is to be consumed as taste or ingenuity may dictate. The usual and most simple mode is to dig a trench 18 inches wide, 12 inches deep, and from four to six feet long. At each end plant a forked stick of equal height, with a stout sapling, from which to suspend the kettles, extending from one to the other.

This, however, is neither the best nor most economical mode, as it consumes much fuel wastes much of the heat, and causes great inconvenience to the cook. An improvement can be effected by easing the sides of the trench with brick, adding a little chimney at one end, and, in place of the forked sticks, using iron uprights and cross-bar, to which half a dozen hooks for hanging kettles are attached.

Besides the allowance from government, however, the company cooks should be furnished, from the " Company Fund," with two large iron spoons, two large iron forks, two stout knives, one tin cullender, and one yard of flannel; also a false tin bottom, closely fitting the kettles; for all of which the cook should be responsible."

Capt. Sanderson also admonishes the troops to be patient and clean. In his "Kitchen Philosophy", he writes "Remember that beans, badly boiled, kill more than bullets; and fat is more fatal than powder. In cooking, more than in anything else in this world, always make haste slowly. One hour too much is vastly better than five minutes too little, with rare exceptions. A big fire scorches your soup, burns your face, and crisps your temper. Skim, simmer, and scour, are the true secrets of good cooking."

Boiled Pork and Bean Soup

From "Culinary Hints for the Soldier" By Captain James M. Sanderson, 1862

Never serve beans until they have been soaked over night. At eight o'clock in the morning, put eight quarts into two kettles, and fill up with clean cold water. Boil constantly, over a brisk fire, for an hour or more, during which many of the beans will rise to the top. At the end of this time, take the kettles off the fire for fifteen or twenty minutes, and then pour off all the water, replacing it with fresh clean water. Add to each kettle a pound of parboiled pork, without rind, and boil continuously for an hour and a half longer.

At quarter past eight o'clock, fill three kettles loosely with pieces of pork weighing from three to five pounds, cover with water, and boil briskly for one hour; then pour all the liquid, and fill up with clean hot water, and boil for one hour and a half longer; then take out all the pork, and lay it aside. Take out also one-half of the beans from the other kettles, placing them aside for breakfast next morning, and add to the remainder the liquor in which the pork was boiled. To each kettle add also two onions chopped or sliced, with plenty of black or red pepper, some salt, and a tablespoonful of vinegar. After fifteen minutes' longer boiling, mash the beans with a wooden stick made for the purpose, and serve, with a slice of pork, in a separate dish. If onions are plenty, mince fine eight or ten of them, fry them in a pan with a little flour and fat, with half a pint hot water, and the same quantity of the liquor in which the pork was boiled. After cooking five minutes, add pepper, salt, and half a glass of vinegar, and pour over the slices of pork.

"The food, while good, was very scant. Breakfast consisted of coffee and a loaf of bread, the latter under ordinary circumstances, with vegetables and other food, would probably suffice for two meals. The loaf was given us at breakfast, and if we ate it all then we went without bread for dinner. If there was any left over we took it to our tents…and saved it for the next meal.
The dinners consisted of a tin cup of soup (generally bean or other vegetable), a small piece of meat…on which a little vinegar was poured to prevent scurvy. My recollection is we had no other meal…[W]e were always hungry, and the chief topic of conversation was the sumptuous meals we had sat down to in other days…"- Luther Hopkins, 6th Virginia Cavalry, writes about the rations at Point Lookout, Maryland

Soldiers might be issued beans when in camp for long periods of time (i.e. Winter Camp) or on garrison duty. Because they took too long to soak and cook, beans were impractical for use while on active campaign, unless the Army had little else to offer. When available and practical for issuance, beans would be used in soups or stews, or to make pork and beans.

Beef Stew

From "Culinary Hints for the Soldier" By Captain James M. Sanderson, 1862

Take the pieces of beef reserved for frying or broiling, and cut them into pieces about two inches square and one inch thick; sprinkle them with pepper and salt, and put them into frying pans, with a little fat; place them over the fire until half cooked; then turn them into camp kettles, adding a handful of flour and six onions cut in quarters to each kettle, with just enough cold water to cover the meat; add also to each kettle two dozen potatoes pared and cut in quarters. Stew slowly over a moderate fire, skimming every now and then, for three hours and a half; then stir in each two table spoonsful of vinegar, and serve smoking hot. All kinds of vegetables—such as leeks, carrots, parsnips, and turnips—can be added to this stew with advantage.

The rations for soldiers in the Confederate army were supposed to follow the guidelines in "Hardee's Rifle and Light Infantry Tactics"; however, the South's armies were frequently short of most of the items listed. The Confederate government made efforts to provide adequate rations for their troops, but blockades, mono-cultural farming, and lack of transportation and supply plagued these efforts.

According to "Hardee's Rifle and Light Infantry Tactics", rations consisted of:

- *20 oz. pork or beef (Beef was either fresh or salted, and pork was always salted.)*

- *12 oz. hard bread (in camp or garrison or 16 oz. of hard bread at sea, on campaign, or on the march)*

- *1 oz. compressed cube of desiccated mixed vegetables or a 1.5 oz. compressed cube of desiccated potatoes if supplemental foods were unavailable*

This would be supplemented by (per 100 rations):

- *8 qts. of beans or peas (however, beans were not issued during campaigns, as they took too long to cook)*

- *10 lbs. of rice or hominy*

- *10 lbs. of green coffee beans or 8 lbs. of roasted coffee beans*

- *10 lbs. of sugar*

- *2 qts. of salt*

- *1 quart of vinegar*

"We have boiled, baked, fried, stewed, pickled, sweetened, salted it, and tried it

in puddings, cakes and pies; but it sets all modes of cooking at defiance, so they boys break it up and smoke it in their pipes!"-E. N. Gilpin, 3rd Iowa Cavalry, writing about desiccated vegetables.

In addition to (or in the absence of) rations, soldiers would forage for food. This might include "capturing" food from a farm or mill, offering to buy food from locals, or finding the food in nature (berries, nuts, hunting/trapping, etc).

"Our rations did not suit us. We wanted a change of diet, but there were strict orders from Col. D. H. Hill that we should not go out foraging. Well, Bill Stone, Alie Todd and myself put on our knapsacks and went to the creek to wash our clothes, but when we got there we forgot to wash. We took a good long walk away from the camp, and saw several shoats. We ran one down, held it so it could not squeal, then killed it, cut it in small pieces, put it in our knapsacks, returned to the creek, and from there to camp, where we shared it with the boys. It tasted good."-Pvt. Louis Leon, Company C, First North Carolina Regiment, Bethal Church, Virginia, June 3, 1861, from his diary.

To Cook Bacon
From "Camp Fires and Camp Cooking, Or Culinary Hints For The Soldier", By Capt. James M. Sanderson, 1862

Bacon should be well washed and scraped and put to soak all night. In the morning, put it to boil slowly; simmering is better. After it has once boiled, throw the water off and fill up with fresh water; then let it simmer for three hours. When thoroughly done, the rind comes off easily, and the meat tastes fresh and sweet.

Frying Bacon
From "Camp Fires and Camp Cooking, Or Culinary Hints For The Soldier", By Capt. James M. Sanderson, 1862

The great secret in frying is to have the fat as hot as fire will make it before putting the article to be cooked into it. The object is to close up the pores of the flesh at once, and prevent the fat from penetrating it, rendering it greasy and indigestible. After the bacon is well soaked, cut it into thin slices, and fry it crisp. If it is cold bacon, slice it into a pan, cover it with bread crumbs—stale bread grated— add very little fat, and put it over a quick fire for four or five minutes; then turn it, and cook the other side.

Bacon German Style
From "Camp Fires and Camp Cooking, Or Culinary Hints For The Soldier", By Capt. James M. Sanderson, 1862

When the bacon is parboiled, clean it thoroughly, taking off the rind and all the bones; put it into clean pans, cutting it into strips, with enough water to cover the bottom of the pan, place it in the oven, and let it bake until the top is browned, basting it with the liquid in the meanwhile to prevent its burning or becoming dry.

Beans for Breakfast
From "Camp Fires and Camp Cooking, Or Culinary Hints For The Soldier", By Capt. James M. Sanderson, 1862

The beans left from the soup of the day before should be put in pans and warmed over the fire, care being taken to prevent them from scorching. In the meanwhile a few onions—say three or four— should be chopped fine and slightly fried, and then strewed over the beans, with pepper and salt, and a tablespoonful of vinegar. In this way they make a first-rate dish for breakfast or supper with bread and coffee.

Beef Soup With Desiccated Mixed Vegetables
From "Camp Fires and Camp Cooking, Or Culinary Hints For The Soldier", By Capt. James M. Sanderson, 1862

The Americans, as a rule, are not fond of soups, unless of the thicker kind; but in no form can meat and vegetables be served together more profitably and more nourishingly. As a matter of economy, it admits of no argument, because every portion is useful, both bone and flesh; and, when properly made, it is wholesome and palatable. On fresh-beef day, if among the rations there are some choice bits—such as sirloin, tenderloin, or rump steaks—cut them into neat slices, and, use for breakfast, broiling them if it can be done; if not, fry them. Save all the bones, if large cut them in pieces and distribute equally among the kettles. If the company numbers seventy men or less, use one large kettle and two smaller ones. Fill them nearly with pieces of meat, from one to three pounds each, not too closely packed; then add water enough to cover it, and place it over a brisk fire, throwing in a large handful of salt to each kettle. As soon as the water begins to boil, and the scum begins to rise, deaden the fire, and skim, carefully and faithfully, every ten minutes, and he very sure that the water does not again come to a boil—it should only simmer; for when the meat is boiling hard the pores of the flesh are immediately closed, the essence of the meat, and all its impurities, are retained within, no scum arises, the meat becomes hard and tough, and the soup thin and watery. If it is only permitted to simmer, the pores are kept open, the blood is drawn out, the juices are extracted, the meat is rendered tender and wholesome, and the soup rich, nutritious, and palatable. In one hour and a half—carefully skimming all the while—the meat should be done; but if it has only simmered, two hours will be better. Then take the meat out, leaving only the bones. An hour previous to this, however, break up a tablet of desiccated vegetables as small as possible, and divide them into as many portions as there are kettles of soup. Place each portion in a separate pan, and fill with fresh clean water, standing them near the fire until thoroughly saturated with water. When the meat is taken out, put the vegetables in, and let them boil gently two hours longer, during that time carefully skimming off all the fat which rises to the surface. Then season with pepper and salt, and a tablespoonful of vinegar, and serve out.

Both the French and American desiccated vegetables come in tablets. The former being twice as large as the latter, it will therefore be necessary to use one of the French or two of the American tablets for a company, which will be found amply sufficient, as they swell up to sixteen times their bulk in a compressed state.

The fat taken from the soup is valuable—first for selling, next for frying, but principally because you don't swallow it in your soup.

To Prepare Coffee

From "Camp Fires and Camp Cooking, Or Culinary Hints For The Soldier", By Capt. James M. Sanderson, 1862

Of all the articles of diet afforded the soldier none is more important or popular than his coffee. The open tin pans used for roasting it are singularly unfit, wasting, even when regularly burnt, the fragrance or aroma, which forms the chief virtue of the drink. To obtain a small roaster, coffee -mill, and strainer, should be the first effort of the cook, and the best outlay of the company fund. If, however, circumstances prevent that, use what is given to the best advantage. In roasting coffee, great care must be bestowed to prevent its burning. To avoid this, some use a little fat, and others add a tablespoonful of sugar; and all stir it constantly, over a very slow fire. When well browned, cover immediately with a damp cloth, and allow it to cool; then grind it, passing it through the mill twice. The kettles in which it is to be prepared should be perfectly cleaned, and scoured inside and out with ashes and hot water, scalding them before using. The water should be fresh and perfectly clear. Fill the kettles very nearly to the top, and place them over a brisk fire to boil. Whilst boiling, throw in the coffee, which should be slightly moistened before with warm (not hot) water; and, stirring it into the water, let it boil up briskly for two minutes; then dash in a cup of cold fresh water, and take it to the fire immediately. Let it stand five minutes, to allow the grains to settle, and then pass it slowly through a flannel strainer into another kettle, from which it is served. By this mode alone can the coffee be prevented from being impregnated with the dust formed by grinding it, and make it palatable and wholesome. A number of men may have to be served, measure out carefully so many rations of water, adding five for leeway, so that it may lose nothing in strength or quantity.

Brazilian Stew
From "Camp Fires and Camp Cooking, Or Culinary Hints For The Soldier", By Capt. James M. Sanderson, 1862

Take shins or legs of beef; cut them into slices or pieces two or three ounces in weight, or about the size of an egg; dip them in vinegar, and throw them into a kettle, with a dozen onions sliced, but no water. Let it stand over a very slow fire from three to four hours; then season with pepper and salt, and serve hot. Some boiled pota— toes, sliced or quartered, will be a great addition; but the principal thing to be observed is that the fire be a moderate one.

Bubble and Squeek
From "Camp Fires and Camp Cooking, Or Culinary Hints For The Soldier", By Capt. James M. Sanderson, 1862

This is an old and favorite mode of getting rid of bits of corned beef among good housewives at home, and can be advantageously introduced into camp. Any pieces of cold corned or salt beef that may be on hand should be cut into slices and sprinkled with pepper; then put them in a pan, with a little grease or fat, and fry them slightly. Boil some cabbage, and squeeze it quite dry; then cut it up very fine, and serve a piece of beef with a spoonful of cabbage, first seasoning it with pepper, salt, and vinegar.

Corned Beef and Cabbage
From "Camp Fires and Camp Cooking, Or Culinary Hints For The Soldier", By

Capt. James M. Sanderson, 1862

The salt beef furnished the army is of the very' best character; rather too highly impregnated with salt, perhaps—a fault easily remedied, however, by soaking in fresh water over night. When about to boil it, renew the water, which should be clean and cold, and place it over a moderate fire for three hours and a half, skimming it carefully every fifteen minutes. By this means only can the salt and blood be drawn from it, and the meat rendered tender. After it has been on the fire at least two hours, add as much cabbage as will fill the pot to each kettle, taking out a portion of the water, so as to be able to get in enough for the whole company, or dividing the meat into more kettles if necessary. Boil gently for an hour and a half after adding the cabbage.

To Boil Hominy

From "Camp Fires and Camp Cooking, Or Culinary Hints For The Soldier", By Capt. James M. Sanderson, 1862

Whatever be the size of the kettle, fill it half full of hominy, covering it with water so as nearly to fill it to the top; 'throw in a handful of salt, and boil it, over a very moderate fire, for at least an hour, stirring it constantly to prevent scorching.

To Fry Hominy

From "Camp Fires and Camp Cooking, Or Culinary Hints For The Soldier", By Capt. James M. Sanderson, 1862

Should you have too much of it boiled for one meal, place the balance in shallow dishes—mess pans being the handiest—and let it grow cold. When it is to be used, cut it into slices about half an inch thick and three inches long; have your fat as hot as fire can make it; then slip your slices into it, and fry it until it obtains a golden brown color on both sides. When you take it out, lay it on cloths, and let the fat drain off; and, when serving, sprinkle a little salt over it.

Pea Soup

From "Camp Fires and Camp Cooking, Or Culinary Hints For The Soldier", By Capt. James M. Sanderson, 1862

For some unexplained reason, this article is by no means popular with the troops, and large quantities are constantly returned to the commissary as company savings. This, it is believed, would not be the case if the proper mode of cooking them was known, as they are not only quite as nutritious as beans, but have always been considered by epicures much more delicate.

To use them properly, they should first be washed; then boiled for at least one hour, in a kettle with a false bottom. For a company, seven or eight quarts should be boiled in double the quantity of water. In default of a false bottom, they must be constantly stirred, to prevent scorching. When quite soft, strain off the water, divide them into three or four portions, according to the number of the kettles, and add them to the pork soup, previously described, instead of the desiccated vegetables, adding at the same time two large onions, sliced, to each kettle. Let it boil slowly for two hours, skimming now and then; and before serving out, season liberally with black pepper, some salt, and a dash of vinegar. They should be well mashed with a pounder before serving.

Pork Soup With Vegetables

From "Camp Fires and Camp Cooking, Or Culinary Hints For The Soldier", By Capt. James M. Sanderson, 1862

This soup is good for a change, and quite economical. Take four pounds of clear pork, without rind or bone; cut it into pieces about one inch square; put into a pan a little fat, which must be as hot as possible, and throw in enough pork to cover the bottom, which is to be fried quite brown, and turned into another pan whilst the balance is being fried. Have three camp kettles filled with clean water; boil it, and add to each kettle one-third of the fried pork, with a handful of salt. Let it boil moderately for fifteen minutes, and in the meanwhile, having soaked the desiccated vegetables, add one-third to each kettle, and continue boiling, not too fast, for one hour and a half. Season with pepper, salt, and a little vinegar, and if there is any stale bread to be had, three or four loaves should be cut into pieces two inches square, or less, and divided equally in the three kettles. After fifteen minutes' slow boiling the soup is ready to serve. Whatever fat floats on the top, before the bread is added, should be carefully removed.

To Make Tea

From "Camp Fires and Camp Cooking, Or Culinary Hints For The Soldier", By Capt. James M. Sanderson, 1862

Have the kettles as clean and as bright as they can be made, and let the water be free from all impurities; boil it over a bright, clear fire, and, when it boils briskly, add the tea, which should, one minute previous, be slightly steeped in boiling water, in a perfectly covered vessel. Let it remain on the fire one minute, covering the kettle with a clean pan, bottom upwards, or a close-fitting cover with-a very small hole in it; then remove it, and stand it near the fire five minutes before serving.

"Says I, "Colonel Field, I desire to introduce you to my father, and as rations are a little short in my mess, I thought you might have a little better, and could give him a good dinner." "Yes," says Colonel Field, "I am glad to make the acquaintance of your father, and will be glad to divide my rations with him. Also, I would like you to stay and take dinner with me," which I assure you, O kind reader, I gladly accepted. About this time a young African, Whit, came in with a frying-pan of parched corn and dumped it on an old oil cloth, and said, "Master, dinner is ready." That was all he had. He was living like ourselves-- on parched corn."- Pvt. Sam Watkins, Co, H, 1st Tennessee Infantry

Hardtack Pudding

From "Recollections of a Drummer-Boy", By Harry Kieffer, 150th Regiment Pennsylvania Volunteers.

"But the great triumph of the culinary art in camp was a hardtack pudding. This was made by placing the biscuit (hardtack) in a stout canvas bag, and pounding bag and contents with a club and a log, until the hardtack was reduced to a fine powder. Then you added a little wheat flour, the more the better, and made a stiff dough, which was rolled over on a cracker box lid, like a pie crust. Then you covered this all over with a preparation of stewed dried apples, dropping in here and there a raisin or two. The whole was then railed all over together, wrapped in a cloth, boiled far an hour or so, and eaten with wine sauce. The wine was, however, usually omitted, and hunger inserted instead."

"After chasing him (a rat) backwards and forwards, the rat finally got tired of this foolishness and started for his hole. But a rat's tail is the last that goes in the hole, and as he went in we made a grab for his tail. Well, tail hold broke, and we held the skin of his tail in our hands. But we were determined to have that

rat. After hard work we caught him. We skinned him, washed and salted him, buttered and peppered him, and fried him. He actually looked nice. The delicate aroma of the frying rat came to our hungry nostrils. We were keen to eat a piece of rat; our teeth were on edge; yea, even our mouth watered to eat a piece of rat. Well, after a while, he was said to be done. I got a piece of cold corn dodger, laid my piece of the rat on it, eat a little piece of bread, and raised the piece of rat to my mouth, when I happened to think of how that rat's tail did slip. I had lost my appetite for dead rat. I did not eat any rat. It was my first and last effort to eat dead rats.” - Pvt. Sam Watkins, Co, H, 1st Tennessee Infantry at Chattanooga, Tennessee

12. PERFUMES, SOAPS, HAIR OILS AND SACHETS

Antique Oil

From “The Lady's Receipt-Book; a Useful Companion for Large or Small Families”, By Eliza Leslie, 1847

This is a fine oil for the hair. Mix together, in a clean glass vessel, half a pint of oil of sweet almonds, and half a pint of the best olive oil. Then scent it with any sort of perfume.

To give it the colour and odour of roses, infuse, in the mixed oil, a small, thin muslin bag of alkanet chips, and set it in a warm place, till coloured of a beautiful pink. Then remove the bag of alkanet, and perfume the oil with ottar of roses. Put it immediately into a bottle, and cork it well.

For a violet perfume, infuse, in the above quantity of the mixed oils, an ounce of the best orris powder. Let it stand, in a warm place, for a week; then pour the whole into a strainer, press out the liquid, and bottle it.

For an orange perfume, scent the oil with essence of neroli, or orange-flowers. For jasmine, with extract of jasmine.

For bergamot, with essence of bergamot.

To Cleanse and Soften Hair
From "The Arts of Beauty: Or, Secrets of a Lady's Toilet", By Lola Montez, 1858

Beat up the white of four eggs into a froth and rub that thoroughly in close to the roots of the hair. Leave it to dry on. Then wash the head and hair clean with a mixture of equal parts of rum and rose water. This will be found one of the best cleansers and brighteners of the hair that was ever used.

Cologne Water
From "The Virginia Housewife", By Mary Randolph, 1836

Three quarts spirits of wine, six drachms oil of lavender, one drachm oil of rosemary, three drachms essence of lemon, ten drops oil of cinnamon--mix them together very well.

Cologne Water
From "Directions for Cookery, in its Various Branches" By Eliza Leslie, 1840

Procure at a druggists, one drachm of oil of lavender, the same quantity of oil of lemon, of oil of rosemary, and of oil of cinnamon; with two drachms of oil of bergamot, all mixed in the same phial, which should be a new one. Shake the oils well, and pour them into a pint of spirits of wine. Cork the bottle tightly, shake it hard, and it will be fit for immediate use; though it improves by keeping. You may add to the oils, if you choose, ten drops of the tincture of musk, or ten drops of extract of ambergris.

For very fine cologne water, mix together in a new phial oil of lemon, two drachms; oil of bergamot, two drachms; oil of lavender, two drachms; oil of cedrat, one drachm; tincture of benzoin, three drachms; neroli, ten drops;

ambergris, ten drops; attar of roses, two drops. Pour the mixture into a pint of spirits of wine; cork and shake the bottle, and set it away for use.

Another receipt for cologne water is to mix with a pint of alcohol, sixty drops or two large tea-spoonfuls of orange-flower water, and the same quantity of the essential oils of lemon,

lavender, and bergamot.

Columbian Soap

From "The Lady's Receipt-Book; a Useful Companion for Large or Small Families", By Eliza Leslie, 1847

Blanch, in scalding water, two ounces of bitter almonds. Beat them in a mortar with an ounce of gum camphor, till completely mixed; putting in, with every almond, a morsel of the camphor. Then beat in an ounce and a quarter of tincture of benjamin, and remove the mixture to a bowl. Afterwards, having shaved down a pound of the best white soap, beat that also in the mortar; mixing with it, gradually, as you proceed, the above ingredients, till the whole is thoroughly incorporaied. Divide it into equal portions, and roll it with your hands into the form of balls. This soap will be found very fine.

If you wish to have it in cakes, after you have shaved down the white soap, put it into a clean jar, cover it, and set the jar into a pot of boiling water, placed over the fire. When the soap is melted, remove it from the fire; and when it begins to cool, (but is still liquid,) stir in the other ingredients that have been mixed together as above. Then mould it in little square tin pans, and set it to cool. When quite cold, take it out of the pan, and wrap each cake in paper.

French Hungary Water

From "The Lady's Receipt-Book; a Useful Companion for Large or Small Families", By Eliza Leslie, 1847

Take two large handfuls of the flowers and young leaves of rosemary; with a handful of lavender-blossoms; half a handful of thyme-blossoms; and half a handful of sage. Mix them well; put them into a large glass jar or bottle, and pour on a quart of inodorous spirits of wine. Then put in, as a colouring, some small bits of alkanet tied in a thin muslin bag. Cork the bottle closely, and shake it about for a while. Let it infuse during a month, exposed to the heat of the sun. Then strain it, and transfer it to smaller bottles.

Honey Soap

From "Confederate Receipt Book. A Compilation of Over One Hundred Receipts, Adapted To The Times", By West & Johnston, 1863

Cut into thin shavings two pounds of common yellow or white soap, put it on the fire with just water enough to keep it from burning; when quite melted, add a quarter of a pound of honey, stirring it till it boils, then take it off and add a few drops of any agreeable perfume. Pour it into a deep dish to cool, and then cut it into squares. It improves by keeping. It will soften and whiten the skin.

Honey Water (Wash for the Hair)

From "The Arts of Beauty: Or, Secrets of a Lady's Toilet", By Lola Montez, 1858

Essence of Ambergris 1 drop, Musk 1 drop, Bergamot 2 drops, Oil of Cloves 15 drops, Orange flower water 4 oz, Spirits of wine 5 oz, Distilled water 4 oz. All these ingredients should be mixed together left about fourteen days then the whole to be through porous paper and bottled for use.

Hungarian Water

From "The Virginia Housewife", By Mary Randolph, 1836

One pint spirits of wine, one ounce oil of rosemary, and two drachms essence of ambergris.

Fine Lavender Water

From "The Lady's Receipt-Book; a Useful Companion for Large or Small Families", By Eliza Leslie, 1847

Mix together, in a clean bottle, a pint of inodorous spirit of wine; an ounce of oil of lavender; a tea-spoonful of oil of bergamot; and a table-spoonful of oil of ambergris.

Lavender Water

From "The Virginia Housewife", By Mary Randolph, 1836

Put a pint of highly rectified spirits of wine, to one ounce of essential oil of lavender, and two drachms of ambergris; shake them well together, and keep it closely stopped.

Lip Salve

From "Directions for Cookery, in its Various Branches" By Eliza Leslie, 1840

Put into a wide-mouthed bottle four ounces of the best olive oil, with one ounce of the small parts of alkanet root. Stop up the bottle, and set it in the sun, (shaking it often,) till you find
the liquid of a beautiful crimson. Then strain off the oil very clear from the alkanet root, put it into an earthen pipkin, and add to it an ounce of white wax, and an ounce and a half of the best mutton suet, which has been previously clarified, or boiled and skimmed. Set the mixture on the embers of coals, and melt it slowly: stirring it well. After it has simmered slowly far a little while, take it off; and while still hot, mix with it a few drops of oil of roses, or of oil of neroli, or tincture of musk.

Macassar Oil

From "The Lady's Receipt-Book; a Useful Companion for Large or Small Families", By Eliza Leslie, 1847

This popular and pleasant unguent for the hair can (*as we know*) be prepared at home, so as to equal, in efficacy and appearance, any that is for sale in the shops; and at less than one-third the expense. Take half an ounce of chippings of alkanet root, which may be bought at a druggist's, for a few cents. Divide this quantity into two portions, and having cleared away any dust that may be about the alkanet, put each portion of the chips into a separate bit of new bobbinet, or very clear muslin. In tying it, use white thread, or fine white cotton cord; as a coloured string may communicate a dirty tinge to the oil. Put these little bags into a large glass tumbler, or a straight-sided white-ware jar, and pour on half a pint of the best fresh olive oil. Cover the vessel, and leave it undisturbed, for several days, or a week; taking care not to shake or stir it; and do not press or squeeze the bags. Have ready some small, flat-bottomed phials, or one large one, that will hold half a pint. Take out carefully the bags of alkanet, and lay them on a saucer. You will find that they have coloured the oil a bright, beautiful crimson. The bags will serve a second time for the same purpose. Put into the bottom of each phial a small quantity of any pleasant perfume; such as oil of orange-flowers; jessamine; rose; carnation; bergamot; oil of rhodium; oil of ambergris; or oil of cloves, mixed with a little tincture of musk. Then fill up each phial with the coloured oil, poured in through a small funnel; and, corking them tightly, tie a piece of white kid leather over the top. To use macassar oil, (observing *never to shake the bottle*,) pour a little into a saucer, and, with your finger, rub it through the roots of the hair.

Millefleurs Perfume
From "The Lady's Receipt-Book; a Useful Companion for Large or Small Families", By Eliza Leslie, 1847

Mix together an ounce of oil of lavender; an ounce of essence of lemon; an ounce and a quarter of oil of ambergris; and half an ounce of oil of carraway. Add half a pint of alcohol, or spirits of wine, which should be of the inodorous sort. Shake all well together. Let it stand a week, closely corked, in a large bottle. You may then divide it in small bottles.
By mixing this perfume with equal quantities of olive oil, and oil of sweet almonds, instead of alcohol, you will have what is called millefleurs antique oil, which is used to improve the hair of young persons.

Oil of Flowers
From "Directions for Cookery, in its Various Branches" By Eliza Leslie, 1840

A French process for obtaining essential oils from flowers or herbs has been described as follows:--Take carded cotton, or split wadding and steep it in some pure Florence oil, such as is quite clear and has no smell. Then place a layer of this cotton in the bottom of a deep china dish, or in an earthen pipkin. Cover it with a thick layer of fresh rose leaves, or the leaves of sweet pink, jasmine, wall-flower, tuberose, magnolia blossoms, or any other odoriferous flower or plant from which you wish to obtain the perfume. Spread over the flower-leaves another layer of cotton that has been steeped in oil. Afterwards a second layer of flowers, and repeat them alternately till the vessel is quite full. Cover it closely, and let it stand in the sun for a week. Then throw away the flower-leaves, carefully press out the oil from the cotton, and put it into a small bottle for use. The oil will be found to have imbibed the odour of the flowers. Keep the scented cotton to perfume your clothes-presses.

To Perfume Linen
From "The Practical Housekeeper; A Cyclopedia of Domestic Economy", By Elizabeth Fries Ellet, 1857

Rose-leaves dried in the shade, or at about four feet from a stove, one pound; cloves, caraway-seeds, and allspice, of each one ounce; pound in a mortar, or grind in a mill; dried salt, a quarter of a pound; mix all these together, and put the compound into little bags.

Pot Pourri
From "The Practical Housekeeper; A Cyclopedia of Domestic Economy", By Elizabeth Fries Ellet, 1857

This is a mixture of dried flowers and spices not ground. Dried lavender, one pound; whole rose-leaves, one pound; crushed orris, coarse, half a pound; broken cloves, two ounces; broken cinnamon, two ounces; broken allspice, two ounces.

To Remove Black Specks or Flesh Worms
From "The Arts of Beauty: Or, Secrets of a Lady's Toilet", By Lola Montez, 1858

Sometimes little black specks appear about the base of the nose or on the forehead or in the hollow of the chin, which are called flesh worms and are occasioned by coagulated lymph that obstructs the pores of the skin. They may be squeezed out by pressing the skin and ignorant people suppose them to be little worms. They are permanently removed by washing with warm water and severe friction with a towel and then applying a little of the following preparation: Liquor of potassa 1 oz, Cologne 2 oz, White brandy 4 oz. The warm water and friction alone are sometimes sufficient.

Rose Sachet
From "The Practical Housekeeper; A Cyclopedia of Domestic Economy", By Elizabeth Fries Ellet, 1857

Rose heels or leaves, one pound; santal wood, ground, half a pound; otto of roses, a quarter of an ounce.

Scented Bags
From "Directions for Cookery, in its Various Branches" By Eliza Leslie, 1840

Take a quarter of a pound of coriander seeds, a quarter of a pound of orris root, a quarter of a pound of aromatic calamus, a quarter of a pound of damask rose leaves, two ounces of lavender blossoms, half an ounce of mace, half an ounce of cinnamon, a quarter of an ounce of cloves, and two drachms of musk-powder. Beat them all separately in a mortar, and then mix them well together. Make small silk or satin bags; fill each with a portion of the mixture, and sew them closely all round. Lay them among your clothes in the drawers.

To Prepare Cosmetic Soaps for Washing the Hands
From "The Virginia Housewife", By Mary Randolph, 1836

Take a pound of castile, or any other nice old soap; scrape it in small pieces, and put it on the fire with a little water--stir it till it becomes a smooth paste, pour it into a bowl, and when cold, add some lavender water, or essence of any kind--beat it with a silver spoon until well mixed, thicken it with corn meal, and keep it in small pots closely covered--for the admission of air will soon make the soap hard.

To Make Soap
From "The Virginia Housewife", By Mary Randolph, 1836

Put on the fire any quantity of lye you choose that is strong enough to bear an egg--to each gallon, add three quarters of a pound of clean grease: boil it very fast, and stir it frequently--a few hours will suffice to make it good soap. When you find by cooling a little on a plate that it is a thick jelly, and no grease appears, put in salt in the proportion of one pint to three gallons--let it boil a few minutes, and pour it in tubs to cool--(should the soap be thin, add a little water to that in the plate, stir it well, and by that means ascertain how much water is necessary for the whole quantity; very strong lye will require water to thicken it, after the incorporation is complete; this must be done before the salt is added.) Next day, cut out the soap, melt it, and cool it again; this takes out all the lye, and keeps the soap from shrinking when dried. A strict conformity to these rules, will banish the lunar bugbear, which has so long annoyed soap makers. Should cracknels be used, there must be one pound to each gallon. Kitchen grease should be clarified in a quantity of water, or the salt will prevent its incorporating with the lye. Soft soap is made in the same manner, only omitting the salt. It may also be made by putting the lye and grease together in exact proportions, and placing it under the influence of a hot sun for eight or ten days, stirring it well four or five times a day. *(Author's Note: Lye is a caustic substance and needs to be used with safety goggles, gloves, a face mask and proper ventilation! It can be purchased on-line from soap making hobbyist websites.)*

To Perfume Soap
From "The Lady's Receipt-Book; a Useful Companion for Large or Small

Families", By Eliza Leslie, 1847

Take half a pound or more of the best white soap. Shave it down with a knife. Put the shavings into a clean white-ware jar; cover the top closely, and secure the cover by tying down a cloth over it. Set it into a large kettle or sauce-pan of hot water. The water must not come up near the top of the jar. It is well to place a trivet in the bottom of the kettle for the jar to stand on, so that a portion of the water may go under it. Place the kettle over the fire, or in a hot stove, and keep it boiling hard, till the soap in the jar within is thoroughly dissolved. It must become liquid all through, and have no lumps in it. Stir it well when done; and add, while warm, a sufficient portion of any nice perfume to scent it highly. For instance, oil of bitter almonds; extract of verbena; tincture of musk, or ambergris; oil of rhodium; oil of bergamot, lavender, jessamine, rose, cinnamon, cloves, &c. Having well stirred in the perfume, transfer the melted soap to gallicups, or little square tin-pans, and set it away to cool and harden. Afterwards, take out the cakes of soap, and wrap each cake closely in soft paper. Put them away where the air cannot reach them.

Vinegar of the Four Thieves
From "The Virginia Housewife", By Mary Randolph, 1836

Take lavender, rosemary, sage, wormwood, rue, and mint, of each a large handful; put them in a pot of earthen ware, pour on them four quarts of very strong vinegar, cover the pot closely, and put a board on the top; keep it in the hottest sun two weeks, then strain and bottle it, putting in each bottle a clove of garlic. When it has settled in the bottle and become clear, pour it off gently; do this until you get it all free from sediment. The proper time to make it is when the herbs are in full vigour, in June. This vinegar is very refreshing in crowded rooms, in the apartments of the sick; and is peculiarly grateful, when sprinkled about the house in damp weather.

Violet Perfume
From "Directions for Cookery, in its Various Branches" By Eliza Leslie, 1840

Drop twelve drops of genuine oil of rhodium on a lump of loaf-sugar. Then pound the sugar in a marble mortar with two ounces of orris root powder. This will afford an excellent imitation of the scent of violets. If you add more oil of rhodium, it will produce a rose perfume. Sew up the powder in little silk bags, or keep it in a tight box.

MEASUREMENTS AND DEFINITIONS

<u>Bain Marie</u>- A container holding hot water into which a pan is placed for slow cooking. Used for melting chocolates, etc. Similar to a Double-Boiler.

<u>Bitter Almonds</u>-A variety of the common almond, and is injurious to animal life, on account of the great quantity of hydrocyanic acid it contains, and is consequently seldom used in domestic economy, unless it be to give flavour to confectionery; and even then it should he used with great caution. A single drop of the essential oil of bitter almonds is sufficient to destroy a bird, and four drops have caused the death of a middle-sized dog. (From "The Book of Household Management").

<u>Burdock</u>-An herb. The entire plant is edible and is a popular vegetable in Asia, particularly in Japan.

<u>Cochineal</u>-A red color additive derived from a scale insect called the cochineal scale *(Dactylopius coccus)*. Cochineal is a naturally occurring compound, used for hundreds of years. Today, it is still used in many food and cosmetic products and is known by different names, including cochineal, carmine, carminic acid, Natural Red 4, and E120.

<u>Demijohn</u>-A bulbous narrow necked bottle holding from 3 to 10 gallons of liquid.

<u>Desiccated Vegetables</u>- Dehydrated vegetables. Carrots, onions, and celery were dehydrated and compressed into pucks that were then boiled and eaten in camp.

<u>Dorure</u>-Yolks of eggs well beaten.

<u>Drachm</u>- A unit of weight formerly used by apothecaries, equivalent to 60 grains or one eighth of an ounce.

<u>Faggot</u>-A small bunch of parsley and thyme and a bay-leaf tied up.

<u>Fortnight</u>-Two weeks.

<u>Gill or Jill</u>-One quarter pint (Liquid Measure) or Eight Tablespoons.

<u>Green Borage</u>- Known as the bee plant, used to prepare green sauce, garnish salads, etc., adding a "cucumber-like" aroma to recipes.

<u>Gum-Arabicked</u>- Acacia gum. A natural gum consisting of the hardened sap of various species of the acacia tree.

<u>Hot Oven</u>-400-425 degrees F.

<u>Indian Meal</u>-Corn meal.

<u>Isinglass</u>-A pure, transparent or translucent form of gelatin, obtained from the air bladders of certain fish, especially the sturgeon: used in glue and jellies and as a clarifying agent.

<u>Jelly Bag</u>-"How to Make A Jelly-Bag-The very stout flannel called double-mill, used for ironing-blankets, is the best material for a jelly-bag: those of home manufacture are the only ones to be relied on for thoroughly clearing the jelly. Care should be taken that the seam of the bag be stitched twice, to secure it against unequal filtration. The most convenient mode of using the big is to tie it upon a hoop the exact size of the outside of its mouth; and, to do this, strings should be sewn round it at equal distances. The jelly-bag may, of coarse, be made any size; but one of twelve or fourteen inches deep, and seven or eight across the mouth, will be sufficient for ordinary use. The form of a jelly-bag is the fool's cap." (From "The Book of Household Management").

<u>Loaf Sugar</u>- Refined sugar molded into loaves or small cubes or squares. A large conical mass of hard refined sugar.

<u>Lye</u>- A caustic substance. It must be used with safety goggles, gloves, a face mask and proper ventilation! It can be purchased on-line from soap making hobbyist websites.

<u>Moderately Hot Oven</u>-375 degrees F.

<u>Moderate Oven</u>-350 degrees F.

<u>Moderately Slow Oven</u>-325 degrees F.

<u>Nasturtion-Seed</u>- From a genus of roughly 80 species of annual and perennial herbaceous flowering plants. It has a slightly peppery taste reminiscent of watercress. The unripe seed pods can be harvested and dropped into spiced vinegar to produce a condiment and garnish, sometimes used in place of capers.

<u>Neats</u>- A cow or other domestic bovine animal.

<u>Patna Rice</u>-A variety of long-grain rice, used for savoury dishes.

<u>Peck</u>-Two gallons (Dry Measure).

<u>Pestragon</u>-Vinegar flavoured with tarragon.

<u>Quart (Dry Measure)</u>- Generally about equal in quantity to a pound avoirdupois, (sixteen ounces.).

<u>Quartern</u>-A quarter of any given measurement. For example, a quartern milk equals a quart.

<u>Quick Oven</u>- 375-400 degrees, F.

<u>Race (as in "of ginger")</u>-A root or sprig.

<u>Salamander</u>-A tool made of cast iron with a round, flat, but relatively thick plate attached to a long handle which made it possible to grasp the cooler end of the handle without getting so close to the heat of an open hearth fire. The plate could rest on the two short legs while pushed into the hot coals so that the cook did not have to hold up its ample weight during the heating process. It resembles a metal bread or oven peel except that they are much smaller and shorter than a peel.

<u>Saleratus</u>-Sodium bicarbonate (or sometimes potassium bicarbonate) as the main ingredient of baking powder.

<u>Sal-Prunel</u>- Potassium nitrate fused and cast in balls, cakes, or sticks.

<u>Salt Petre (or "Salt Peter")</u>- Nitrate crystals. No longer used commercially

because it is toxic in quantity. Instead, sodium nitrate or sodium nitrite is used. Saltpetre was also used for gunpowder. You must instead use Prague Powder #1 and #2. You can find them on any website that sells sausage making supplies (casings, stuffers, etc). #1 is also known as pink curing salt, and is a mixture of 1 oz sodium nitrite per pound of salt.

Sauter-To fry very lightly.

Savoury Herbs-Examples include celery, rosemary, parsley, thyme, sage, oregano and marjoram.

Scrag- The lean end of a neck of mutton or veal.

Slow Oven-300 degrees, F.

Spikenard Root-Known commonly as wild or false sarsaparilla, in part for the root's mild, pleasant, licorice like flavor, and has been often used as a substitute for sarsaparilla. It can be purchased on-line.

Subcarbonate of Soda-Also known as "Washing Soda". It is not to be confused with baking soda, despite being closely related.

Suet- A form of animal fat, similar to lard, but usually sold in shredded form. Suet is the solid white fat found around the kidneys and loins of beef, sheep and other animals. Your butcher should be able to get this for you.

Tamis or "Tammy"-A strainer of thin woollen canvas, or silk, used for straining soups and sauces.

Tartaric Acid-A white crystalline diprotic organic acid. The compound occurs naturally in many plants, particularly in grapes, bananas, and tamarinds. It is also one of the main acids found in wine. Tartaric acid can be added to food when a sour taste is desired. It can be purchased at grocery stores or on-line.

Tin Kitchen-A type of roaster.

Tincture-Liquid extracts.

Treacle, or Molasses-Treacle is the uncrystallizable part of the saccharine juice drained from the Muscovado sugar, and is either naturally so or rendered uncrystallizable through some defect in the process of boiling. As it contains a large quantity of sweet or saccharine principle and is cheap, it is of great use as an article of domestic economy. Children are especially fond of it; and it is accounted wholesome. It is also useful for making beer, rum, and the very dark syrups.

<u>Unbolted Flour</u>-Whole grain flour.

<u>Very Slow-Oven</u>-Below 300 degrees F.

<u>Vinegar a Pestragon</u>-Vinegar flavored with tarragon.

<u>Wine Glass</u>-Four Tablespoons.

<u>Yelk</u>-Yolk of an egg.

<u>Yellow Dock</u>-A perennial flowering plant in the family Polygonaceae, native to Europe and Western Asia. It can be purchased on-line.

BIBLIOGRAPHY

Beecher, Catherine Esther, *Miss Beecher's Domestic Reciept Book: Designed As A Supliment To Her Treastise On Domestic Economy*, Third Edition. New York: Harper & Brothers, 1850.

Beeton, Isabella. *The Book of Household Management*. London: S. O. Beeton Publishing, 1861.

Billings, John D. *Hardtack and Coffee*. Boston: George M. Smith and Company, 1887.

Bury, Charlotte Campbell. *The Lady's Own Cookery Book*, Third Edition. London, 1844.

Chase M.D., Alvin Wood. *Dr. Chase's Recipes, or Information for Everybody*. Ann Arbor, MI: Chase, 1864.

Chesnut, Mary Boykin. *A Diary From Dixie*. New York: D. Appleton and Company, 1905.

Collins, Angelina Maria. *The Great Western Cook Book*. New York: A.S. Barnes & Company, 1857.

Confederate Receipt Book. A Compilation of over One Hundred Receipts, Adapted to the Times. Richmond: West and Johnston, 1863.

Douglas, Henry Kyd. *I Rode With Stonewall*. The University of North Carolina Press, 1940.

Ellet, Elizabeth Fries, *The Practical Housekeeper*. New York: Stringer and Townsend, 1857.

Francatelli, Charles Elmé. *A Plain Cookery Book for the Working Classes*. London: Routledge, Warne, and Routledge, 1852.

Gilpin, E. N. *The Last Campaign A Cavalryman's Journal*. Leavenworth: Ketcheson Printing Company, 1908.

Hardee, Brevet Lieut. Col. W. J. *Rifle and Light Infantry Tactics*. Philadelphia: J. B. Lippencott and Company, 1861

Hopkins, Luther W. *From Bull Run To Appomattox*. Baltimore: Fleet-McGinley Co., 1908.

Kieffer, Harry M. *The Recollections of A Drummer Boy*. Boston: Ticknor and Company, 1889.

Kitchiner, Dr. William. *The Cook's Oracle and Housekeeper's Manual*. New York: J. and J. Harper, 1830.

Leon, Louis. *Diary of a Tar Heel Confederate Soldier*. Charlotte: Stone Publishing Company, 1913.

Leslie, Eliza. *Directions for Cookery, in its Various Branches*. Philadelphia, H.C. Baird, 1840.

Leslie, Eliza. *The Lady's Receipt-Book; a Useful Companion for Large or Small Families*. Philadelphia: Carey and Hart, 1847.

Montez, Lola. *The Arts of Beauty: Or, Secrets of a Lady's Toilet*. New York: Dick and Fitzgerald, 1858.

Moss, Maria J. *A Poetical Cook-Book*. Philadelphia: Caxton Press of C. Sherman, Son & Co., 1864.

Rundell, Maria Eliza Ketelby. *A New System of Domestic Cookery*. Philadelphia : Benjamin C. Buzby, 1807.

Sanderson, J. M. *The Complete Cook*. Philadelphia: J. B. Lippincott, 1864.

Sanderson, Capt. James R. *Camp Fires and Camp Cooking; or, Culinary Hints for the Soldier*. Washington: Government Printing Office, 1862.

Taylor, Lt. Gen Richard. *Destruction and Reconstruction: Personal Experiences of the Late War*. New York: D. Appleton and Company, 1883.

Thomas, Jerry. *How To Mix Drinks, Or The Bon Vivant's Companion*. New York: Dick and Fitzgerald, 1862.

Watkins, Sam R. *Co. Aytch A Confederate Memoir of the Civil War*. New York: Simon & Schuster, 2003.

Kindig, Bruce R. *Courage and Devotion A History of Bankhead's/Scott's Tennessee Battery in the American Civil War*. Bloomington: Author House, 2014.

Smith, Andrew F. *The Tomato In America: Early History, Culture and Cookery*. Columbia: University of South Carolina Press, 1994.

"Civil War Diaries of Van Buren Oldham" Dieter C. Ullrich, ed. Originals at Special Collections/University Archives, Univ. of Tennessee at Martin. https://www.utm.edu/departments/special_collections/E579.5%20Oldham/text/vboldham_1863.php (Accessed 18 January 2018).

"Billy Yank and Johnny Reb Letters" Wordpress.com. https://billyyankjohnnyreb.wordpress.com/ (Accessed 18 January 2018).

"Diary of a Confederate Soldier" Southern Historical Society Papers, Volume 10. http://www.perseus.tufts.edu/hopper/text?doc=Perseus%3Atext%3A2001.05.0123%3Achapter%3D7.66 (Accessed 18 January 2018).

INDEX

ABOUT THE AUTHOR

David W. Flowers earned his Bachelor's of Science, with a Minor in Sociology and additional hours in Education from Illinois State University. In 2016 and 2017, David was honored with the "Grand Cook of the Year" award from Civil War Talk (civilwartalk.com) for his research in original Civil War era recipes. The American Civil War has been a passion, culminating in a lifetime of study, travel to battlefields and actively participating in Civil War reenactments on the local and National levels since 2005. Since the 1980's, he has taught classes ranging from Career Counseling, Pre-K, Junior High School and GED/HiSET coursework to youth involved in the Criminal Justice system. Combining a love of cooking, reenacting and Civil War history, it came natural for his kitchen and backyard fire pit to exude the smells and tastes of the 1860's. He resides in Illinois with his wife, Monica and son, David.

Made in United States
Cleveland, OH
16 December 2024

11983295R00116